Female Voices from
the Worksite

Female Voices from the Worksite

The Impact of Hidden Bias against Working Women across the Globe

Edited by
Marquita R. Walker

LEXINGTON BOOKS
Lanham • Boulder • New York • London

Published by Lexington Books
An imprint of The Rowman & Littlefield Publishing Group, Inc.
4501 Forbes Boulevard, Suite 200, Lanham, Maryland 20706
www.rowman.com

6 Tinworth Street, London SE11 5AL, United Kingdom

British Library Cataloguing in Publication Information Available

Library of Congress Cataloging-in-Publication Data

Names: Walker, Marquita R., 1950- editor.
Title: Female voices from the worksite / edited by Marquita R. Walker.
Description: Lanham : Lexington Books, [2020] | Includes bibliographical references and index. | Summary: "This collection examines narratives expressed by women as they maneuver through social, cultural, economic, and political landmines during the search for gender equality in their respective work fields"—Provided by publisher.
Identifiers: LCCN 2020039112 (print) | LCCN 2020039113 (ebook) | ISBN 9781793628749 (cloth) | ISBN 9781793628756 (epub)
Subjects: LCSH: Sex discrimination in employment. | Women—Employment. | Equal pay for equal work. | Sexual division of labor.
Classification: LCC HD6060 .F46 2020 (print) | LCC HD6060 (ebook) | DDC 331.4/133—dc23
LC record available at https://lccn.loc.gov/2020039112
LC ebook record available at https://lccn.loc.gov/2020039113

Contents

Acknowledgments

I always thought I could do anything. My assumption was if I worked hard enough and long enough at something, I would succeed. Though I have worked hard and long over the course of my career, I now realize my assumption was incorrect. Now I know no matter how fast I dance, there will be barriers I cannot traverse, goals I cannot achieve, and mountains I cannot climb simply because I am female, and I am one of the lucky ones. I live in the United States, am white, and have a decent education and career. Yet, my achievements are valued at 80 percent of my male counterparts who complete the same achievements. What is wrong with this picture?

The insidious nature of hidden and indirect bias against women in the workplace will continue to erode, harm, and hold back half of the world's population because of social and cultural mores, economic policies, and political ideologies against women. There have been some inroads made over the course of past decades, at least in the United States, in the form of antidiscrimination laws to correct these imbalances, but good luck in climbing the uphill battle of proving intent if you experience discrimination in the workplace; for the most part, these indirect biases remain embedded in the consciousness of both men and women based on outmoded belief systems and archaic and traditional ways of thinking about gender roles and resurface in the form of career impediments, wage disparities, and biased language in vetting, hiring, training, and retention policies.

I owe debts of gratitude to this manuscript's contributors who provide insights into women's experiences of personal and professional devaluation and exploitation resulting from indirect and hidden biases. Their expertise and knowledge in conducting studies which reflect the struggles of women in various industries worldwide speaks to the pervasive nature of hidden biases. This is a global phenomenon which continues to suppress the creativity and ingenuity of millions of women. Just think to what heights we could soar if women were provided the same opportunities and supports as men. Then, perhaps, women could do anything.

This book is dedicated to my daughter, Dana, and my granddaughter, Abigale. It is for them and others like them I try to ferret out, expose and correct hidden workplace biases in the hope the future world in which they live will seriously consider more gender balanced opportunities and compensation.

Introduction

Marquita R. Walker

Female voices from the worksite (2021) is an edited volume of qualitative research reflecting the voices of women who have faced covert and overt discrimination on the job and the challenges/barriers they face(d) from employers, coworkers, and unions. This research emphasizes the reoccurring themes of devaluation, exploitation, and dehumanization of female workers resulting from unconscious or implicit bias which directly and indirectly impacts the ability of women to succeed and thrive on worksites predominantly guided by social and institutional policies/laws/rules which evolved through a patriarchal and gendered division of labor. These women's voices speak to the daily struggles they face in various industries when trying to maintain a decent standard of living and progress in their careers while dealing with inflexible and long work hours, masculine workplace cultures, employers' stereotypical attitudes, and the absence of work-life balance initiatives. This volume is divided into three parts. The first part explores the explained and unexplained bias associated with the gender wage gap as a measure of success in the labor market. The second part speaks to the way language is used to indirectly devalue women in the workplace, and the third part focuses on institutional structures which reinforce women's secondary status through legislation and policies.

EXPLAINED AND UNEXPLAINED REASON FOR THE GENDER WAGE GAP

Women currently make up 47 percent of the total U.S. workforce (U.S. Bureau of Labor Statistics 2019a), earn 80.5 percent of what men earned in 2017 (Fontenot 2018), and 81.1 percent of what men earned in 2018 (Current

Population Survey 2019). The Bureau of Labor Statistics (2018b) reports that women over the age of sixteen working full-time salary or wage jobs, considered as thirty-five hours or more per week, earned a median weekly income of $770 as compared to a median weekly income of $941 for men (2). Younger women, ages sixteen to twenty-four, earned $499 per week while younger men, aged sixteen to twenty-four, earned $547 per week; women's weekly earnings increased through age sixty-four to $856 while men's weekly earnings topped out at $1,098 (1). Generally speaking, Asian women and men earn more than their White, Black, or Hispanic counterparts (2018b, 3), and women's educational attainment outpaces men's (2018b, 5). Women are more concentrated in office and administrative support roles and professional and related occupations such as health care and education and less affiliated with construction, production, or transportation occupations (2018b, 6). In 2017, two million women or 13 percent of women employed full time filled "the three most common jobs for women . . . registered nurse ($1143), elementary and middle school teacher ($987), and secretary or administrative assistant ($735)" (2018b, 7).

The gender pay gap has a significant economic impact over the course of women's lifetimes. In 2017, 13 percent of American women and 9 percent of men ages sixteen to sixty-five were living below the federal poverty level, and 11 percent of women and 8 percent of men ages sixty and older were living in poverty (Miller 2018, 5; Fontenot 2017). Women suffer from wage discrimination because their salary history is used to set their wages for subsequent jobs; compounded over a lifetime, the cumulative effect of women's decreased earnings results in fewer social security, life insurance, and disability benefits (Fischer 2013). Social security tends to be the mainstay of income for people over sixty-five years of age and reduced social security income catapults women into poverty more than men. This problem is exacerbated with age. According to Fischer (2013), "Without Social Security benefits, 32 percent of men aged sixty-five to seventy-four would be in poverty, as would 48 percent of men aged seventy-five and older; 41 percent of women aged sixty-five to seventy-four and 58 percent of women aged seventy-five and older would also be in poverty" (12).

This snapshot of women's placement relative to men's placement in the labor market calls into the question the reasons men's earnings outpace women's earnings across the board. If earnings or wages are the criteria by which we gauge and reward success in the labor market, then the earnings/wage gap between men and women is an indicator of disparity between sexes. The Bureau of Labor Statistics reflects that "Women's-to-men's earnings ratio varied by race and ethnicity. White women earned 81.4 percent as much as their male counterparts, compared with 90.8 percent for Black women, 72.5 percent for Asian women, and 83.2 percent for Hispanic women" (U.S.

Bureau of Labor Statistics 2019b). To what can this wage gap be attributed and what can be done to close this gap? Why and how have women's efforts to succeed in the labor market been stymied? Though some movement to narrow the wage gap can be explained by the downward or static trend in men's earnings since 1979 which have reflected little to no change (2018b, 96), there still exists a chasm between men's and women's earnings which isn't easily explained. This collection of case studies seeks to explore why this gap continues to exist, how the gap affects women in various occupations, how women, as agents, perceive their labor market roles, how social and economic institutions such as markets, governments, unions, and families contribute to this gap, and offers some recommendations to narrow or eliminate this discrepancy.

THE EXPLAINED WAGE GAP

Human Capital Investment

Earnings differentials between men and women have long existed and are partly explained by the investment of human capital, the education, and training and work experience individuals amass during their lifetimes, which makes them more valuable employees, increases their skill levels, and strengthens their appeal to employers (Blau 2017; Becker 1985). Men's higher compensation as an "explained" part of the wage gap suggests men have made greater investments in human capital and are, therefore, more highly rewarded for those investments. Blau (2017) also notes the narrowing of the male-female wage gap due to the convergence of education and experience peaked around 1980 and has since slowed. Women's substantial advances in certain occupations such as law and medicine have closed the wage gap to some extent, but generally women lag behind men in earnings even when accounting for increased human capital investments in education and work experience (Leith 2014; Goldin 2014b). For instance, women in top-level positions, CEOs, board members, or executive officers, hold small percentages of those positions (Catalyst 2019). Other explanatory factors for the explained wage gap include "the family division of labor, compensating wage differentials, discrimination, falling rates of collective bargaining, and issues relating to selection into the labor force"(Blau 2017, 790–791).

Family Division of Labor

The traditional male/female dichotomies within familial structures often dictate family members' roles. Women, typically responsible for caregiving obligations, anticipate shorter work lives outside their domestic realm, and expect interruptions in their work life such as having and caring for children. This results in a disinvestment of human capital, fewer labor market experiences, and depreciation, over time, of lifetime earnings. Often women self-select into industries, education, health care, retail, and hospitality, which require less specific and more general human capital investment. For instance, women tend to gravitate toward nurturing jobs, teaching, nursing, and food and cleaning service, because the skills required for these positions are less costly to acquire and transferable once acquired. Employers, who often bear some of the cost of firm-specific training such as in the building trades, may shy away from hiring those with general skills, primarily women, because of uncertainty about worker productivity which would impact their return on investment (Blau 2017; Becker 1993; Gough 2013).

Women bear the brunt of family care. While women are more likely to be married and have dependent children, they are also more likely to earn low wages and work fewer paid hours than men. Men, on the other hand, who are likely to be married and have dependent children, earn higher wages and work longer hours (Rose 2004). Some argue women work fewer paid hours by choice, and as more women graduate from college and the economy shifts toward the service industry and away from manufacturing, that the wage gap will simply disappear. There is little evidence to conclude that will happen if women, bearers of progeny, must interrupt their working careers in the paid labor force resulting in a lifetime earnings' reduction. A study by Rose (2004) concluded, "The average woman earned only $273,592 while the average man earned $722,693, leaving a gap of 62 percent over [a] 15-year period" (2). The study explored 1983–1998 data from the Panel Study of Income Dynamics (PSID) which included 1,614 women and 1,212 men, aged twenty-six to fifty-nine, "who had at least one year of positive earnings during that period" and reflected one in three women and one in fourteen men experienced poverty during this time period (Rose 2004).

Compensating Wage Differentials

The theory of compensating wage differentials suggests less desirable jobs, those with increased risk factors or undesirable working conditions, must pay more to attract workers, and more desirable jobs, those with better benefits or working conditions, can pay less to attract workers (Glauber 2011). Some of the wage gap is explained because women are often relegated to or tend to gravitate toward traditional nurturing jobs associated with lower risk and are paid less for those positions. Blau and Khan (2017) write, "Women have been found to be more risk averse than men on average, which could lower their relative wages" (791), and psychological factors "such as self-confidence may contribute to a worker's productivity" (837). "Ample anecdotal evidence exists that women give greater importance in their choice of job to its value to society and to personal interactions, and less importance to money and prestige than men" (Fortin 2008, 886).

Discrimination in the Labor Market and the Pre-Labor Market

Covert labor market discrimination is difficult to measure, yet the effects are visible in the persistent earnings wage gap between men and women, the most reported form of discrimination. According to the Pew Research Center (2019), "four-in-ten working women (42%) said they have experienced gender discrimination at work, compared with about two-in-ten men (22%) who said the same" (np). About 39 percent of women report they have taken significant time away from work for family obligations; 42 percent report they have reduced their work hours for caregiving responsibilities; and 27 percent report they have quit work to accommodate work-life balance (Graf 2019).

Employer discrimination in the labor market falls into two categories: statistical discrimination, when employers assume all women are less productive and less committed because some women of childbearing age may interrupt their work lives to bear and care for children, and taste discrimination, when employers, and possibly coworkers and customers, prefer working with childless women (Gough 2013). Tastes are ascribed as the reasons individuals choose to live/work apart from others and would require a premium to interact with them (Goldin 2014a, 313), so women gravitate toward different occupations than men and are paid less than men. Tastes discrimination holds than men separate themselves from women in the workplace in order to maintain power, influence, status, money, and turf. Entry into all male professions by women is seen as "polluting" (Goldin 2014a, 314) because society might view the "standard of admission" to the male-dominant workplace as being compromised. The outcome of statistical and taste discrimination is the same, "women who differ *only* with respect to their parental status will be treated differently by employers" (Gough 2013, 331).

Mothers typically earn between 5 and 10 percent less per child than women who are childless (Gough 2013). Motherhood then is a critical factor in the wage differential between men and women; this factor is known as the "motherhood penalty" (Gough 2013, 328). According to Budig (2011), "not all mothers incur the same wage penalties for children and that mothers who can least afford to lose wages are the ones incurring the largest proportionate penalties" (725). Though the lack of childcare "fails all families with its high costs, limited availability, and often low quality" (Fredrickson 2015, 170), it disproportionately affects families least able to absorb the costs (Fass 2009). This penalty is likely exacerbated for women of color (Budig 2010).

The gendered division of labor is "unstable and unsustainable" (Rose 2004, 5) and has a direct impact on women's lifetime earnings, social security and retirement benefits, educational attainment, and entrance into poverty. Obviously if women's incomes were higher, they and their families would experience a higher standard of living. Reduced lifetime earnings prevent women from acquiring sufficient resources for retirement (Rose 2004). Glauber (2010) writes that all else being equal, "female-dominated jobs pay less than male-dominated or integrated jobs" (116).

Fredrickson (2015) writes: "One of the easiest ways to fall from middle class into poverty, or from poverty into destitution, is to have children" (148). The majority of mothers in the United States are in the paid labor force (Crouse 2015, xi). According to Crouse (2015), the participation rates of never-married mothers with children under eighteen increased from 42.2 percent in 1975 to 71.5 percent in 2012; the participation rates of divorced, widowed, or separated mothers rose from 62.8 percent in 1975 to 80.2 percent in 2012; and the employment rate for all mothers has now plateaued for married mothers with a spouse present at 65 percent, divorced, widowed, and separated mothers at 71.8 percent, and never-married mothers at 59.6 percent (III-31). When single mothers are dependent on only their earnings, they are 25 percent more likely to fall into poverty, need public assistance, or be forced into bankruptcy (Fredrickson 2015).

"The gendered discrimination in the labor market is self-reinforcing" (Rose 2004, 5). Married women who are not heads of households are able to take lower wage jobs because it makes economic sense for the lower wage earners in the family to care for children, while single, widowed, or divorced women without other supports are channeled into low-wage jobs because employers assume women will interrupt their work cycle for childbearing/childrearing. Employers may offer part-time work to women in lieu of full-time work with time off for childcare (Gough 2013). Family leave policies are legislatively relegated to selective employees. For instance, the Family and Medical Leave Act (FMLA) (2018a), enacted in 1993 under the Clinton Administration, provides twelve weeks of unpaid leave in a twelve-month period for births and adoptions and other family healthcare needs. But only employers with fifty or more employees who have worked 1,150 hours in a previous year are required to provide FMLA benefits. These restrictions discount around 40 percent of private sector workers (Saad-Lessler 2017, np). FMLA is an unpaid benefit, so "only 14 percent of workers had access to paid family and medical leave in 2016" (Saad-Lessler 2017, np; Bureau of Labor Statistics 2016) because workers are required to take any paid benefits, such as vacation or sick pay time, prior to using FMLA benefits. Most women simply cannot afford to take the time off even if they are eligible. Consequently, the women who most need these FMLA benefits are ineligible or unable to take them.

Falling Rates of Collective Bargaining

Women's participation in the labor force continued to rise significantly after WWII for several reasons (Goldin 2006). Much household work, traditionally the purview of women, was reduced because of technological innovations such as electric washing machines, dryers, and vacuum cleaners. Women were better able to control their own reproductive rights as a result of birth control measures and court decisions legalizing abortion. Consequently, women were able to delay marriage and childbearing and pursue education and careers (Blau 2017). The passage of Title IX of the Civil Rights Act, which theoretically prohibited discrimination in educational institutions, led to the increased admission of women in higher education; changing social norms begat more support for female education which strengthened girls' desires for college entrance as their high school math and science scores paralleled boys' scores. Increased education and skill sets for women increased their income and led to fewer births and divorces. Consequently fewer women found themselves as single heads of households in poverty (Walker 2014).

THE UNEXPLAINED WAGE GAP

An unexplained or "residual" portion of the wage gap, "often termed 'wage discrimination' since it is the difference in earnings between observationally identical males and females" (Goldin 2014b, 1093), remains in question. These unobservable differences are attributed to direct gender bias and discrimination (Miller 2018). Are women penalized for simply being women? Blau (2017) writes this unexplained wage gap may emerge from psychological attitudes influenced by the labor market context; for instance, "anticipated treatment of women in the labor market may affect their aspirations" (791). Some suggestions as to the causes of this gender wage gap are women's inability or lack of desire to negotiate wages (Leith 2014), women's need for flexibility within work schedules for child birth, childrearing obligations, and family responsibilities (Goldin 2014b), women's inclination to be less competitive and more risk averse than men (Blau 2017), and employers' and customers' preferences for dealing with men (Lips 2013).

Occupation and Industry Segregation

Occupation and industry segregation account for an unexplained portion of the gender wage gap (Miller 2018; Blau 2017). At an early age, boys and girls are socially conditioned in gender-specific ways which often follow them through their lives. These trajectories funnel women into nurturing and support jobs and channel men to maintenance and production roles. This resulting "occupational segregation" means women tend toward lower-paying jobs with limited opportunities for promotion, often deemed as "women's work," while men tend toward higher- paying jobs with unlimited promotional opportunities (Miller 2018). Occupational segregation somewhat narrowed from 1960 to 2000 because women moved into male-dominated jobs such as construction but has since remained static for all races (Hegewisch 2014). During that period, the wage gap closed to some extent but has remained stable since then.

The wage gap remains irrespective of female-dominated or male-dominated occupations when gauged on a median hourly basis. On average, men and women "worked more hours in predominately male occupations than workers in predominately female occupations" (Hegewisch 2014, 15) yet men's pay for medium hours worked exceeded women's pay for medium hours worked. According to Rose and Hartmann (2004), "there is a clear penalty for working in female-dominated occupations" (16). "Men also suffer a wage penalty for working female-dominated occupations compared to what they could earn in male-dominated occupation at the same skill level" (Rose 2004, 15).

The Glass Ceilings

Women occupy fewer positions of authority than men in larger companies; "fewer than 3 percent of top executives of Fortune 500 companies are women" (Alkadry 2011, 743). The conservative nature of women's advancement into managerial positions occurs even though legislation in the form of Equal Employment Opportunity (EEO) mandated the illegality of discrimination because of race, color, religion, sex, gender identity, sexual orientation, national origin, age, disability, or genetic information (1964). Alkadry (2011) finds covet pay discrimination is directly related to the strength of the authority women have over employees they supervise and their associated financial responsibility (740). Bosse (2012) calls this the "second glass ceiling," an obscure and hidden barrier which hinders women from rising to the top of the hierarchy because they are assigned "less supervisory and financial authority than men" (Alkadry, 2011, 743) and primarily only have power over subordinates in routine tasks (Hopcroft, 1996). Alkadry (2011) posits this second glass ceiling is more attributable to the responsibilities assigned than to hierarchical levels. Bosse (2012) suggests some women leave corporate management positions in which they encounter this "glass ceiling" (Morrison 1992, xi), a constraint on their ability to rise through the corporate ladder and enter into their own small business arrangement in which they will have more autonomy and receive greater benefits only to encounter a "second glass ceiling" (53), another form "of systemic gender bias that constrain[s] their performance" (53) by compromising their ability to raise capital.

Flexibility

The term *flexibility* suggests workers and employers can mediate hours worked based on their wants and needs either through reduced working hours or scheduling working hours in a flexible way. "Workers value flexibility, which is costly for employers to provide" (Flabbi 2012, 1). Golden (2014) focuses on workforce interruptions, either temporary or permanent, and posits reduced or increased hours of work are dependent on "personnel economics" (818) with women placing a higher value on temporal flexibility than men and employers determining the cost of providing flexible hours in terms of increased searching, hiring, training, and organizing for additional workers. Consequently, the flexibility penalty is higher in jobs where substitute workers cannot easily satisfy clients' needs in a timely manner, such as doctors or attorneys, and lower in jobs where substitute workers can easily replace other workers (Blau, 2017). The penalties for working shorter hours and workforce interruptions, such as taking time off for childbirth and childrearing, continue to have an impact on the wage gap years after the interruption and seem to be bigger at the top of the wage distribution than at the bottom (Blau, 2017). One example is female lawyers, who worked shorter hours, worked part-time, or took time off for childbirth/rearing, earned less than male counterparts who had no work interruptions (Noonan, 2005).

Golden (2014) suggests reduced hours or part-time work's effect on the wage gap translates into a "part-time penalty" (821) which primarily affects women who hold the bulk of part-time jobs; women, as primary caregivers, may self-select into part-time positions for the flexibility offered and accept the corresponding lowered wage (Schaffer, 2019). Women also have fewer opportunities for upward job mobility and remain on the sidelines in fashioning the policies favorable to themselves. Women occupy fewer leadership positions in the financial, building trades, and manufacturing industries, yet overwhelmingly make up the bulk of workers in the hospitality, healthcare, and teaching industries.

Examples of implicit bias against women abound within the policies which dictate employment relationships. For example, small business has been called the backbone of the American economy. Lascocco (2012) suggests the reason female small business owners are less successful than male business owners is the societal responsibilities for home, family, and community placed on women who must balance their commitments between work and family. Goldin (2014) writes the gender pay gap " is a reflection of the lower earnings women receive relative to men in almost all occupations" (1101) and suggests the difference is a result of flexibility within the work schedule due to the arrival of children and their care. Rose (2004) reports "women are much more likely than men to reduce or interrupt their time in paid work to deal with family responsibilities, resulting in a dramatic impact on their earnings" (1). Men make no such trade-off, so their economic pursuits are less riddled with home/family challenges making them free to pursue and improve their access to "contracts, capital, and business skills" (Loscocco 2012, 210).

PART I: THE GENDER WAGE GAP

The following chapters consider the subordinate placement of women workers in their industries as the result of rigid cultural roles resulting in female exploitation and devaluation.

Chapter 1: Anil Duman writes about "Precarious Employment Intersecting with Gender: Are Women Punished More?" Duman argues skilled and unskilled Turkish female workers suffer penalties for workforce participation; unskilled female workers suffer because of higher degrees of exploitation in comparison to their male counterparts while skilled female workers' qualifications are undervalued, and culturally, they must subscribe to rigid gender roles in conjunction with their household duties.

Chapter 2: Anu Mariam Philipose uses a narrative framework in her interviews with three tea workers entitled "Women Tea Workers of Munnar: Daily Negotiations with the Restrictive Spaces." Philipose situates the women tea pluckers on the lowest rungs of the tea commodity chain in which they are viewed by society as "outsiders" and must negotiate their daily existence with male overseers. The narrative exposes the juxtaposition of women's resistance strategies within their restricted workspace which cleaves to its colonial past and the comradery among the women tea pluckers as they form bonds of solidarity to counter restrictions on their social mobility, create their own networks for unpaid care activities, and support each other as best they can.

Chapter 3: Nisha Viswanathan uses a narrative approach when exploring gender-based disparities in medicine. In "Gender-Based Differences in the Medical Field: The Female Physician Story," Viswanathan argues female physicians, a majority of medical school applicants and matriculants, are, compared to their male peers, less likely to find equality in the clinic, burn out more quickly, underpaid, at greater risk for discrimination in the workplace, and deprived of career opportunities. She discusses the discriminatory factors drawn from female physicians' stories and makes policy recommendations to foster equality between male and female physicians in the medical field.

Chapter 4: Saniye Dedeoglu and Asli Sahankaya Adar contribute "Voicing the Invisible: Women's Home-Based Work and Labor in Istanbul's Garment

Industry" in which they examine women's home-based piecework in the Turkish garment industry and emphasize the gender inequalities underlying export success of that industry through the reproduction of gender ideology and norms by ensuring the articulation of women's subordinate position with the social organization of garment production and the mobilization of kinship relations.

PART II: THE USE OF LANGUAGE TO DEVALUE WOMEN IN THE WORKPLACE

Centuries of human evolution have not self-corrected the status of male as primary and woman as secondary. Our historical documents, language, and culture continue to reflect the male-dominate female-subservient dichotomy. Take for instance the textbooks and literature which record human history. Students in history classes read about frontier fathers but never read about frontier mothers. Were there no women on the frontier working and fighting alongside male family members and friends to conquer the wild west? The lack of gender inclusivity in textbooks is part of a "hidden curriculum" (Stromquist, 1998) in which "stereotypes of males and females are camouflaged by the taken-for-granted system of gender stratification and roles and this constrains girls['] *and* boys' visions of who they are and what they can become" (Blumberg 2008, 347). Textbooks, with which students spend a great deal of time and from which instructors take a great deal of content, emphasize the dominancy of male characters through pictures and stories while female images and stories are often conspicuous by their absence. There is little interest and a high cost in rewriting textbooks to favor gender inclusivity, so gender-stereotype reinforcement is likely to continue (Blumberg, 2008). Blumberg (2008) surmises that almost all studies "concluded that textbooks have not adequately reflected the range of women's roles and occupations in the real world" and consistently reflect women as "underrepresented," "accommodating," and "passive conformists" (347).

Students are conditioned from an early age to embrace an unconscious bias toward the primacy of males and the inferiority of females. Male bias saturates our spoken and writing language in every day communications, print and broadcast media, pop culture, and historical accounts, and reinforces and reproduces gender stereotypes of females as "communal/warm[th]" and men as "agentic/competent" (Menegatti 2017, 1). Linguistically, nouns and pronouns referring to women are derivatives of male nouns and pronouns: man becomes woman and he becomes she. Even the masculine terms *men* and *mankind* are said to subsume both sexes and all genders thus eliminating women from humanity. Menegatti (2017) theorizes our lexical choices "not only reflect [our] stereotypical beliefs but also affects recipients' cognition and behavior, [and] the use of expressions consistent with gender stereotypes contributes to transmit and reinforce such [a] belief system and can produce actual discrimination against women" (1). Gender stereotypes are automatically triggered by gender-specific words even in people who believe they have no bias against certain groups, so simply by conforming to gender rules in a specific language, individuals associate gender bias with normalcy.

Job-Related Language

Male-centric language, the use of he versus the gender-inclusive s/he, is shown to "lower [a] sense of belonging" and be "less motivation[al], to women during job interviews" (Stout 2011, 757). Stout (2011) explores the linguistic bias in the everyday use of pronouns when using male referents to acknowledge an entire group even though the group contains males and females. This type of subtle gender-exclusive communication ostracizes the female group that feels actively "ignored and excluded" (Stout 2011, 758) even though gender-exclusion is not the intent of the speaker. In the study conducted by Stout (2011) exploring male bias in job advertising language, "both women and men perceive the use of gender-exclusive language as sexist, women feel more ostracized, less motivated, and less identified with a job when it is described using gender-exclusive versus gender-inclusive language" (761). The use of gender-exclusive language may well fit into the phenomenon of ostracism as posited by Williams, Forgas, and von Hippel (2005) who explain social ostracism and social exclusion threaten a target's self-esteem or "how we perceive others to perceive our goodness and worth" (Williams 2005, 22).

Take, for instance, the way women are referenced in letters of recommendation, job evaluations, job interviews, and the wording of job openings and the job selection process. Gender-related words such as *superb, outstanding, and remarkable* (Madera 2009, 1591), are used more in recommendations for male applicants to graduate school and for faculty openings than for female applicants even though there were no differences in qualifications (Madera, 2009). Female applicants are described as being kind, agreeable, and helpful while male applicants are described as being forceful, confident, and ambitious. Consequently the "research showed that communal characteristics mediate the relationship between gender and hiring decisions in academia, suggesting that gender norm stereotypes—and not necessarily the sex of applicants—can influence hireability ratings of applicants" (Madera 2009, 1598) resulting in more male applicants than female applicants being hired. Even when the number of adjectives used to describe communal or agentic traits was small, over time the cumulative effect is compounded and can have detrimental effects on women's academic opportunities (Madera, 2009; Eagly, 2000).

Gaucher (2011) contends gendered wording favoring masculinity maintains, reinforces, and perpetuates group-based inequality from an institutional perspective and acts as a mechanism for inequality maintenance (109). This mechanism, functioning as social dominance theory, is "deeply embedded within the social structure . . . [and is easily] overlooked by society at large" (Gaucher 2011, 109). A closer look reveals gendered words in job advertisements "serves as a covert institutional practice—one that is very subtle—that ultimately serves to reinforce existing gender inequalities, keeping women out of areas that men (the dominate group) typically occupy" (Gaucher 2011, 111).

Another approach to reinforcing gender inequalities through gendered wording is theorized by Eagly (1987) who posits original gender roles have conditioned individuals to stereotype men as agentic and women as nurturing. This social role theory predicts gender inequality results from an "inference-based perceptual process whereby gendered language emerges within advertisements depending on which gender predominates" (Eagly, 1987).

Rudman (1999) poses there is a "backlash effect" (Rudman 1999, 1004) for women who exhibit agentic traits anathema to their stereotypical persona. When women in job evaluations were found to violate prescriptive norms, what women ought to be like, rather than descriptive norms, what women are like, they were sanctioned more severely by being demoted because the higher standard of interpersonal skills such as sensitivity and niceness associated with what women ought to be like were perceived to be unmet (Rudman, 1999). In other words, women who possess stereotypical masculine traits such as assertiveness, decisiveness, and forcefulness are often penalized because they do not fit into the stereotypical communal female role. Because the prescriptive rules in employment relations have been established by those in power and those in power tend to be men, there is a built-in bias against women who seek to break out of their normal stereotypical roles and assert dominance over traditional men's turf and power. Because "men are dependent on women for sex, for sexual reproduction, for child-rearing and as homemakers, all of which give men strong motives to control women's behavior" (Rudman 1999, 1005), men in power seek to maintain their status and influence by replicating supportive roles for women without which their male dominance is questioned (Glick, 1999).

This spectacle of backlash played out on national television during the job interview of Brett Kavanaugh for Justice of the U.S. Supreme Court in September 2018. Undergirded by the #MeToo movement, a 2017 groundswell of opposition to male sexual assault and harassment against women, particularly those in the workplace, Dr. Christine Blasey Ford testified before

Congress that Brett Kavanaugh, nominee for the job of Justice of the U.S. Supreme Court, had sexually assaulted her when they were in college. Her testimony was considered, tearful, logical, and well-reasoned and backed by scientific descriptions of how memory works. She presented facts as she could best remember them in a reasoned tone which gave pause to those watching that she obviously was traumatized by the event and carried with her still the emotional and psychological scars of the assault.

Kavanaugh, on the other hand, was rude, critical, loud, demeaning, assertive, and argumentative when providing his account against the accusations and, in several instances, became belligerent toward senators asking him questions. His anger was on full display. The result was a 50–48 senate confirmation vote for his ascension to the highest court in the United States. This decision made by primarily right-leaning white male senators could not have happened without adherence to a conservative structural institution in power which values males over females, construes aggressive male behavior as preferential to communal female behavior, and wishes to ensure for future decades that social and economic status is reproduced through policies/laws/rules which value the standard of white male primacy by which all others are judged.

Male dominance is also a counterforce for economic and social change. As women enter the workforce in increasing numbers and demand equal rights, wages, and benefits, the maintenance of the male dominant-female secondary status quo becomes a necessary component for dominant groups to control. Women, too, often buy into and accept this female communal stereotype and push back against women who violate the stereotype even at the expense of their own subordination (Rudman, 1999). Consequently, men who behave in stereotypical agentic fashion during job interviews are perceived as being "masterful" (Rudman 1999, 1006), while women, though judged competent during a job interview, may be perceived as less communal, and, therefore, "denied the job or promotion on the basis of company policy" (Rudman 1999, 1006). If jobs are awarded because of agentic merit and the worth of agentic female applicants is undervalued because they are considered less communal, then women face an untenable situation in job attainment and advancement. When women have to constantly fight the unconscious bias built into job interviews, evaluations, and job promotions, they cannot achieve economic or social parity and will continue to be at the bottom of the economic heap, their worth undervalued and exploited, and they will be less able to contribute to advancements which make the world a better place (Rudman, 2001).

The following chapters explore how societal and cultural perceptions and the language used to describe those perceptions of what women "ought to be" has a profound effect on women's ability to advance within their career, take positions of leadership, and conscript higher wages.

Chapter 5: Elizabeth Hoffmann and Chris Sahley write, "How Students Think about Women Professors: Enforcement of Hegemonic Femininity in Students' End-of-Term Evaluations." Hoffmann's study suggests women professors in Science, Technology, Engineering, and Math (STEM) suffer an erosion of their professional power because they receive lower than their male counterparts' numeric scores on students' end-of-term evaluations, and are evaluated by their students on their ability to conform to norms of hegemonic femininity as well as being fair in the classroom. The findings reflect student evaluations of female professors, demonstrate the tensions between gender norms and professional status, and may impact career progression when used as a metric for promotion and tenure decisions.

Chapter 6: Fatma Fulya Tepe and Per Bauhn explore "Explicit and Implicit Career Impediments for Women: The Case of Turkish Engineering Academia" from a phenomenological perspective. Interviews with sixteen women from the Turkish engineering academy uncover new research which suggests implicit career impediments do exist in Turkish academies and prevent women from rising to the top in their chosen field. Female academicians, aware of these implicit biases, developed coping strategies to deal with sexist career obstructions.

PART III: INSTITUTIONAL STRUCTURES WHICH REINFORCE WOMEN'S SECONDARY STATUS

Though formal laws against discrimination as a result of the Civil Rights Act of 1964 have reduced some forms of explicit bias, there still exist implicit biases equally detrimental to women's career progression (Cortina, 2013; Jones, 2016), acceptance into masculine workplace cultures (Schein, 1973; Heilman, 2012), abilities, skills, knowledge, and emotions as perceived by employers (Brescoll, 2008; Heilman, 2012), social status approval (Heilman, 2012; Eagly 1987, 2000; Rudman, 2004), and work-life balances (Kossek, 2006). Indirect bias, an automatic, involuntary, and uncontrollable unconscious process which flavors and colors an individual's thoughts, feelings, and actions against a social object, usually a person or a group, is the result of past experiences which have conditioned an individual to think about, chose options, or reflect negatively or positively about some group, person, phenomenon, event, or situation (Rudman 2004). The presence of indirect bias contributes to the inequity we find when noting women receive fewer extrinsic rewards such as making less money than men, receiving fewer promotions than men, and living in poverty more than men.

Clearly, seven decades of legislation to eradicate discrimination in the workplace has been ineffectual in correcting imbalances for many women who find the workplace inflexible when dealing with caregiver obligations, receiving promotions for career progression, earning comparable salaries as men for the same job, remaining underrepresented in STEM professions, and finding agencies and organizations lack commitment to changing unconscious gender and stereotypical perceptions about women in employment decisions and opportunities (U.S. Equal Employment Opportunity Commission, 2013).

Indirect bias leads to institutional bias which is the tendency to discriminate and leads to institutional discrimination which the act of discrimination. Agencies and organizations do not set out to incorporate indirect bias into their decision-making laws/policies/rules, but because primarily men in leadership positions make decisions affecting the agency's or organization's operation through financial, employment, benefit, and worksite decisions, the masculine acculturation they have experienced throughout their lives permeates the ways they think about themselves and others and drives decision making toward an unbalanced allocation of resources and results in inequitable power relationships which relegate women to secondary social and economic status. The top-of-the-heap, virile, aggressive, and testosterone-laden nature of male dominance is certainly not a new phenomenon and is traced to the hunter-gatherer society of yesteryear when men's physical prowess dominated the hunting scene while women gatherers planted and harvested crops and cared for offspring (Perez 2019). Little credence is given to the important and necessary role of women as communal mediators or their necessary cooperation to establish protection for group survival, and there exists less documentation of women's roles as warriors or artists.

Gender Bias Origins

Gender stereotypes evolved from the different social roles males and females adopted in order to sustain life through procreation and childrearing and protect themselves from external threats such as marauders, life-threatening weather events, and lack of sustenance (Eagly, 2000). Early origin theories center on the "basic or ultimate causes of sex differences" (Eagly, 1999, 408) which foster the age-old question of whether the chicken or egg came first; do psychological differences dictate social roles or do social roles dictate psychological differences. The first origin theory speaks to psychological roles which foment social roles based on the different sex-specific mechanisms of men and women such as physical protector and bearer of progeny. These primeval environments were built around procreation considered to be the main cause of sex-differentiation in sexual roles and behavior. Consequently associating men with physical prowess in protecting and providing for themselves and others and women with childbearing and nurturing abilities in order to ensure linage continuation led to different sex-typical roles in the home and at work (Eagly, 1999).

The second origin theory speaks to social structure roles of physical protector and bearer of progeny which lead to psychological differences and suggest the social roles men and women inhabit force them to accommodate to those roles. Changing social and cultural environments across the spectrum result because of "technological, ecological, and other transformations" (Eagly 1999, 409), and men and women adapt and respond to these "restrictions and opportunities" (Eagly 1999, 409) through sex-differentiated behavior leading to a societal division of labor between the sexes. The social structure origin theory takes into account the biological and physical differences of men and women as a mechanism which filters them into different social roles; men's physical prowess historically allowed them to do the heavy lifting while women's ability to nurse and care for children thrust them into caregiver roles. This division of labor in which men's roles led to assertive, aggressive, and controlling dominant behavior and women's roles led to accommodating, cooperative, and conciliatory behavior created efficiencies within society based on sex-specific skill sets. These sex-specific roles fostered expectations about socially approved male and female behaviors and the desirable attributes associated with each sex led to stereotypes of what men and women ought to be and how they should behave (Eagly, 1999).

From these stereotypical sex-specific roles emerges a gendered division of labor to which males and females are expected to conform. Individuals internalize gender roles as a part of acculturation in society and self-regulate their behavior to conform to familial and societal pressures to receive economic and societal rewards such as monetary compensation for work and acceptance within the group. Because individuals wish to maximize their own utility and achieve the most success in the most efficient manner, the assumption is that individual social interaction, as governed and constrained by social structures and institutions, such as families, organizations, markets, and governments, will lead to the most efficient outcomes in terms of economic, societal, and cultural preservation. This social view of how men and women are expected to act transfers to the worksite and is evident in the number of women in caregiving, nurturing, and lower-skilled jobs such as teaching, hospitality, and retail which tend to pay lower wages and have fewer benefits versus the number of men in highly skilled jobs such as construction and finance which tend to pay higher wages and have better benefits.

The following chapters deal with institutional reforms which address gender inequality. Institutional structures such as government policies and practices are often complicit in perpetuating and reinforcing gender inequality by shaping employment dynamics through indirect or unconscious bias.

Chapter 7: Lygia Sabbag Fares and Ana Luíza Matos de Oliveria explore how austerity measures implemented in 2017 by the Brazilian government impacted gender inequality in the Brazilian labor market. Their chapter, entitled "A Feminist Perspective on the 2017 Labor Reform in Brazil: Impacts on Higher Education Facility," seeks to explain the outcomes of reform measures two years out from the implementation of the measures on issues such as economic and non-economic benefits. They propose preliminary conclusions about the reform and its impacts on the perpetuation of gender inequalities at work.

Chapter 8: Marquita R. Walker and Armand Chevalier focus on indirect bias as a cause of historically generated gendered oppression leading to the marginalization and underrepresentation of women in the building trades in "Gender Equality in the Building Trades: International Laws' and Cultural Legitimacy's Effect on Indirect Bias." Situated in political economy theory, Walker and Chevalier argue the historic marginalization of women has a deleterious effect on the current hiring and retention of women in trades, and they make recommendations to correct these injustices.

Chapter 9: Zeynep Ceren Eren Benlisoy contributes to the gender discrimination literature through an exploration of the neoliberal re-structuring of global agri-food relations on small producers in rural Turkey by using a socialist-feminist perspective and feminist methodology that prioritizes women's agency/qualitative research techniques, fieldwork, participant observation, and in-depth interviews to construct "Gendered Agribusiness, Feminization of Work, and the Seeds of Empowerment: The Case of Women of the *Greenhouse*, Western Anatolia, Turkey." She concludes women of the *Greenhouse*, whose work is culturally feminized and serves as a reserve army of cheap labor, find and use coping strategies to transform and change their lives by undermining the role of male breadwinners, challenging the patriarchal barriers to increase their bargaining power, feeling self-confident, and establishing an alternative social network of their own.

Chapter 10: Lynn Duggan, Gracia Clark, and Marquita R. Walker analyze women's experiences in the building trades through the lens of tokenism in "Gender Dynamics in Midwestern Building Trades: Tokenism and Beyond." Their findings support the theory of tokenism which suggests higher sex ratios of women in construction would foster a climate more supportive of women and confirm hegemonic male organizational culture continues to discourage women's entry and retention in the building trades.

REFERENCES

1964. Title VII of the Civil Rights Act of 1964. In *42 U.S. code, chapter 21, section 1311*. Washington, DC: U.S. Equal Employment Opportunity Commission.

2018a. *Family and Medical Leave Act*, edited by US Department of Labor. Washington, DC: Wage and Hour Division.

2018b. *Highlights of women's earning in 2017*. Washington, DC: US Bureau of Labor Statistics.

Alkadry, M., & Tower, L. 2011. "Covert pay discrimination: How authority predicts pay differences between women and men." *Public Administration Review* 71(5):740–751. doi: 10.1111/j.1540-6210.2011.02413.x.

Becker, G. 1993. *Human capital: A theoretical and empirical analysis with special reference to education*. 3rd ed. Chicago and London: University of Chicago Press. Original edition, 1964.

Becker, G., & Tomes, N. 1985. "Human capital and the rise and fall of families." *Journal of Labor Economics* 4(3):Part 2: The family and the distribution of economic rewards.

Blau, R., & Khan, L. 2017. "The gender wage gap: Extent, trends, and explanations." *Journal of Economic Literature* 55(3):789–965. doi: 10.1257/jel.20160995.

Blumberg, R. 2008. "The invisible obstacle to educational equality: Gender bias in textbooks." *Prospects* 38(3):345–361. doi: 10.1007/s11125-009-9086-1.

Brescoll, V., & Uhlmann, E. 2008. "Can and angry woman get ahead? Conferral, gender, and expression of emotion in the workplace." *Psychological Science* 19(3):268–275.

Budig, M., & Hodges, M. 2010. "Difference in disadvantage: Variation in the motherhood penalty across white women's earnings distribution." *American Sociological Review* 75(5):705–728. doi: 10.1177/0003122410381593.

Bureau of Labor Statistics. 2016. *Table 32: Leave benefits: Access, civilian workers, March 2016*. Washington, DC: Bureau of Labor Statistics.

Catalyst. 2019. "Quick take: Women's earnings: The wage gap." Accessed August 7, 2019. https://www.catalyst.org/research/womens-earnings-the-wage-gap/.

Cortina, L., Kabat-Farr, D., Leskinen, E., Huerta, M., & Magley, V. 2013. "Selective incivility as modern discrimination in organizations: Evidence and impact." *Journal of Management* 39(6):1179–1605. doi: 10.1177/0149306311418835.

Crouse, G., & Waters, A. 2015. *Welfare indicators and risk factors: Fourteenth report to congress*. Washington, DC: Office of Human Services Policy.

Current Population Survey. 2019. *Table 39: Median weekly earnings of full-time wage and salary workers by detailed occupation and sex*. Bureau of Labor Statistics.

Eagly, A. 1987. *Sex differences in social behavior: A social-role interpretation*. Hillsdale, NJ: L. Erlbaum Associates.

Eagly, A., & Wood, W. 1999. "The origins of sex differences in human behavior." *America Psychologist* 54(6):408–423.

Eagly, A., Wood, W., & Dickman, A. 2000. "Social role theory of sex differences and similarities: A current appraisal." In *The developmental psychology of gender*, edited by T. Eckes & H. M. Trautner. Mahwah, NJ: Erlbaum.

Fass, S. 2009. *Paid leave in the states: A critical support for low-wage workers and their families*. New York, NY: National Center for Children in Poverty.

Fischer, J., & Hayes, J. 2013. *The importance of social security in the incomes of older Americans: Differences by gender, age, race/ethnicity, and marital status*. Washington, DC: Institute for Women's Policy Research (IWPR).

Flabbi, L., & Moro, A. 2012. "The effect of job flexibility on female labor market outcomes: Estimates from a search and bargaining model." *Journal of Econometrics* 168(1):81–95.

Fontenot, K., Semega, J., & Kolla, M. 2017. *Income and poverty in the United States: 2017.* Washington, DC: US Census Bureau, Current Population Survey.

Fontenot, K., Semega, J., & Kolla, M. 2018. Table A-4. In *Number and real median earnings of total workers and full-time, year-round workers by sex and female-to-male earnings ratio: 1960 to 2017,* edited by Income and Poverty in the United States: 2017. Washington, DC: U.S. Census Bureau.

Fortin, N. 2008. "The gender wage gap among young adults in the United States: The importance of money versus people." *The Journal of Human Resources* 43(4):884–918.

Fredrickson, C. 2015. *Under the bus: How working women are being run over.* New York: The New Press.

Gaucher, D., Friesen, J., & Kay, A. 2011. "Evidence that gendered wording in job advertisements exists and sustains gender inequality." *Journal of Personality and Social Psychology* 101(1):109–128. doi: 10.1037/a0022530.

Glauber, R. 2011. "Women's work and working conditions: Are mothers compensated for lost wages?" *Work and Occupations* 39(2):115–138. doi: 10.1177/0730888411422948.

Glick, P., & Fisk, S. 1999. "Sexism and other "isms": Interdependence, status, and the ambivalent content of stereotypes." In *Sexism and stereotypes in modern society: The gender science of Janet Taylor Spence,* edited by J. Langlois, W. Swann, & L. Gilbert, 193–221. Washington, DC: American Psychological Association.

Goldin, C. 2006. "The quiet revolution that transformed women's employment, education, and family." *American Economic Review* 96(2):1–21.

Goldin, C. 2014a. "A pollution theory of discrimination: Male and female differences in occupations and earnings." In *Human capital in history: The American record,* edited by C. Frydman, L. Boustan, & R. Margo, 313–348. Chicago: University of Chicago Press.

Goldin, C. 2014b. "A grand gender convergence: Its last chapter." *American Economic Review* 104(4):1091–1119. doi: 10.1257/aer.104.4.1091.

Gough, M., & Noonan, M. 2013. "A review of the motherhood wage penalty in the United States." *Sociology Compass* 7(4):328–342. doi: 10.1111/soc4.12031.

Graf, N., Brown, A., & Patten, E. 2019. *The narrowing, but persistent, gender gap in pay.* Washington, DC: Pew Research Center.

Hegewisch, A., & Hartmann, H. 2014. *Occupational segregation and the gender wage gap: A job half done.* Washington, DC: Institute for Women's Policy Research (IWPR).

Heilman, M. 2012. "Gender stereotypes and workplace bias." *Research in Organizational Behavior* 32:113–135. doi: 10.1016/j.robb.2012.11.003.

Hopcroft, R. 1996. "The authority attainment of women: Competitive sector effects." *American Journal of Economics and Sociology* 55(2):163–184.

Jones, K., Peddie, C., Gilrane, V., King, E., & Gray, A. 2016. "Not so subtle: A meta-analytic investigation of the correlates of subtle and overt discrimination." *Journal of Management* 42(6):1588–1613. doi: 10:1177/0149206313506466.

Kossek, E., Lautsch, B., & Eaton, S. 2006. "Telecommuting, control, and boundary management: Correlates of policy use and practice, job control, and work-family effectiveness." *Journal of Vocational Behavior* 68:347–367. doi: 10.1016/j.jvb.2005.07.002.

Leith, L. 2014. "Why do women still earn less than men?" *Monthly Labor Review* 137:1.

Lips, Hilary M. 2013. "The gender pay gap: Challenging the rationalizations. Perceived equity, discrimination, and the limits of human capital models." *Sex Roles* 68(3):169–185. doi: 10.1007/s11199-012-0165-z.

Loscocco, K., & Bird, S. 2012. "Gendered paths: Why women lag behind men in small business success." *Work and Occupations* 39(2):183–219. doi: 10.1177/0730888412444282.

Madera, J. 2009. "Gender and letters of recommendation for academia: Agentic and communal differences." *Journal of Applied Psychology* 94(6):1591–1599. doi: 10.1037/a0016539.

Menegatti, M., & Rubini, M. 2017. "Gender bias and sexism in language." *Communication*:1–24. doi: 10.1093/acrefore/9780190228613.013.470.

Miller, K., & Vagins, D. 2018. *The simple truth about the gender pay gap.* Washington, DC: American Association of University Women (AAUW).

Morrison, A., White, R., & Van Velsor, E. 1992. *Breaking the glass ceiling: Can women reach the top of America's largest corporations?* Reading, MA: Addison-Wesley.

Noonan, M., Corcoran, M., & Courant, P. 2005. "Pay differences among the highly trained: Cohort differences in the sex gap in lawyer's earnings." *Social Forces* 84(2):853–872.

Perez, C. 2019. *Invisible women: Data bias in a world designed for men.* New York, NY: Abrams.

Rose, S., & Hartmann, H. 2004. *Still a men's labor market: The long-term earnings gap.* Washington, DC: Institute for Women's Policy Research (IWPR).

Rudman, A., & Glick, P. 1999. "Feminized management and backlash toward agentic women: The hidden costs to women of a kinder, gentler, image of middle managers." *Journal of Personality and Social Psychology* 77(5):1004–1010. doi: 10.1037/0022-3514.77.5.1004.

Rudman, A., & Glick, P. 2001. "Prescriptive gender stereotypes and backlash toward agentic women." *Journal of Social Sciences* 57(4):743–762.

Rudman, L. 2004. "Social justice in our minds, homes, and society: The nature, causes, and consequences of implicit bias." *Social Justice Research* 17:129–142.

Saad-Lessler, J., & Bahn, K. 2017. *The importance of paid leave for caregivers.* Washington, DC: Center for American Progress.

Schaffer, D., & Westenberg, J. 2019. "Time flexibility, women's wages, and the gender wage gap." *Atlantic Economic Journal* 47(2):217–239.

Schein, V. 1973. "The relationship between sex role stereotypes and requisite management characteristics." *Journal of Applied Psychology* 57(2):95–100. doi: 10.1037/h0037128.

Stout, J., & Dasgupta, N. 2011. "When he doesn't mean you: Gender-exclusive language as ostracism." *Personality and Social Psychology Bulletin* 37(6):757–769. doi: 10.1177/0146167211406434.

Stromquist, N., Lee, M., & Brock-Utne, B. 1998. "The explicit and the hidden school curriculum." In *Women in the third world: An encyclopedia of contemporary issues*, edited by N. P. Stromquist & K. Monkman, 397–407. New York: Garland Publishing Inc.

U.S. Bureau of Labor Statistics. 2019a. "Employed persons by occupation, sex, and age." In *Labor force statistics from the Current Population Survey*, edited by Annual Averages Household Data, 9. Washington, DC: US Department of Labor.

U.S. Bureau of Labor Statistics. 2019b. "The Economics Daily." In *Current population survey*, edited by Median weekly earnings for second quarter 2019 increased by 3.7 percent over the year. Washington, DC: US Department of Labor.

U.S. Equal Employment Opportunity Commission. 2013. *EEOC women's work group report*. Washington, DC: US Equal Employment Opportunity Commission.

Walker, M. R. 2014. *The daily grind: How workers navigate the employment relationship*. Lanham, MA: Lexington.

Williams, K., & Zadro, L. 2005. "Ostracism: The indiscriminate early detection system." In *The social outcast: Ostracism, social exclusion, rejection, and bullying*, edited by J. Forgas K. Williams & W. von Hippel, 19–34. New York, NY: Psychology Press.

Part I

THE GENDER WAGE GAP

Chapter 1

Precarious Employment Intersecting with Gender

Are Women Punished More?

Anil Duman

INTRODUCTION

A growing share of populations both in the developed and developing parts of the world are going through labor market transformations including the growth of nonstandard forms of employment. These range from part-time work to temporary contracts to informal sector jobs, and even though there are important differences with regards to risks and uncertainties they contain, all these non-standard forms of employment are demarcated as precarious. Not only do such jobs mean lower wages and fewer social security benefits, they also are claimed to have negative health consequences (Vosko, 2009; Kim et al., 2008). While precarious employment is on average rising across the globe, there are still vital differences in terms of their composition and which social groups are mostly affected by these changes. For example, it is well documented that women are overrepresented in part-time jobs almost in every economy, and in most developed countries, the incidence of temporary employment is higher for female workers (ILO, 2016). The uneven distribution of atypical jobs across gender has several explanations. In some countries, flexibilization reforms are passed with the goal of encouraging female labor force participation. Gendered divisions of labor and traditional norms about caregiving responsibilities of women reduce their bargaining power. Moreover, such beliefs intensify the existing stereotypes about productivity and effort in the labor market and cause occupational segregation (Vosko, 2009; Grimshaw, 2011).

There are various studies underlining the differences between standard and non-standard forms of employment in terms of wages, social security benefits, working hours, health outcomes, training opportunities, and collective bargaining (Duman, 2019; Gash and McGinnity, 2007). The greater representation of women in precarious jobs means that gender inequalities could be worsened in the absence of remedial policies. However, in many developing countries such as Turkey, non-standard forms of employment are still not dominated by women. This is mainly due to the low female labor force participation rates, especially for women with less than university degree. Yet, in these countries females still can be overrepresented in other types of precarious positions such as employment in the informal sector and unpaid family work. Moreover in most of these societies, there are rigid gender roles, and a traditional division of labor continues to dominate the policy making as well as the practical outcomes in the labor markets. For example, women in Turkey have much lower rates of participation in the formal sector employment, which is the result of lack of education, inadequate childcare services, and patriarchal culture (İlkkaracan, 2012). However, there are a lot of women in the informal sector whose jobs range from seasonal agricultural work to home-based production. The prevalence of family-related and home-based work is attributed to the consideration of these as an extension of women's domestic obligations and not clashing with the family duties including child and elderly care (Tartanoğlu, 2018). While there are differences in precariousness of female workers according to their educational and cultural backgrounds, prioritizing household responsibilities and various forms of discrimination by the employers are common to all.

In this chapter, we argue that even when women do not constitute the majority of precarious employment as in the Turkish case, the consequences are still disproportionately negative for them in comparison to their male counterparts with similar jobs. Overall, our investigation points out several disadvantages for female workers in the Turkish labor market. Women have much lower possibilities of finding waged and salaried work, which can be seen from the low female participation rates and declining full-time employment. If they become part of the labor force, they pay larger penalties and face discrimination. All the women in precarious employment highlighted the importance of rigid gender roles ascribed to them with regards to household responsibilities. Their caretaking duties intensify the existing poor working conditions and put them in even more disadvantageous positions as opposed to their male counterparts. Their inability to participate in collective bargaining and unionization, biased attitudes in the workplace, and extremely restricted exit options are found to be the other fundamental hindrances experienced by the female workers in precarious employment.

As a result, they suffer from low wages, limited social benefits, and serious threat of job loss risks. While the chapter focuses on Turkey, similar results can be drawn for other developing countries with enduring gender inequalities particularly with respect to distribution of paid and unpaid work. The increase in precarious jobs in such societies disproportionatly hurt women and worsens their already unfavorable economic status. Hence, not only the quantity but also the quality of jobs should be the focus of policy making if the goals are to enhance gender equality and empowering women.

The chapter is divided into four sections. In the second part, we first review the factors behind the higher penalties for women in insecure jobs with an emphasis on undervaluation of female work and gendered division of household responsibilities. Then, we discuss the overall gender differences in the labor market and more specifically precarious employment in Turkey. In the third part, we qualitatively examine the reasons why precarious jobs are more penalizing for women in Turkey based on the interviews conducted among several female employees in temporary and informal positions across different sectors. Three dimensions of precariousness, reconciliation of work and life, attitudes in the workplace, and collective representation and their consequences in terms of wages, benefits, and job security, are considered. The final section offers concluding remarks and discusses the general implications of the findings for other developing countries. Also included are policy suggestions that can help to raise gender equality and improve the working conditions of women.

LITERATURE REVIEW AND PRECARIOUS EMPLOYMENT IN TURKEY

Overview of Precarious Employment and Its Impact on Women

The definitions of *precarious employment* among researchers vary and different scholars emphasize different aspects ranging from low pay to nonstandard character of contracts to limited social benefits and statutory entitlements. Despite the alternative descriptions, precarious employment typically includes all the jobs that are insecure and poorly paid rendering the workers without adequate opportunities to support a household (Rodgers and Rodgers, 1986; Vosko, 2000). Populations in the developed and developing world are going through labor market flucuations. Not only is the proportion of workers under the regulatory and social protective systems in developed countries declining but also the legal definition of *employment* is becoming more blurred with the advancement of solo self-employment, contracted work, and platform economy. In developing countries, informal employment proves to be persistent alongside an increasing share of temporary, seasonal, and subcontracted employment.

The normalization of nonstandard employment across the globe makes it necessary to bridge the concepts of temporary contracts and informality. Even though the proponents of new forms of employment suggest various benefits can accrue to workers such as better reconciliation of work and life and higher control over work schedules, it is shown that non-standard employment, on average, has lower quality and less security than permanent employment, and workers in these jobs face more interrupted careers (Olsthoorn, 2013; Aleksynska, 2018; Duman, 2019).

Flexibilization in labor markets is partly supported to give several disadvantaged groups, such as women, more opportunities for employment. The possibility of combining work and domestic responsibilities and control over working hours and schedules are claimed to be very beneficial for female workers (Evans, 2001). Women across all countries assume a greater share of unpaid work including child and elderly care. It is impossible to separate the reproductive economy from the productive economy to fully grasp the functioning of labor markets. The greater representation of women in non-standard jobs is often explained by the interplay between productive and reproductive economies, and it is argued that women voluntarily opt for part-time and temporary employment so they can reconcile work and household duties (Booth et al., 2002). However, it should be noted that the voluntary nature of non-standard employment is dependent on contextual factors and in a number of countries, women have to select either part-time or temporary positions given the difficulties in finding full-time formal sector jobs (Petrongolo, 2004; Duman, 2019). Furthermore, a significant number of women in non-standard employment report caregiving as the reason they self-select into nonstandard employment as opposed to men, who choose flexible arrangements to advance their education or other personal goals (Cranford et al., 2003). There are crucial differences across gender for selecting into non-standard jobs and the likely outcomes these jobs generate.

A big part of the gender pay gap is attributed to discrimination including occupational segregation. Several forms of discrimination are identified in the literature that can affect gender composition of occupations as well as returns in the labor market. This leads not only certain low-paid sectors and occupations to be dominated by women but also undervaluation of female work and persistence of segregation (Wright et al., 1995). For example, in every country, care services and jobs on short-ladder career professions are largely represented by women; organizational norms and lack of rewards contribute to women earning lower wages than their male counterparts (Young, 2010). Another source of discrimination against women is the belief that female workers behave distinctly and cannot manage stress and demanding tasks (Booth and Nolen, 2012). The gendered assumptions concerning risk behavior and responsibility can severely impede women's career advancements. Women might not be given the tasks essential for career advancement or long-term relationships if they are believed to be less competitive. In addition to the observable differences in education, occupation, and work history, the unexplained portion of the gender wage gap is considerable and increasing (Blau and Kahn, 2017).

Moreover, women might self-select into occupations that enable them to reconcile work and family life and accept lower-paying jobs with flexible hours and other desirable features. But the educational and occupational choices of women could also affect social norms and expectations in return. Employers might statistically discriminate against female workers by considering their average performance rather than individual performance. Employers often project the higher turnover rates for women because of family responsibilities as lack of commitment and offer lower wages. Additionally, societal expectations with respect to gender-specific competences and skills affect the perceptions about productivity of women and their earnings (Meurs and Ponthieux, 2015). We argue that the level of discrimination is even higher in precarious jobs since there are limited legal and collective protections. While gender-based exclusion and incomplete recognition of effort and productivity can occur under any contract type, the negative effects of such attitudes at the workplace are more detrimental in precarious positions since the mechanisms to improve working conditions are weak. Legal and collective protections in temporary and informal jobs are very limited or nonexistent, and imply that women who face discrimination do not have the statutory rights and bargaining power to mitigate the adverse effects.

The last dimension of precariousness is collective representation. Trade unions and collective bargaining have multiple benefits for workers ranging from higher wages to job security. For example, even in Turkey where trade union density and collective bargaining coverage are quite low, there is 14 percent wage premium (Duman and Duman, 2016). Moreover, there is a negative correlation between the regulatory strength of wage-setting institutions and low-paid employment (Lucifora et al., 2005). Collective representation and centralized wage bargaining alleviate some of the negative consequences of precarious employment either by improving the material and social benefits or by decreasing the share of atypical jobs in the economy. Nevertheless, there are various problems in relation to agency and representation of women in trade unions and other forms of workers' organizations. Some argue employees in precarious jobs do not necessarily see trade unions as representing their interests due to insider-outsider divides (Park, 2016). Certain groups such as women are not equally represented in the existing collective bodies.

This is very much related to occupational and sectoral segregation women face as discussed previously. In the majority of the jobs female employees hold, such as low value-added services, unionization is not widespread (Grimshaw, 2011). The combination of poor wages and lack of legal protections is a result and outcome of collective representation making precarious jobs enduring, and since women have a greater share of these positions, they are stuck with unrewarding careers more than their male counterparts. Also, the size of the enterprise is an important driver of collective representation, and women tend to be employed in smaller-sized firms (Kalleberg et al., 2000). Employees of larger firms can unionize more easily, and, in return, can have larger benefits from collective organization due to size. This can promote solidarity and inclusionary attitudes toward members. Since women in precarious employment are less likely to belong to large firms, they receive fewer benefits, if any at all, from collective bargaining and trade unions. Additionally, they have fewer exit options which can impede their ability and willingness to join if there is a hostile stance by the employers toward collective organizations.

Due to caretaking responsibilities, attitudes at the workplace, and lack of collective representation and bargaining power, non-standard employees and particularly women get low wages and benefits and experience high job insecurity. For example, I assert temporary contracts affect earnings differently not only along the distribution but also across gender. Definitely nonstandard forms of work can be unfavourable for both males and females, and in the previous studies, it is widely recognized that atypical contracts decrease earnings across countries even after controlling for a number of individual- and firm-level characteristics (Duman, 2019; Garnero et al., 2016). Nonetheless, we suggest that atypical jobs could affect gender wage gap in numerous ways through altering the careers of men and women distinctly and deepening the already existing gender segregation in the labor market. Female workers are believed to choose non-standard employment to juggle their household and work responsibilities. Such a perception not only locks them into temporary, part-time, and other atypical contractual arrangements but also potentially increases discrimination and undervaluation of women's work. Together with less representation in trade unions and collective bargaining, the negative effects for female workers in nonstandard jobs are intensified and lead to marginalization and deteriorating working conditions. Given the various dimensions of risks related to the security of employment, incomes, and social relations, these jobs can be easily considered as precarious, and their precariousness intersect with gender.

Gender and Precarious Employment in Turkey

Despite the strong legal framework and long history of women's movement, Turkey's performance with regards to various measures of gender equality is gloomy. In 2019, the country ranked as 130th among 153 nations, and its

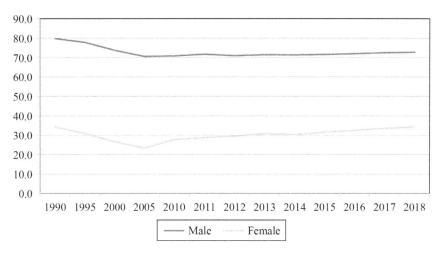

Figure 1.1   Labor Force Participation across Gender. *Source*: Author's calculation based on TUİK (nd).

score was especially low in economic participation and opportunity (WEF, 2020). As can be seen from the figure 1.1 below, female labor force participation has been always below male participation, but the gap persisted over time and in 2018, only 34.2 percent of women were active in the labor market as opposed to nearly 73 percent of men. The stagnation of the manufacturing sector in the 1990s, the resulting decreases in industrial employment, and the frequent economic recessions during the first years of the 2000s were the primary factors behind the fall in female labor force participation. By the 1990s global value chains and outsourcing grew immensely, and Turkish manufacturing companies were integrated into the global economic order through these mechanisms. With subcontracting and outsourcing, a big part of the textile factories in Turkey began to offer home-based schemes and piecemeal work to women instead of offering full-time and formal sector jobs (Ecevit, 1990). However, it should be noted there are crucial variances among women according to their educational background. For example, labor force participation for female university graduates was more than 70 percent while the ratio was less than 25 percent for women with primary schooling (TUİK, nd).

Not only do Turkish women suffer from low labor market participation, but they also are overburdened with household responsibilities. Figure 1.2 presents ratios of time spent on paid and unpaid work by women to men. While all the selected countries perform badly in terms of gender parity, clearly unpaid work allocated to women in Turkey is much worse. Females spend nearly 4.5 times more time on unpaid work compared to men, and 0.37 times on paid work, which show the economic disadvantages they experience. The

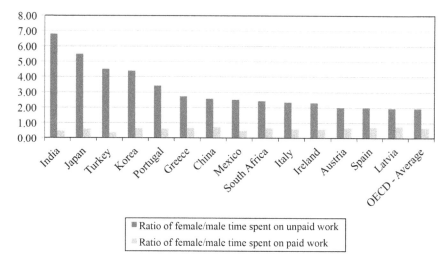

Figure 1.2   Paid and Unpaid Work across Gender. *Source*: Author's calculation based on OECD.Stat. (nd).

male breadwinner model and patriarchal social relations are the bases of the gendered division of labor and for the lack of opportunities for women to take part in waged and salaried economic activities (İlkkaracan, 2012). Like many developing countries with export-led industrialization, Turkey also went through a feminization of labor markets, particularly in cities where women took part in different stages of production processes. But such developments did not alter the severely adverse conditions for women and gender norms. In fact, informal sector employment and the mentioned subcontracting schemes reinforced the patriarchal social relations and gendered division of labor as females were mostly employed in low-paid jobs with limited social benefits and no prospects of advancement.

Nonstandard contracts, temporary, casual, and part-time work are regarded as the main forms of precarious employment in developed countries. However, in developing countries, the work-related risks cannot be adequately captured if the informal sector is not considered. Figure 1.3 shows the share of precarious employment since 2010 in Turkey across gender. All jobs not in the formal sector, permanent, or full-time are included in the category of precariousness. It is evident there is a small reduction in precarious employment for men, which went down from almost 26 percent to nearly 20 percent between 2020 and 2017. The ratio for women has remained stagnant around 25 percent for the entire period with a slight reduction until 2014 and then full recovery. Women with low education are heavily represented among the informal and temporary workers and are the main source of cheap labor for subcontracting firms and service providers. Like other developing countries,

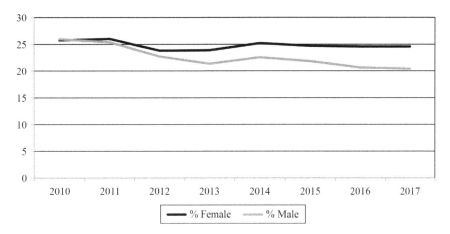

Figure 1.3   Precarious Employment across Gender. *Source*: Author's calculation based on Labor Force Surveys.

poorer socioeconomic status of women decreases their reservation wages and makes them the workforce of choice in labor-intensive sectors (Kidder and Raworth, 2004).

Turkey's manufacturing firms resorted to cost-cutting measures to remain globally competitive, and reduced labor costs through informal arrange-ments and home-based schemes utilizing female workers (Tartanoğlu, 2018; Hattatoğlu and Tate, 2016). Also, internal migration and urbanization in Turkey, which escalated in the 1980s and 1990s, caused low-educated women formerly employed in the agricultural sector to become unemployed as they migrated to cities, further decreasing the reservation wages. Additionally females involved in unpaid family work and home-based care work not regu-lated by legal frameworks and not covered by social security put them into extremely volatile positions and reproduce the socioeconomic inequalities.

Finally, I look at the wage differences between males and females in pre-carious jobs for selected years. As can be observed from table 1.1, men earn more than women for the time period, and the gap increased significantly from 2010 to 2017. While female employees in precarious employment received 92 percent of the wages men received in similar positions in 2010, the ratio went down to 81 percent in 2017. This supports our argument about higher disadvantages for women in precarious jobs. Clearly, temporary contracts and informal sector work decrease the wages for both genders, but the table above indicates that women are disproportionately penalized. Particularly, informal sector employment is a major aspect of precariousness in Turkey since these jobs are not covered by social security and fall out of the scope of regulations. As discussed widely, female employees are respon-sible for household duties and the lack of publicly affordable care services is

Table 1.1   **Average Wages across Gender**

	Male Wage	Female Wage	Ratio of Female to Male Wages
2010	472.02	433.81	0.92
2011	525.26	472.21	0.90
2012	587.35	521.74	0.89
2013	655.39	560.82	0.86
2014	761.52	616.28	0.81
2015	833.77	685.63	0.82
2016	984.32	828.07	0.84
2017	1124.45	909.13	0.81

Source: Author's calculation based on Labor Force Surveys.

a fundamental barrier to their entrance and continuance into the labor market (Orhan-Karaalp, 2017). It is less expensive for women in low-paid jobs to leave the labor market after they give birth since childcare is costly, and there are few publicly funded childcare facilities. Partly due to their caretaking duties and partly due to the absence of enough secure and formal sector jobs, Turkish women opt for atypical forms of employment. However, these jobs increase their vulnerability given the low pay and lack of social security and legal protections. In addition, precarious employment of females in Turkey strengthens the patriarchal social relations as they leave traditional roles of child and elderly care and everyday household tasks to women and aggravate the biased perceptions in the society (Aktaş, 2013).

FINDINGS FROM THE INTERVIEWS WITH WOMEN IN PRECARIOUS EMPLOYMENT

Description of the Interview Process and Participants

To understand the experiences of women in precarious positions and reflect their views on working conditions, I interviewed female employees from different occupations and sectors in Turkey. Interviewing is among the most used methods in qualitative research, and given its flexible structure, it enables us to collect in-depth information about the dimensions of precarious employment under consideration (Sarantakos, 2005). There is no consensus on the meaning of precariousness, but all jobs that deviate from the norm of regular, secure, and permanent wage work can be regarded as such. In line with Rodgers's and Vosko's definitions, questions on reconciliation of work and life, attitudes at the work place, and collective representation are asked to capture the economic, social, organizational, and temporal aspects of precarious employment (Rodgers and Rodgers, 1983; Vosko, 2010). I used purposive sampling defined as the non-probability sampling method based on the characteristics of the population and the research objective (Sarantakos, 2005). Since our main goal is to understand the effects of precarious employment for female workers in Turkey, I talked to five women who have temporary contracts or are in the informal sector. Certainly, there are other employment categories viewed precarious such as teleworkers and participants of the gig economy. However, as discussed in the earlier section, the dominant forms of precarious employment in Turkey are temporary and informal sector jobs. Even though five interviews are not necessarily representative of the Turkish labor market, our findings are still generalizable as they focus on the core dimensions of precarity and its interaction with gender.

For confidentiality reasons, the names of the participants are not revealed, and they are referred by consecutive numbers. Table 1.2 summarizes the profiles of the interviewees. In terms of their age, all interviewees are in the prime working age group, ranging from twenty-eight years old to fifty-two years old. One of the participants is divorced without children and four participants are married with children. Among the mothers, two of them have children below the age of six, which is the typical age to start primary schooling in Turkey. Both stated the children are going to kindergarten but still need to spend some time with grandmothers until the mothers return home from work. On the weekends, all mothers said they are responsible for the household duties including child and elderly care. Two of the participants have university educations, two others graduated from high school, and one participant has a primary school degree. The type of precarious jobs among the interviewees differs as three of them have social security coverage, and their contracts are fixed term. One of the participants is working for an informal firm without contract or social security coverage. The remaining interviewee is called for work whenever there is demand. Lastly, the work experience of the respondents is between five and thirty-two years, and only

Table 1.2   Summary of Participants

	Age	Education	Marital Status	Children	Employment
Interviewee 1	36	University	Married	Yes, under the age of six	Temporary
Interviewee 2	33	High school	Married	Yes, under the age of six	Informal sector and on-demand
Interviewee 3	41	Primary school	Divorced	No	Informal Sector
Interviewee 4	28	University	Married	Yes	Temporary
Interviewee 5	52	High school	Married	Yes	Temporary

one out of the five has a permanent position since the beginning of their labor market history.

DIMENSIONS AND OUTCOMES OF PRECARIOUS EMPLOYMENT

Reconciliation of Work and Life

One of the issues repeatedly voiced to support atypical contracts is the flexibility it provides to employees, particularly accommodations for nonwork-related duties. Control over working hours and schedules are argued to provide women with the opportunities to reconcile their household duties and work (Evans, 2001). However, interview observations suggest no precarious forms of employment are giving the women the mentioned advantages. In contrast, women rely on informal networks to combine their domestic responsibilities and work. According to one of the participants, there is also difference across jobs and her ability to reconcile deteriorated over time. She says:

> In my previous job I was able to work with some flexibility and the boss was nice to let me go whenever there was something that I needed to attend for my kid. The new job requires me to work for much longer hours and now I have to completely rely on my mom and my mother-in-law. They are helpful and love to spend time with their grandkid, however, they are old and don't have the energy to handle a five year old. I wish my current boss is more understanding.

This is partly related to the lax enforcement of labor law in Turkey since overtime is regulated on paper, but there are hardly any penalties for violation. For example, among the Organisation for Economic Co-operation and Development (OECD) countries, Turkey has the highest share of people, 23.3 percent, reporting they work over sixty hours a week (OECD, 2020). Long working hours in precarious jobs without adequate compensation put women in an extremely disadvantageous position as they need to allocate limited amounts of time to their jobs and children.

This point is echoed by another interviewee whose experience highlights the greater risk of precarious employment for women. It is stated that care responsibilities are one of the reasons female workers accept flexible arrangements, yet, when the support mechanisms are missing, they would be trapped in these positions (Young, 2010). She said:

> I didn't know what I would have done if my mom was not picking up my son after school and taking care of him. Some evenings I arrive home at 9 pm

because I cannot leave the office before rush hour and there is always traffic on the bridge. His father works until 6 pm and takes him home but until then someone needs to be with my son. I even tried to hire a part-time caregiver, no luck there though. I know that some of my colleagues are staying at work even later than I do but they are men and are not expected to go back home and take care of their children. It is still the mothers' duty in my society.

The struggle to reconcile work and life is also asserted by another participant, which is mostly attributed to the strong gendered division of labor in Turkey and lack of childcare facilities.

My children are teenagers now and hardly need much attention by their parents. So, things got a little easier for me but I remember the days when I was trying to juggle everything. A full-time job and little kids are not something that a woman can handle lightly. The pre-schools are expensive, and I don't earn enough to afford a good one. I was spending my entire out of work time taking care of my kid, and still consider myself lucky because I was able to find a public pre-school in my neighborhood. Tending children, cooking, cleaning and on top of all that working is what we women do here.

Attitudes at the Workplace

Traditional segregation theories demonstrate women are overrepresented in certain jobs and occupations. Moreover, they are not given the same opportunities as men for lucrative positions even if they have the same levels of human capital (Wright et al., 1995). In addition to the observable instances of discrimination, women can also be subject to prejudices and hostile atmosphere in the workplace (Blau and Kahn, 2017; Meurs and Ponthieux, 2015). Our findings based on the responses are mixed; there are participants reporting their employers are biased and negatively treat them. While there are no references to overt discrimination in terms of lack of promotion or unequal pay for the same job, favoritism and harassment are voiced by two of the participants. Interviewee 4 reports it is not only the employers but also fellow workers giving the sense of exclusion. She says:

My sense is there is an old boy's club in the company and men including superiors hang out a lot. Perhaps I am wrong and no one is having personal relations beyond work but at least that is the impression I am getting from them and their casual way of conversing. I usually go out with my female coworkers to lunch at after work or over the weekends none of us have spare time. If there are social events, we are not invited.

Another interviewee complains about the inappropriate behavior of her boss and his firmness on monitoring them. She explains:

> The owner of the shop is always there checking on us and making us uncomfortable. I have been in this shop for 6 years and he keeps doing this. Not even sure if he doesn't trust us or he is a control freak. I and my coworkers become overtly alert and we try to watch our behavior all the time. I also know that some of my colleagues had other problems with him, not me though. He was asking them to hang out after work and didn't like it when they declined.

There are also participants expressing positive views about the bosses and coworkers. Interviewee 1 is quite content about her work environment, however, feels there is some favoritism in terms of task allocation. She says:

> I cannot complain about the general work environment as everyone more or less has the same type of problems and I don't feel any particular employee is favored. But, whenever there are additional tasks that need to be picked up, usually our male friends are approached by the management. Maybe, this is because the managers are trying to be nice to women thinking that we are already overburdened by other chores. However, it would feel better if they consider us too, especially given that the readiness for extra work seems to be important for promotions and we are not even provided with the chance.

For Interviewee 5, the drawbacks of precarious employment are shared by all the people in the firm, and there is harmony among the coworkers. She explains:

> People in the office are usually very friendly and we try to hang out after work hours whenever we can. But most of the time we end up talking about our problems at work, especially our uncertain futures and how much we want to move to another country, including the superiors.

Given the differentiated opinions on the attitudes at the workplace, it is hard to conclude that all female employees in precarious jobs go through the same discriminatory practices. There is a lot of variation depending on the employer and fellow workers, even for issues that should be regulated by law such as sexual harassment.

Collective Representation

The presence of collective representation through trade unions or work councils can have major effects on wages and nonpecuniary benefits by increasing the bargaining power of their members (Duman and Duman, 2016). Nevertheless, it is argued that women, especially in low-paid jobs, are protected less by the collective bodies in comparison to men (Vosko, 2000; Grimshaw, 2011). The interview results are contradictory with regards to union membership as one of the participants indicates she had no trouble in joining a union, but the union she chose is not able to collectively negotiate wages and working conditions with the firm since it doesn't have the highest number of members.

I am a union member and actually decided to become a member after one of the strikes female workers undertook last year to be part of this organization. It first sparked my interest and then I started to follow more closely their efforts. Unfortunately, my union doesn't have the right to represent us in collective bargaining. Fixed-term contract workers can be included in collective agreements as far as I know but the union I belong doesn't have the membership numbers that is necessary to be in the bargaining table.

With the recent changes in 2015, a union has the right to take part in collective bargaining if it represents at least 1 percent of the workers in an occupation and has the majority of the employees in an enterprise as members (Özkan, 2017). It should be also remembered that in Turkey, workers face serious threats of job loss if they join unions, especially in sectors which are not traditionally unionized.

In sharp contrast to the previous assessment, Interviewee 3 mentions there is no collective representation, and this is for everyone in her firm. She reiterates:

There is no chance of unions even coming to my workplace let alone collective bargaining and representation. The whole country's attitude is horrible on these issues; I don't think it is just my boss or managers. I recently had a friend who was fired because he was trying to organize his fellows in his union. He will go to the court but I am not hopeful about the result, even if he wins how he is going to earn a living. Also, I should say that no union ever contacted me and I didn't hear from my coworkers in other firm in this sector that any union representatives visiting. I wonder if they care about employees like us, people in bad jobs. They seem to rather cooperate with the state and do nothing.

A similar point is raised by Interviewee 2 who asserts that there is no talk of unionization and more broadly no organization that can address grievances. Her explanation is:

Thanks to my friends and family I can survive. My job is nerve wracking and sometimes I am thankful that it is not permanent or full-time. There is no mechanism in the work place that I can complain about the unrealistic demands and whenever I try to speak to the boss, she dismisses my worries and tells me that it is the normal procedure. As an agency worker I don't even know what my rights are.

These responses are quite in line with the arguments made in the literature on how precarious employees do not view trade unions as contributors to job protection and equality (Park, 2016).

Consequences of Precarious Employment: Wages, Benefits, and Job Security

Low wages, limited benefits such as unemployment insurance and paid holidays, and higher job insecurity are among the most distinguishing characteristics of precarious employment (Vosko, 2000; Kalleberg, 2011). The interviewees highlighted job insecurity, no social benefits, and lack of statutory rights as the most crucial problems they are facing. One of the interviewees mentioned her employer is not offering her social security coverage even though there are others in the firm with these benefits and implicitly threatens her with job loss. She clarifies:

I don't have a pension and other type of protections because the employers don't want to pay the social security tax. Whenever I raise the issue, they avoid talking about it and implicitly tell me to look for other jobs if I am not happy. I have to put up with this kind of attitude and my chances are so small in the job market. I don't have a good education, I am getting older, and my employers know that I won't be able to find another job in this crisis times. There are others who are registered to social security but honestly I don't know how they managed to get those deals.

In Turkey, over 33 percent of the employees are in the informal sector without legally binding contracts and social security registration, and the ratio is slightly higher for women, which implies they face greater losses.

Another participant raises concern about the temporal risks, particularly the uncertainty regarding the continuity of employment and protection against job loss (Rodgers and Rodgers, 1986). She emphasizes the problem of finding suitable employment and how the risks grew due to increasing unemployment rates in Turkey as well as low wages. She says:

I don't think I have many options. I could try to get a job in one of the local agencies but I don't think any of them are hiring, if anything they are laying people off right now. This is very worrisome for me. I have little savings and have to rely on them if I am fired. There is no safety net, no pensions. There are many other people like me but there are also people with better jobs and they are not more qualified than I am. And they don't have to look after kids or their in-laws. My family is helping but I want to earn enough money on my own and I don't want to feel persistently anxious. I don't even have the energy and time to search for an additional job to make ends meet.

It is evident that not only is she suffering from irregularity of work but also from not having social security protection and low earnings. This observation can be generalized in the Turkish context since female workers with temporary and informal sector jobs experience significant reductions in their wages, especially among the low educated (Duman, forthcoming).

For one of the interviewees, the deteriorating working conditions and low pay are the key difficulties in her current job.

Initially I was working as a bank teller. The job started at 8 am and sometime went until late at night. When I became pregnant, it became very difficult to meet the requirements and the managers were not helpful at all. After I gave birth, they didn't offer me paid leave and I was basically let go. I had a lot of health problems at the time and was away from the job market for a while. After I returned, I only could do jobs that were mediocre and didn't pay well. Having a family is expensive, and the prices are skyrocketing over the last years. We struggle to pay for our fixed expenses let alone going on vacations or saving. The employers want us to work constantly with little money.

However, another participant evaluates her situation more positively, especially in relation to the broader labor market conditions in Turkey. She says:

I consider myself lucky although my job is not a good one, at least I have one. The university graduates are not able to find employment nowadays or work for minimum wage. I also make minimum wage, which is of course not sufficient to have decent living standards. Yet, I feel the young people with college degrees should get more. So, I am not looking for a different job and don't know if I will do that in the future.

CONCLUSION AND POLICY RECOMMENDATIONS

This chapter assesses the relationship between nonstandard employment and gender in terms of precariousness and variation of negative consequences between women and men. The majority of the literature posits precarious jobs are disproportionately allocated to female workers;. I reviewed the case of Turkey, an example of a labor market with relatively equal proportions of men and women in atypical positions. Observations reflect Turkish women experience low benefits and wages and higher job loss risks. Additionally, women experience greater difficulties in finding waged and salaried work, and after they find such work, they pay larger penalties and face discrimination. Interview results indicate women's rigid gender roles and caretaking responsibilities put them in extremely disadvantageous positions. Their work is undervalued, and they face discrimination at the workplace. They do not have control over their work schedules and cannot easily reconcile paid and unpaid duties. The impact of structural conditions in the Turkish labor market as well as the lower representation of women in trade unions means reservation wages are quite low and exit options are highly restricted. Therefore, the non-standard jobs become precarious jobs for women, and they experience larger penalties in terms of earnings, job security, and benefits in comparison to men in Turkey.

It is well known there are various barriers hindering women's labor force participation and employment opportunities in Turkey. From the supply side, household responsibilities including child and elderly care heavily fall on women. Also, there are still educational gaps across genders in Turkey especially at the upper secondary level. From the demand side, discrimination in the labor market, constraints for entrepreneurship, and lack of access to finance are important. Our chapter revealed another impediment, non-standard employment, locking women into these positions and generating precarious working conditions that intensify the already existing gender norms. In addition to the widely studied policy recommendations of regulation and enforcement of equal pay, I argue employment protection legislation should take gender aspects into consideration and have stricter restrictions on atypical contracts for potentially disadvantaged groups. Making contracts securer and accommodating them with proper income and labor market policies such as publicly funded childcare aiming to facilitate the entrance and continuation of work can be effective ways to reduce gender inequalities.

Finally, Turkey has a large share of informal employment which is quite comparable to many other developing countries. In economies where formal and informal sectors coexist, the statutory rights and social security coverage are quite limited, and employers can exploit workers further by switching to informal sector production. I recommend social security eligibility requirements be relaxed and employment protection legislation (EPL) extended to the workers who do not have contracts. This can be partly done by shifting the registration and protection framework from an employee to enterprise-based system. The Turkish labour market is largely segregated into well-protected and well-paid jobs and informal and precarious jobs. Thus, de jure measures of job protection are relevant only for a fraction of the employees whereas all types of unregistered workers and smaller firms are not covered by the EPL. Given that low-educated women have a higher share of informal sector employment, particularly in certain low-paid occupations, the extension of social security and EPL could considerably improve their working conditions and benefits. The absence of collective representation and low union density in Turkey make legal protections even more relevant. Also, it should be noted that not only de jure measures but enforcement of the regulations are equally important to improve the quality of jobs in developing countries.

While this research focuses on Turkey, similar results can be drawn for other developing countries with enduring gender inequalities particularly with respect to the distribution of paid and unpaid work. The increase in precarious jobs in such societies disproportionally hurts women and worsens their already unfavorable economic status. Precarious employment is an outcome of multiple factors including the type of contract, sector, occupation, and legislation. Even though negative outcomes are visible for both genders, women suffer more because of the biased gender values and discrimination. If the goals are to enhance gender equality and empowering women, then not only the quantity but also the quality of jobs should be the focus of policy making.

REFERENCES

Aktaş, G. (2013) "Üretiyorum Öyleyse Varım: Buldan'da Ev Eksenli Çalışan Kadınların Aile ve Toplumsal Yaşamda Görünmeyen Emeği." *Sosyal ve Beşeri Bilimler Dergisi*, 5(1): 258–267.

Aleksynska, M. (2018) "Temporary employment, work quality, and job satisfaction." *Journal of Comparative Economics*, 46(3): 722–735.

Blau, F. and Kahn, L. (2017) "The gender wage gap: Extent, trends, and explanations." *Journal of Economic Literature*, 55(3): 789–865.

Booth, A., Francesconi, M. and Frank, J. (2002) "Temporary jobs: Stepping stones or dead ends?." *Economic Journal*, 112(480): 189–213.

Booth, A. and Nolen, P. (2012) "Choosing to compete: How different are girls and boys?." *Journal of Economic Behavior and Organization*, 81(2): 542–555.

Cranford, C., Vosko, L. and Zukewich, N. (2003) "The gender of precarious employment in Canada." *Industrial Relations*, 58(3): 454–482.

Duman, A. (2019) "Wage penalty for temporary workers in Turkey: Evidence from quantile regressions." *Developing Economies*, 54(4): 283–310.

Duman, A. (forthcoming) "Non-standard employment and wage differences across gender: A quantile regression approach."

Duman, A. and Duman, A. (2016) "Türkiye'de Sendika Üyeliğinin Kamu ve Özel Sektördeki Ücretler Üzerindeki Etkileri." *Çalışma ve Toplum*, 48(1): 11–30.

Ecevit, Y. (1990) "Kentsel Üretim Sürecinde Kadın Emeğinin Konumu ve Değişen Biçimleri." In S. Tekeli (ed). *Kadın Bakış Açısından 1980'ler Türkiye'sinde Kadınlar*. İstanbul: İletişim, pp. 105–115.

Evans, J. M. (2001) "Firms' contribution to the reconciliation between work and family life." *OECD Occasional Papers*, No. 48.

Garnero, A., Giuliano, R., Mahy, B. and Rycx, F. (2016) "Productivity, wages and profits among Belgian firms: Do fixed-term contracts matter?." *International Journal of Manpower*, 37(2): 303–322.

Gash, V. and McGinnity, F. (2007) "Fixed-term contracts-the new European inequality? Comparing men and women in West Germany and France." *Socio-Economic Review*, 5(3): 467–496.

Grimshaw, D. (2011) "What do we know about low-wage work and low-wage workers? Analyzing the definitions, patterns, causes and consequences in international perspective." *ILO Working Paper*, No. 28.

Hattatoğlu, D. and Tate, J. (2016) "Home-based work and new ways of organizing in the era of globalization." In R. Lambert and A. Herod (eds). *Neoliberal Capitalism and Precarious Work: Ethnographies of Accommodation and Resistance.* Cheltenham: Edward Elgar, pp. 96–124.

İlkkaracan, İ. (2012) "Why so few women in the labour market in Turkey?." *Feminist Economics*, 18(1): 1–37.

ILO (2016) *Non-Standard Employment Around the World.* Geneva: ILO.

Kalleberg, A. (2011) *Good Jobs, Bad Jobs: The Rise of Polarized and Precarious Employment Systems in the United States, 1970s to 2000s.* New York, NY: Russell Sage.

Kidder, T. and Raworth, K. (2004) "Good jobs and hidden costs: Women workers documenting the price of precarious employment." *Gender and Development*, 12(2): 12–21.

Kim, M., Kim, C., Park, J. and Kawachi, I. (2008) "Is precarious employment damaging to self rated health? Results of propensity score matching methods, using longitudinal data in South Korea." *Social Science and Medicine*, 31(3): 1982–1994.

Meurs, D. and Ponthieux, S. (2015) "Gender inequality." In *Handbook of Income Distribution*, Vol. 2A, pp. 983–1119, United States, North America: Elseviar. DOI 10.1016/b978-0-444-59428-0.09990-2.

OECD (2020) "Hours worked." Available at: https://data.oecd.org/emp/hours-worked. htm?fbclid=IwAR2dowe4rJOmyPZOdnckrL52AzrG5jT4wSkn0JeVv0sbjBSTm _96ZcbSMao#indicator-chart (accessed 15 March 2020).

OECD.Stat. (nd) "Time spent in paid and unpaid work, by sex." Available at: https:// stats.oecd.org/index.aspx?queryid=54749 (accessed 15 March 2020).

Olsthoorn, M. (2013) "Measuring precarious employment: A proposal for two indicators of precarious employment based on set-theory and tested with Dutch labor market-data." *Social Indicators Research*, 119(1): 421–441.

Orhan-Karaalp, H. S. (2017) "What are the trends in women's labour force participation in Turkey?." *European Journal of Sustainable Development*, 6(3): 303–312.

Özkan, U. R. (2017) "Translating from multiple sources: Labour legislation reform in Turkey." *International Labour Review*, 156(2): 287–302.

Park, J. (2016) "A collective voice in an insecure world." In Y. Cooper (ed). *Changing Work: Progressive Ideas for the Modern World of Work.* Brussels: Fabian Society, pp. 57–64.

Petrongolo, B. (2004) "Gender segregation in employment contracts." *Journal of the European Economic Association*, 2(2–3): 331–345.

Rodgers, G. and Rodgers, J. (1986) *Precarious Jobs in Labour Market Regulation: The Growth of Atypical Employment in Western Europe*. Brussels: Free University of Brussels.

Sarantakos, S. (2005) *Social Research*, 3rd ed. Basingstoke: Palgrave.

Tartanoğlu, S. (2018) "The voluntary precariat in the value chain: The hidden patterns of home-based garment production in Turkey." *Competition and Change*, 22(1): 23–40.

TUIK (nd) "Isgucu Istatistikleri." Available at: http://www.tuik.gov.tr/PreTablo.do?alt_id=1007 (accessed 24 February 2020).

Vosko, L., MacDonald, M. and Campbell, I. (2009) *Gender and the Contours of Precarious Employment*. London: Routledge.

Vosko, L. F. (2000) *Temporary Work: The Gendered Rise of a Precarious Employment Relationship*. Toronto: University of Toronto Press.

WEF (2020) "Global gender gap report." Available at: http://www3.weforum.org/docs/WEF_GGGR_2020.pdf (accessed 24 February 2020).

Wright, E. O., Baxter, J. and Birkelund, G. E. (1995) "The gender gap in workplace authority: A cross-national study." *American Sociological Review*, 60(3): 407–435.

Young, M. C. (2010) "Gender differences in precarious work settings." *Industrial Relations*, 65(1): 74–97.

Chapter 2

Women Tea Workers of Munnar

Daily Negotiations with the Restrictive Spaces

Anu Mariam Philipose

BACKGROUND

There are many studies[1] based on the workers in tea estates in India, but very few are positioned from the workers' perspectives. Most of the studies have taken on a top-down approach which recognizes that the workers are being exploited but discounts their role as active agents. One cannot make full sense of these workers' lives unless their voices are given due importance, placing their lived experiences first. Engaging with a phenomenological approach, the chapter tries to address this gap precisely by placing itself in the everyday lives of women workers and attempting to understand their perspectives on work, the various choices they make, as well as their strategies of daily negotiations with their circumstances.

Set within the tea plantations of Munnar in Kerala, a southern state in India, this chapter explores the challenges of work in the context of a workplace-household continuum. This becomes particularly pertinent in the setting of the chapter, as the women workers, who form the predominant share of laborers in the lowest rung of the chain, live in houses allotted to them within the premises of the estate. Even though the field site is unique in various respects, the precarious conditions of the workers here and their active negotiations with them could bear resemblances at large to other contexts as well.

The chapter consciously adopts a phenomenological approach in finding answers to the layers of meaning attached to the term "work" and other related concepts used by women workers in the tea estates. At times, some of these views appear contradictory as they denote the different shades of interpretation of the same concept by the women. However, these subjective experiences and interpretations of the workers become the window to their everyday lives, survival strategies, and negotiations. "Women revert to memory, narrative and voice as tools for reconstructing their emotions, thoughts and experiences in making sense of their own constitution as embodied, gendered beings. It is through her embodiment that woman both experiences and articulates herself" (Thapan 2009, 5).

This chapter presents the narratives of three workers, Letchmi, Rajani, and Vijayamma[2], who are at varying stages of their life cycles and have entered their jobs under different circumstances. I visited them multiple times between 2017 and 2019. Even though the in-depth interviews were structured to an extent, the conversations were mostly guided by the respondents themselves. The topics of discussion ranged from their everyday practices, memories, and matters concerning their family members to their political views and general views on the society and their belief systems. These conversations provided insights into their embodied experiences in the context of their daily routines.

The first section of the chapter contains an examination of the gendered division of labor and it briefly touches on the history of the estates as well. The discussion on the order within the estates started in this section continues to the second with a description on the household settings present there. The description of the three workers' profiles and the detailed discussion on their various views are covered in the next section which is further divided into five smaller subsections. The first subsection covers the personal histories of the workers and their entry into the jobs. The next three subsections cover their views on work, the order within the estates, and their choice/ need to work, respectively. The importance placed by the workers on being able to provide for their next generation and their everyday negotiations are described in the next two subsections, respectively. The chapter then concludes.

THE GENDERED DIVISION OF
LABOR IN THE ESTATES

The tea estates in Munnar, in which the study has been conducted, are under the Kannan Devan Hill Plantations Company Private Limited (KDHPCL). The beginnings of this plantation can be traced back to 1877 and was a part of one of the first and largest tea plantations owned by the European planters in Kerala. These tea plantations have a history of engaging "unfree" labor for which various sources were tapped—laborers released from the traditional sectors as a result of the abolition of slavery, distressed migrants from drought-hit areas, and even the very tribal folks who were thrown out of their homes when large tracts of forest areas were cleared to make way for the plantations (Raman, 2010). In the plantations, a large number of families were recruited or lured by benefits like housing, for which they initially were loaned a small sum. Never able to repay the loan later, these workers were never free to leave the employment making them "bonded" or "indentured" laborers.

Initially, women and children were involved in plucking tea leaves, while men were involved in other jobs in the plantations. The logic behind this division was often reduced to the standard explanation that they had "nimble fingers" which were right for the job. However, this practice of employing women and children in large numbers was an important factor that kept the wages low in the plantation, apart from the abundant supply of laborers. The value of work done by these categories of laborers has always been viewed as low and inferior to that of their male counterparts in the estate and society, and their wages were seen as only supplementary to the family income. This patriarchal view was used by the planters to their own benefit. Resistance against these unjust practices was minimal as the workers were not in a position to bargain at the time. While the old ways of the plantation such as employing minors and indentured laborers were discontinued, there are certain path-dependent practices which continue on the tea estates even to this day.

In the present context, in terms of the organization in the tea estates, the tea pluckers are at the bottom of the hierarchy. These tea pluckers are almost always women workers, and they also form the majority of workers in the estates. They mostly use large shears to harvest leaves and resort to hand plucking only when the leaf growth on the tea bushes are minimal. The next level in the hierarchy is that of the supervisor, followed by field officers and higher levels of management in the estate, and finally, that of the larger company that owns the estates. At the supervisory level, there is no discrimination, at least by official policy—the recently introduced qualification tests ensure that both men and women are given opportunities in filling up the post. In reality, however, most supervisors are still men. Moreover, very few women in these parts possess the required qualification of passing the tenth grade within the specified age category. Beyond the supervisory level, the positions of field officers and above are filled by men only. At the level of field officer, men even dress in a way that resembles that of the English planters to distinguish themselves from the rest of the workers below them.

The strict gendered division of labor that evolved in the workplace ensures that men are employed in the more "skilled" jobs. The discussions on the gendered division of labor in both paid and unpaid work have not been new.[3] The German Feminist School looks into the creation of surplus from both paid and unpaid work. The main focus of the "sectoral sexual division of labour,'" as termed by Custers, is to keep a control over women (Custers, 1997).

Lindberg's study on cashew workers in Kerala reveals how the activities of roasting and shelling of cashew nuts, which are considered to be "dirty" activities, have become increasingly feminized over the years (Lindberg, 2001). This account is similar to the one suggested by Mies regarding the division of tasks in agricultural activities in the state of Andhra Pradesh, India (Mies, 1986). However, Lindberg's analysis of the condition of women cashew workers in Kerala also shows that these workers have undergone the process of "effeminisation" (Lindberg, 2001). This process, she argues, is broader than the "housewifization" thesis (Mies, 2014). Not only are the workers treated as "housewives" in this case, but they are also expected to conform to the perceptions of the society regarding dressing, behaving, and acting in "womanly" ways.

Not unlike the strict gendered division of labor within the estate's work-force, the same continues for the workers even in their individual lives, within the settings of their households. In certain articulations of their views, the participants of the study have also shown signs of pressure to conform to the norms of being a "morally upright woman." Their acceptance of the division of labor on gendered terms at the various scales could be a result of the internalization of these patriarchal values, which can be seen in their narratives later.

LIVING SPACES OF WORKERS

Most of the present-day workers are either third- or fourth-generation descendants of the earlier workers who had migrated from the neighboring state of Tamil Nadu. A majority of these workers also belong to socially disadvantaged lower castes, viz. Scheduled Castes (SCs) and Other Backward Castes (OBCs)[4]. Workers mostly live inside the estates in their allotted houses, a practice which has been in place since the plantations were established and families were recruited in large numbers. These estate houses are extremely small, containing just one room which serves as the living room and the bedroom, a kitchen, a bathroom, and a toilet. A "line," as it is locally referred to, means a group of houses built together in a row. These line houses are formed by simple partitions between them, and thus, two houses would share a common wall. Typically, there are six or eight such houses in a row forming a "line." There are many such rows of houses, mostly on different levels on the ground as the terrain is hilly, and each one of these "lines" is connected by a flight of stairs. This spatial arrangement of the household units in the estates becomes crucial in the formation of support networks for the women, giving them the much-needed space for negotiations and maneuver.

THREE WOMEN TEA WORKERS

The three women workers chosen for this chapter are all tea pluckers and live in these houses provided to them by the company. Despite the similarities in the nature of their job and schedules associated with it, Letchmi, Rajani, and Vijayamma, being at different stages of their life cycles, have nonidentical patterns and intensities of work. Apart from the other differences in their backgrounds, they also significantly vary in their educational qualifications and household incomes.

Letchmi who is twenty-six years old is one of the youngest workers in her neighborhood and belongs to OBC. She is also one of the very few workers who has completed twelfth grade. Although she is more fluent in Tamil, she speaks Malayalam and can read and write basic English. She lives with her husband, also a worker at the estate, and two children, aged five and seven. Rajani is forty-one years old and also lives with her husband and two children. Her son is an auto-rickshaw driver and is the only other earning member in the family, besides her. She belongs to SC, and speaks only Tamil. Vijayamma is sixty years old and also belongs to the same caste as Rajani. She had retired from her permanent job as a tea plucker in the estate two years ago. As her son's limited income as a maintenance worker in the tea estate could not sustain the household, she started working her old job again on a temporary basis. Her work schedules and timings mostly remain the same as before, when she used to be a permanent worker. Besides the two earning members, her pregnant daughter-in-law makes the third member of the household.

The three workers featured in this chapter shared their personal histories, backgrounds, details of their work, and their opinions on various topics, providing insights into their daily lives as well as their choices and negotiations on an everyday basis. In the following subsections, these are discussed in detail.

Personal Histories and Entry into Job

Rajani is a third-generation worker and started working as a tea plucker in the estate where she grew up soon after she failed her eighth grade. Her mother and her friends helped her to perfect her skills of leaf plucking using her hands. She stopped working for a few years when she got married and moved into her husband's home, another house in the workers' lines. Her husband's family has been living in the same house for two generations, as her husband's grandmother and mother were also tea pluckers. Her mother-in-law made decisions related to her work. Initially, she was asked not to work at the estate but to cook for the large family of seven. Between looking after her young children and the household chores, she recalls having hardly any time to consider taking up an external job as well. After her children started attending the nearby school and when the size of the family reduced after her husband's siblings moved out, her mother-in-law decided it was time for her to take up the job of a tea plucker. So, at twenty-four, she started working again as a tea plucker.

Letchmi had considered other jobs, especially with the new resorts operating in the town, but decided to become a tea plucker as none of the other jobs pays her as much as the present job. Although she is a fourth-generation tea estate worker, she considers her job which she started almost three years ago as part of a transit phase. She aspires to become a supervisor someday. Although it is mostly men who are supervisors, she points out examples of a few women who have made it to the post in the recent years after the exam has been introduced. She told me that she was preparing hard for the test on her off-days, even with her two young children at home. She also told me that one needs to have the right contacts with the trade union to help get placed as a supervisor. She really hopes to crack the test, move upward, and accomplish what the other older women workers in her family could not do.

Vijayamma had come to Munnar after her marriage at the young age of fifteen. She only has a primary-level education. Her family in Tamil Nadu arranged the marriage through their caste connections to her husband who was ten years older. Vijayamma who had never seen tea plantations was quite new to the way of life in Munnar when she arrived, and was amazed to see how a family of eight (at the time) fit into such a small house. After her eldest two children, both daughters, were born, she started working as a tea plucker in the estate. Her mother-in-law taught her how to pluck leaves using her hands for the first time, and within a month, she became a skilled tea plucker with good speed in harvesting leaves. Except for the one and a half years she took off when she was pregnant with her son, she has been working since she was twenty-two years old.

Inferences from the chapter participants' descriptions of their personal histories, suggest these women entered the job of leaf plucking because of the lack of permanent and alternative job opportunities in the sleepy hills of Munnar. In a nonnuclear patrilocal family, the woman's decision to enter a job depends on the views held by the extended family members as well. In the case of the two older respondents, their entry into the jobs was particularly affected by the positions held by the other elder women in the family who also happened to be working in the estates as tea pluckers. With only middle school and primary school levels of education, respectively, Vijayamma and Rajani also did not have the skills required for many alternative job opportunities within the locality. The idea of working as a tea leaf plucker was an option toward which they "naturally" inclined, as the families have been living within the estates in the company-owned houses for generations. Letchmi's decision to work as a tea plucker was an option most women of her age in the neighborhood refused to consider and was made after weighing the alternative job opportunities and the potential incomes arising out of them. Like Vijayamma and Rajani, she started her job after her children were born and hopes she can move out of her present job in a few years' time either within or outside the estate as she has completed school—an advantage she has over the older workers. The increasing availability of job opportunities for the younger generation may make this possible because of the changing nature of the town itself which now features a resort area with a steady inflow of tourists every year. With most women achieving higher levels of education than the previous generations of women tea workers, they aspire to work outside the estates or not work at all.

Views on Work

Waged employment and unpaid work are interconnected for women tea workers in the estate. The logistics of the job sites to the tea pluckers' households is spatially significant. The identity of being a woman in the estate requires for one to not shirk "responsibilities" at home. A quick peek into the tea pluckers' everyday routines shows that each one of them tries to finish off their chores at home, which include cooking both lunch and breakfast for the entire families, before leaving for work at 7:30 a.m., on normal days, or just after 6:00 a.m., on days in the peak season of leaf harvest. They try to come back in for lunch, whenever possible, mainly to attend to some of the unfinished work at home. After coming back from work at around 5:30 p.m., they do not have much time to relax and immediately start preparing dinner for the family. Being in a close-knit community where your neighbors are also your coworkers, there is an added pressure to conform to the norms of the society for a woman to be seen as a *good, responsible, and morally upright person..*

Tea plucking is one of the most physically demanding jobs on the estate involving the repeated motion of hands to use the large shears and carry large sacks of plucked tea leaves up and down the slopes of the hills even during difficult weather conditions. When asked about their "work," the women first talked about their "waged work" and its physically daunting dimensions.

The most difficult part of the job is to carry sacks of leaves which may weigh an average of 50 kgs. The rainy seasons are the worst. The weight of the bag just goes up with the leaves being wet. And the final weight of the leaves calculated for wages is often very less after deducting the standard weight of water in the leaves. (Rajani, on asked about the most difficult part of her waged work)[5]

The repeated motion of the right hand while shearing the top layer of leaves for many years results in shoulder pains. For the last couple of years, I cannot even move my hands during winters. I cannot work at all on those days when my hands are not functional. (Vijayamma speaks)

For Letchmi, the presence of her two young children means additional care and household activities to undertake. She says:

The peak seasons of harvest always leave me exhausted all the time. It takes meticulous planning and execution to leave the house at 6 or 6:30 in the morning after finishing all the cooking and other household chores till I come back from work at 5:30 or so in the evening. I would be seeing my kids for the first time in the day when I return in the evening and I still will not have the time to spend with them as I will be involved in cooking for dinner and preparing vegetables and other chores for the next day.

Each of them stands at a different point in their life cycle as well as in their years of experience on the job, prompting them to highlight different aspects of the same job as the most challenging part to them. Although Vijayamma and Rajani also talk about their responsibilities regarding household chores later, their primary concerns had more to do with the physically demanding aspects of their jobs which have had a clear impact on their health over the years. Letchmi, who is also the youngest of the three, first expresses her concerns regarding managing both household and job work, more than the others. With regard to providing care activities for her children, she bears an unevenly large burden compared with her husband. Solely responsible for household chores, besides her more physically demanding waged job conditions, the young mother oftentimes finds herself completely exhausted during the peak seasons of harvesting tea leaves.

Much of the physical hardships faced by these women, with respect to the demands of the household activities are worsened during the peak seasons of harvest. However, the three women view household chores and their responsibilities regarding them differently. Vijayamma and Letchmi recognize they are "working" at home and often complained about the lack of time to complete their chores. They do not expect anyone else in the family to help with most of the work. Vijayamma's daughter-in-law used to help out earlier, but her complicated pregnancy has prevented her from getting involved with the work at home anymore. In Letchmi's case, the most help she can expect from her husband is in helping her children get ready for school during the peak seasons when she has to leave home early. Rajani, on the other hand, does not even consider her housework as "work." Rajani associates "work" with something physically difficult. She does not believe there could be "light" work. For her, "work" is restricted to her job for which she is paid in wages. She believes it is a woman's duty to look after the affairs of her home. She, therefore, considers her household chores as part of her "responsibility" of being a "good married woman" and does not even complain about them.

The varied views on what ought to be considered as "work" and the low expectation of receiving help from other family members show the degree of internalization of patriarchal ideals prevalent in the community among the three participants. This was also visible during the conversations regarding their monthly incomes. Rajani and Letchmi mention they are the primary earners of their families in hushed tones. In Letchmi's case, she purposefully downplays her income figures in her husband's presence. This could suggest the attempt of the women to conform to the accepted societal view to consider the husband as the primary earner in the household as the ideal situation, even though in many households in the estates, the women earn more than their spouses. In my position as an outsider to their community, they were not happy to divulge this less-than-ideal situation of earning more than their husbands. It is also interesting to note that their higher incomes did not translate into a higher bargaining power for Letchmi and Rajani regarding the various household decisions.

Views on the Order within the Estates

The tea estates serve as both the workers' jobsites and their homes. Their view of the estates and the order within them often invoke mixed feelings from them for the same reason. The earlier generations of workers found themselves bound to the estates due to their debts and they also pulled in their children to work in the estates early itself. However, with the present generation of workers, they do not have a binding to be in the estates or to continue the same job as their elders in the family. The provision of a house for the permanent employees seems to be the most important incentive, both financially and emotionally, that keeps them rooted to the place. Some of them do not wish to even move away from the place, even if they had alternate job opportunities. Rajani mentions that she cannot even imagine a different life without the presence of these tea bushes.

Although being able to work is considered the most important asset for a worker in the estate, there is a reverence to nature and to even their jobs that sustain them observed among the workers. This is quite an odd position, while considering their own critical views of the job mentioned earlier in the context of its physically demanding nature. For these women, the physical space of their houses provided by their employer served as a home to more than a generation of workers in their families. Vijayamma says that she sees the hills of the tea plantations as *a blessing that nurtured her and her family for all these years.*

The company that owns both their place of living and jobsite also takes up the role of a "benevolent" patriarch that ensures loyalty from the workers. For instance, workers have yearly quotas on rice and tea (calculated for the entire family living in a household), along with other essentials such as blankets and firewood supplied from the company's side, through the mediation of the trade unions. Apart from a few concessions on the rates, these essentials are being paid for by the workers themselves in installments and are usually deducted from their wages. Only Letchmi knew about the exact amounts being deducted from her wages every month as she was more educationally qualified than others. But in general, the whole act masquerades as a kind gesture from their employer which makes it extremely hard to raise their voice against the issues they face. Vijayamma even says that *the company has been good to all and it looks after us.*

They have internalized the unequal structure of the company and have even accepted their position at the base of the hierarchical ladder in the estates. On the topic of the gendered division of labor within the estates, the study participants mention that they do not find the arrangement problematic. Vijayamma tells me this has been the way things have always functioned within the estate. She also considers the men's jobs, even that of maintenance workers, as more difficult than the women's jobs. While Letchmi views that the supervisory posts require better-skilled workers, she believes she will be able to do the job and aspires to be one in the future.

The positions of these women in the estates as workers and their views on their present jobs have been overwhelmingly determined by nonmonetary factors. While they have emotional ties to the place, they are also guided by the patriarchal values of the society they live accepting their positions in the estate at the lowest rung of its hierarchal order. With very bleak chances of promotion, even for a relatively more educated and younger woman worker like Letchmi, they do not attempt to question the order of things within the estates. The gendered division of labor at the jobsite is as accepted just as the one observed in the households.

On the Choice/Need to Work

While the above discussion throws light on the emotional ties of the workers to the place and the job, this is an attempt to elaborate their grip on their household financial situations as they continue working in this physically demanding and comparatively low-paying job. Kathi Weeks (2011) in her introduction to her book starts off with a question "Why do we work so long and so hard?" (Weeks 2011, 1). This subsection follows a similar note and asks the question whether the workers perceive if they really have a choice regarding their work. This is important to explore as it is a giveaway into their willingness to seek higher pay or better conditions at work.

An earlier socioeconomic survey conducted on a larger sample of tea pluckers in the estates in Munnar revealed that the average monthly income for a permanent employee was approximately Rs 8,500 per month (roughly about $120).[6] Their incomes go into servicing the various needs of the family. In most cases, the income would have been sufficient to meet the everyday expenses of the family under normal circumstances. However, they are also expected to spend on social occasions, including weddings, births and deaths, sometimes even for their extended families and neighbors, and during the times of various festivals. This, combined with unforeseen expenditures like that of health shocks, pushes the households into a constant cycle of debt with both formal and informal credit channels. The reasons are many, as could be seen in the discussion of the life stories of the three respondents here, but the households in the estate are heavily indebted at almost all times.

In Vijayamma's case, her husband's alcoholism and his eventual death almost eighteen years ago pushed the family into a debt trap involving repeated borrowing from various sources, pawning, and even selling whatever little assets (mostly gold) she and her family owned. Her husband had a few years left in his service before his retirement at the time of his death. Although her son took up a job on the tea estates soon after that, the household's debt only kept mounting. Her husband's alcoholism and medical bills had already severely dented the family's financial situation. The expenses incurred on both her daughters' weddings and the birth of her three grandchildren further pushed her to take multiple loans with exorbitant interests. Vijayamma lost most of her gold jewelry she had pawned earlier as she could not pay back the loans taken with her wages. She cannot afford not to have a job even after her retirement. She returned to the same job as a temporary worker as she did not know where else to look for employment. "Who would want to employ a retired tea-plucker for a job outside the estates?," she asks. Currently, she and her son try to raise additional income by selling milk from their recently bought cows. Even as they have improved their financial situation, they are yet to be freed from the debt cycle.

For Letchmi's family, apart from the expenses for her children's education, their major expenditure is the contribution to the health expenses of both their parents. Letchmi and her husband have both taken many loans in the past for the same reason. Their household comparatively does much better in terms of income, with both the spouses working and the additional income earned every month from selling milk from the cows they own. As there is a common facility provided by the company, they could easily maintain the cows despite their limited space in the house. They manage to earn a little more than Rs

20,000 (approximately $300) a month from all their sources, during the non-peak season. However, the household expenses, which include monetary support to her husband's old parents, mostly exceed their income in most months. They try to restrict their loan sources to the cooperative societies run by the trade union they are a part of, but Letchmi had had to pawn her gold jewelry thrice in the past as well.

Three years back when Rajani's daughter secured a seat for an undergraduate degree in computer science in a college in the state of Tamil Nadu, she immediately knew her daughter had to study no matter the costs involved. She sent her daughter to college after arranging her stay in a relative's place nearby. Her income from her job hardly keeps the family afloat, with the loans taken earlier for the expenses of her daughter's education. She augments her income with the occasional contract job she gets in the resorts nearby. The main source of earning more money for her, however, is to harvest more tea leaves, especially during the peak seasons. Rajani recalls suffering many injuries and physical pain from carrying large loads of tea leaves, the result of her necessity to earn more money to meet household expenses. Despite all these efforts to arrange extra funds, she never remembers a time the family was out of debt. They have exhausted all possible sources of borrowing, jokes Rajani at one point during the conversation. Rajani has sometimes taken out a loan to service a previous one, and has often pawned her gold jewelry in one of the numerous pawn shops or "financiers," as these are called, located in the town. As long as her health allows her to work, she does not see these mounting debts as problematic. She looks forward to every peak season of tea harvest, despite her health issues, to pay back the loans.

With the unavoidable social and family commitments each of the workers face, the wages they receive do not even cover their bare essential needs. They have little choice but to continue working for as long as they can to solve their financial situations. The workers rely on their labor as the best way to solve their financial issues. Their only comfort is in knowing their hard work goes toward securing a better future for their children and grandchildren, a conscious choice they make.

Providing for the Next Generation

While there are financial and emotional reasons involved for the workers to continue their strenuous jobs, the thought of contributing to the improvement of the lives of their children seems to be the main motivating factor that sustains them in their routine hard work in the long run. This subsection discusses the workers' narratives on this aspect.

Letchmi expresses her desperate desire to earn as much extra income as possible from her job while she is young and healthy in order to save for her children's future. One of her main aspirations in life is to enable her children to get a good education. She does not want her children to work in the estates unless it is a managerial position. Letchmi and her husband have already decided to send their younger son to the English-medium school in Munnar when he reaches grade 1. They cannot afford to send both the children to such a school, and they have made the hard choice between educating their son instead of their daughter; their choice shaped by the preferential treatment for the son in the family.

Rajani is very proud of her daughter who just completed her degree. She keeps mentioning that her daughter is the only one who has earned a degree in the family. Her daughter, whom I have met on a few occasions, is unhappy about her mother's decision to not let her work after finishing her college. When asked, Rajani explains that she does not want her daughter to be away from home for too long in order to arrange her marriage soon. Rajani, using all her connections, is actively looking for a groom for her daughter. She really hopes her daughter does not have to ever work like she did in her life.

Vijayamma regrets she could not provide the best for her children. Constrained by her large debts, she did the best she could to marry off her two daughters, and she is happy they are settled comfortably in Tamil Nadu, although the expenses of the weddings immersed her in deeper financial troubles. She worries for her son who has to work and pay off the debts of the family. She hopes to turn the tables of fortune for her son's child who would be born in a few months.

The desire for providing for the next generations pushes these women to immerse themselves in work. They constantly engage and negotiate with their limited circumstances for the sake of their children. This is similar to the concept of "intergenerational pathway of empowerment" proposed by Kabeer and Khan in the context of Afghan women who try everything they can to make their daughters' futures better (Kabeer and Khan 2014, 20).

Everyday Negotiations

When the hegemony is internalized, it is not easy to openly question it and organize large-scale protests against the issues the workers face[7]. However, this does not mean that these women workers do not negotiate with their given circumstances. It is more common and easier for workers to engage in smaller acts of everyday negotiations. While they constantly engage and articulate their differences or even resort to their own strategies to overcome hurdles in everyday lives, not all of them are met with success.

The workers have managed to form their own networks along the same divisive lines that are used to suppress their upward mobility. As discussed earlier, most workers belong to socially disadvantaged caste categories and speak only Tamil. They do not often get much support and are often looked down upon by outsiders to the estates, especially by people speaking the state language of Malayalam. Despite being settled in Munnar for a long time and over generations, and even constituting the majority in many localities, the Tamil-speaking population is generally "othered" by the rest of the society. The newer generations of workers like Letchmi try to overcome the language barrier by speaking both the languages. However, it has been rather difficult for them to integrate into the society. The workers consider the estates as a safe space and their home emotionally. Although there are competition and surveillance among the groups of women laborers working together, they have also developed strong ties of friendship among themselves and mostly look out for each other.

Letchmi depends on her neighbors to watch her children at times, especially on the off-days when she is busy preparing for her tests. Other women in her neighborhood, who are all older than her, are extremely supportive of her test preparation as well. Vijayamma leaves her neighbors in charge to look after her pregnant daughter-in-law when she is away. She finds the presence of her neighbors a great relief during such times. Women workers who are double burdened with both their paid and unpaid work find a great deal of comfort in getting a helping hand in the provision of care activities for the young and old dependent members of the family through these informal support networks. These women have formed their own networks, based on their caste, locality, or any other commonalities that they share, for the provision of such care activities.

The commonalties in their financial woes and health issues have brought them even closer. Women workers have formed their own smaller groups, mainly for the purpose of borrowing money from the government project of Kudumbasree, which mostly includes microfinance operations. While the success of the microfinance model is debatable, it is more important to see this association as a form of solidarity and as an act of negotiation on the part of the workers to deal with their economic issues. Letchmi, Rajani, and Vijayamma are all part of the Kudumbasree units in their localities.

While resistance forms a significant part of it, their negotiations are not all about resistance alone. They also include acts and expressions of survival for merely getting by more smoothly. These extend to the physical spaces they live in as well. Worker households try to accommodate themselves as conveniently as possible within their limited economic means. To get around the limitation of the small living spaces, Rajani's family has built extensions to the main structure of the house. They have enclosed the veranda with a roof that serves as a shed for her son to park his auto-rickshaw. At other times, the space is used for overnight guests. Vijayamma uses cloth curtains to create separate spaces within the living room to accommodate her son's family with more privacy.

While these are acts of negotiations that could be seen in the physical space, there are many which are much more subtle. It was not uncommon to listen to these women joke about their issues and share a laugh while I was doing my fieldwork. Even talking and laughing among themselves in the workplace become acts of resistance in their own way. Recognizing the problems associated with their jobs and talking about the same are extremely crucial in a setting like this where one assumes that the internalization of patriarchal values is complete. They are not oblivious to the physical hardships and toll on their health incurred from their jobs, but they still choose to continue with the same, after weighing the options they have in front of them, for the sake of their children or even grandchildren, as in Vijayamma's case.

CONCLUDING REMARKS

Through their own narratives of their life experiences, it becomes evident that Rajani, Letchmi, and Vijayamma display remarkable determination to face the challenges of their circumstances even during very difficult times. They understand that the most important asset they have is their own labor. As women workers, they rely on their labor power to work twice as hard to meet and balance the requirements of their job and household responsibilities. Even though they are aware of the hardships involved, they look forward to working as a means to provide for their next generation. As they live within the estates, their views regarding their job and the employer are mixed. They perceive the estates as their rightful home for generations and as a safe space from the rest of the society where they are "othered." While they regard their jobs as difficult, they also respect the company like a "benevolent patriarch." The image is a remnant of the colonial past, carefully constructed and sustained by the company that owns the estates. As suggested in the literature, tapping into the already established patriarchal norms of the society has proved helpful to the company in maintaining the status quo as well as the gendered division of labor, without much resistance.

While the women workers do not find fault with a lot of arrangements within the estates as they try to largely conform to the societal expectations of "what they ought to be" as women and workers, they still negotiate with their circumstances. Negotiations happen at various levels in the lives of the workers. Even the crammed living spaces within the estates that have been a cause of worry for them were negotiated with, physically, by way of extensions and separations within the houses. However, this very living arrangement of "house lines" has also helped them to form strong ties with other neighboring workers in the estates. The women workers have a strong sense of camaraderie among them and help each other on a daily basis. Through the provision of care activities for other households and forming their own networks for support including financial benefits, the female tea pluckers of Munnar's hills negotiate with their restrictive spaces of work and living. In a lot of ways, the insights from the field open up new layers of meanings to the concept of workspace–household continuum, proving once again, the need to employ a phenomenological approach in understanding the dimensions of work and domestic life in different sectors and settings.

NOTES

1. For a broad overview, see Bhadra (2004), Bhowmik (2011, 2015), Kar (1984), Prasanneswari (1984), and Raman (2010).

2. The names have been changed to preserve the anonymity of the respondents of the study.

3. For instance, see Acker (1990), Mies (1982, 1986) for a broad overview. Another study worth mentioning in the context of the division of labour is Priti Ramamurthy's account (2004) of looking at the commodity chain from a feminist perspective.

4. As part of the larger survey initially conducted between 2017 and 2019 among 300 worker households in the two chosen estates in the plantations, it was found that 44 percent of the households belonged to the Scheduled Castes (SCs), 37 percent to the Other Backward Castes (OBCs), 15 percent belonged to other economically backward classes, and 4 percent belonged to other categories.

5. There is a standard reduction in the weight of the leaves, of about 18 percent of the total weight, employed by the company. It goes up on rainy days.

6. This is based on the survey conducted by the author among 300 workers in two estates owned by the KDHPCL in Munnar, during various periods from December 2017 to December 2019. The said monthly wages is an approximation of the average figures for various months, taking into consideration the variations in the weight of the tea leaves harvested both in peak and lean periods. It is subjected to individual biases and should only be considered as an approximation.

7. The women workers, however, successfully managed to come together for a large strike without the backing of any political party to demand for higher wages in 2015 and even established Pembilai Orumai, a women's collective which is now formally registered as a trade union. See Kamath and Ramanathan (2017) for a detailed discussion on the strike itself. While the act of coming together and organizing the strike were commendable, the momentum of the collective did not last long. Their internalized patriarchal values were used by the interested parties to create divisions within the collective. The popularity of the women's trade union initiative, Pembilai Orumai, has been receding over the years, truly catering to the vested interest of capital in suppressing the voice of the women's collective.

REFERENCES

Acker, Joan. 1990. "Hierarchies, Jobs, Bodies: A Theory of Gendered Organizations." *Gender & Society* 4(2): 139–58.

Bhadra, Mita. 2004. "Gender Dimensions of Tea Plantation Workers in West Bengal." *Indian Anthropologist* 34(2): 43–68.

Bhowmik, Sharit K. 2011. "Ethnicity and Isolation: Marginalization of Tea Plantation Workers." *Race/Ethnicity: Multidisciplinary Global Contexts* 4(2): 235–53.

Bhowmik, Sharit K. 2015. "Living Conditions of Tea Plantation Workers." *Economic and Political Weekly* L(46&47): 29–32.

Custers, Peter. 1997. *Capital Accumulation and Women's Labour in Asian Economies*. New Delhi: Vistaar Publications.

Kabeer, Naila, and Ayesha Khan. 2014. "Cultural Values or Universal Rights? Women's Narratives of Compliance and Contestation in Urban Afghanistan." *Feminist Economics* 20(3): 1–24.

Kamath, Rajalakshmi, and Smitha Ramanathan. 2017. "Women Tea Plantation Workers' Strike in Munnar, Kerala: Lessons for Trade Unions in Contemporary India." *Critical Asian Studies* 49(2): 244–56.

Kar, R. K. 1984. "Labour Pattern and Absenteeism: A Case Study in Tea Plantation in Assam, India." *Anthropos* 79: 13–24.

Lindberg, Anna. 2001. "Class, Caste, and Gender among Cashew Workers in the South Indian State of Kerala 1930–2000." *International Review of Social History* 46(2): 155–84.

Mies, Maria. 1982. *The Lace Makers of Narsapur: Indian Housewives Produce for the World Market*. London: Zed Press.

Mies, Maria. 1986. "Indian Women in Subsistence and Agricultural Labour." In *Women Work and Development Series No. 12*. Geneva: International Labour Organization.

Mies, Maria. 2014. *Patriarchy and Accumulation on a World Scale: Women in the International Division of Labour*. London: Zed Books.

Prasanneswari. 1984. "Industrial Relation in Tea Plantations: The Dooars Scene." *Economic and Political Weekly* 19(24/25): 956–60.

Ramamurthy, Priti. 2004. "Why Is Buying a 'Madras' Cotton Shirt a Political Act? A Feminist Commodity Chain Analysis." *Feminist Studies* 30(3): 734.

Raman, Ravi. 2010. *Global Capital and Peripheral Labour: The History and Political Economy of Plantation Workers in India*. London and New York: Routledge.

Thapan, Meenakshi. 2009. *Living the Body: Embodiment, Womanhood and Identity in Contemporary India*. New Delhi: SAGE.

Weeks, Kathi. 2011. *The Problem with Work: Feminism, Marxism, Antiwork Politics, and Postwork Imaginaries*. Durham and London: Duke University Press.

Chapter 3

Gender-Based Differences in the Medical Field

The Female Physician Story

Nisha Viswanathan

HISTORY OF FEMALE PARTICIPATION IN THE MEDICAL PROFESSION

Historically, female participation in the medical profession was poorly documented prior to the 1800s. There are textual references to female medical practitioners in Ancient Greece with free-standing medical practices where they performed both surgical and obstetrical care (Mead, 1938). After the dissolution of the Roman Empire, little evidence remains proving the ongoing existence of female physicians.

The Catholic beliefs regarding women's inferior status in society led to few formal medical educational opportunities for women during the Middle Ages, forcing many women to become healers and midwives, professions that made them prone to accusations of witchcraft (Brooke, 1997). Ultimately, the creation of licensure and guilds pushed women into more ancillary roles in medicine, such as nursing.

By the nineteenth century, women had taken a renewed interest in joining the medical profession as doctors. Small groups of women were able to attend foreign medical schools or participate in unlicensed apprenticeships. In 1849, Elizabeth Blackwell became the first woman to receive a medical degree in the United States. She struggled to find employment due to poor societal acceptance of female physicians and had to spend her early medical career practicing out of her home. In 1857, she founded the New York Infirmary for Women and Children, which created opportunities for female physician practice in the subsequent decades (Bernstein, 1992). By the late nineteenth

43

century, female admission to medical schools started to increase, with around 12,000 women attending U.S. medical schools by the turn of the century.

Published in 1910, "A Medical Study in the United States and Canada" by Abraham Flexner provided a scathing analysis of all higher medical education institutions in North America, noting that the worst-quality education was provided at female medical colleges (Flexner, 1910). This study unfortunately had a major negative impact on female access to medical education, leading to the closure of one-third of American medical schools, disproportionately affecting female students (Bernstein, 1992).

Subsequently, female enrollment in medical schools remained low well into the 1960s. Many medical schools also openly stated a preference for male applicants and had internal quotas for female enrollment (Walsh, 1990).

Big changes were afoot for female medical education by the 1970s with the onset of the feminist movement. Title IX passed and became law in the summer of 1972. It stated, "No person in the United States shall, on the basis of sex, be excluded from participation in, be denied the benefits of, or be subjected to discrimination under any educational program or activity receiving Federal financial assistance." This directly impacted medical education, and by 1974 women accounted for 23 percent of all medical students (Jolly, 1988).

This increase in female matriculants to medical school has continued since the 1970s. In 2018, the Association of American Medical Colleges (AAMC) announced that women now comprised the majority of medical school applicants and matriculants for a second year in a row, with promising increases among racial minority groups such as blacks and Hispanics (AAMC, 2018). According to a 2017 Athena Health study, women now comprise 60 percent of all physicians under the age of thirty-five (Johnson, 2018).

THE PROBLEM

Numerical parity in the classroom has not translated however to equality in the clinic room. Until the last decade, there has been a paucity of research on the gender-based differences in the medical profession.

Central to this discussion is the disparity in income between female and male physicians. Traditionally a high-income profession, physician salaries tend to vary depending on specialty, practice type (academic versus private practice), years of experience, and reimbursement rates. Furthermore, other factors, including faculty rank, clinical trial participation, and grant funding also influence a physician's yearly salary.

In 2014, *Journal of the American Medical Association Internal Medicine* presented the most compelling evidence that gender-based differences in physician incomes did exist despite accounting for the factors noted above. While the study was limited to academic practice settings, the results revealed that there were significant differences in physician salary only explained by physician sex. The largest absolute adjusted sex differences in salary were seen in the surgical and procedural specialties, namely orthopedic surgery, OB/GYN, and cardiology (Jena et al., 2014). This data was supported by other studies which showed income disparities among physician-researchers, with one study calculating that accounting for all other factors if a female researcher were to become male she would earn $12,000 more per year (Jagsi et al., 2012).

There are many reasons cited as contributing to this gender-based income inequality. Among these include that female physicians are by and large younger than their male colleagues, there are differences within choice of specialties, and that female physicians are less likely to negotiate early in their careers, leading to an overall lower lifetime earning potential.

Notably, these salary differences start early in a physician's career. As recently as 2018, recently graduated male residents in internal medicine were offered on average a starting salary of at least $17,000 more than their female colleagues (Saunders et al., 2018). This is consistent with data in other non-medical professional fields which have shown male applicants are rated more positively and offered greater starting salaries when applying for a new position. This difference is seen whether hiring committees are composed of primarily men or primarily women, which denotes a strong cultural bias at play (Issac et al., 2009). Additionally, studies in other fields show blinding an applicant's name, thereby hiding their gender, changes a committee's perception of their achievements (Budden et al., 2008).

The prevailing method for payment in medicine is based on the number of clinical, patient-facing hours. Most departments utilize a method of payment to their medical providers based on relative value units (RVUs) which quantify how much their time is worth based on what type of clinical service is being performed. For example, doing open heart surgery for coronary bypass is given 40 RVUs, while seeing an established patient in clinic for a fifteen-minute visit is billed as 0.67 RVUs. Payment is adjusted accordingly.

Many believe this is an equitable system that does not carry inherent gender bias. On close review of the RVU system, some discrepancies do appear. For example, urologists, who primarily work with the male urogenital tract and are overwhelmingly male providers, and urogynecologists (Uro-GYNs), who focus primarily on female urogenital issues and are predominantly female providers, overlap in their surgical purview with similar procedures performed by either field. A complete urethrectomy, or the complete removal of the tube that allows one to urinate, is compensated as 16.85 RVUs for urologists and only 13.72 for Uro-GYNs. Similar comparisons of other procedures reveal 84 percent of the time the urologist's compensation is higher (Benoit et al., 2016).

Research is another source of income in medicine if a physician does not wish to be a full-time clinician. Unfortunately, opportunities for grant funding for research are limited and studies reveal similar results to their clinical peers that women are less likely to be chosen to renew grants or receive as much grant funding by the National Institutes of Health (NIH) (Kolehmainen et al., 2018).

Of all the theories to explain these salary differences, the most frequently cited factor is that many female physicians enter their childbearing years during the most crucial early years of their medical career. Physician-mothers take at least three months, if not longer, for maternity leave, with additional time for appointments or unforeseen medical complications requiring complete bedrest. Once they return to the workplace, physician-mothers often require additional accommodations, which include providing lactation rooms, breast milk storage options, and time in their busy schedule for pumping. This can equate to seeing fewer patients and the perception of not working as hard by their peers.

This idea of fewer hours worked equaling less pay was challenged in a 2017 study published in *Journal of American College of Cardiology*. In a study of over 2,600 participants, cardiologists' salaries were evaluated based on their various subspecialties, number of half days worked, and RVUs generated. In a multivariate analysis, female physicians were more likely to be working less than full time as compared to their male colleagues (79% vs. 90%). Yet, on reviewing their productivity female physicians should have been paid on average greater than $31,000 more per year. The study analysis revealed "an independent association between sex and salary" (Jagsi et al., 2016).

Worse, many female physicians note increased discrimination in the workplace related to their maternal status. Salary discrepancies were frequently mentioned, but additional reasons included unfair treatment by staff and peers, being held to a higher standard, and not being involved in administrative decision making (Adeisoye, 2017).

Most notably female physicians carry maternal responsibilities that extend far beyond the physical responsibility of childbearing and subsequent maternity leave. Female physicians have still been found to disproportionately bear the responsibilities of domestic tasks and parenting. The NIH found that its male physician-researchers worked on average sever hours more per week doing research and spent twelve fewer hours than their female peers on domestic tasks or parenting.

Additionally, female physicians tend to bear the responsibility of sick care for their children, forcing many of them to take unpaid leave. This likely stems from the fact that female physicians statistically are more likely to have spouses who work full time (86%) as opposed to male physicians whose spouses tend to have lower rates of full-time employment (44%). In fact, male physicians' spouses are four times as likely to work part time or not at all (Jolly et al., 2014).

These results have been replicated among surgeons. Male surgeons were less likely to be married to a fellow physician (27%) as compared to the female colleagues (43%), less likely to be married to a fellow surgeon (5%) as their female colleagues (27%), were twice as likely to have a spouse that stayed at home, and were more likely to have had their first child earlier in their careers than their female colleagues. Worse, female surgeons noted their career provided conflict with their partner greater than 50 percent of the time leading to increased exhaustion, higher depressive scores, and lower quality of life scores than their male peers (Dyrbye et al., 2011).

All of this research shows there has been limited change for female physicians in over thirty years. Studies from the 1990s show female physicians often noted they had fewer departmental funding opportunities and less access to secretarial support, which directly correlated with fewer publications and an overall slower career growth (Carr et al., 1998). Interestingly, this is consistent with findings that when men ask for reduced time for familial responsibilities within their departments they were rated as poorer workers and were penalized with fewer promotions or salary increases (Rudman et al., 2013). This makes clear the reality that domestic responsibilities do affect a physician's ability to develop their career.

In 2019, Medscape's *National Physician Burnout & Depression Report* published that female physicians are burning out at twice the rate of their male peers. *Burnout* is defined as "long-term, unresolvable job stress that leads to exhaustion and feeling overwhelmed, cynical, detached from the job, and lacking a sense of personal accomplishment"(Kane, 2019). These results carry major societal implications as physician burnout carries a substantial financial burden as well, with $4.6 billion lost to physician turnover annually. In addition, burnout leads physicians to scale back their clinical hours which exacerbates the increasing need for medical providers nationally (Han et al., 2019).

These confluences of factors may explain the change in female physician practice habits over time. Female physicians with children are more likely than their male peers with children to consider changing their work status for family needs. This reflects itself in the statistic that shows 40 percent of female physicians are likely to go part time or leave the workforce within six years of training completion (Frank et al., 2019). In addition, female physicians with children have been found to work almost eleven fewer hours than female physicians without children (Ly et al., 2017).

Despite these alarming statistics, few departments have made constructive changes to their care delivery models. Given the disproportionate number of male physician-leaders who often have non-working spouses, there may be poor understanding by hospital leadership of the challenges of the dual-working household. Lack of recognition of the problem then flares existing gender gaps in salary and opportunity, perpetuates cultural stereotypes of female gender roles, and prevents the creation of targeted interventions to create inclusivity in the medical field.

METHODS

Given the literature on gender-based differences in the medical field, there is a greater need to understand not only to identify the factors that perpetuate the disparities in the male and female physician experiences, but also understand from those women who have succeeded how they have made this possible.

Nine female physician-leaders at academic institutions underwent semi-structured interviews regarding their career paths and what factors they believed contributed to their professional success. The physicians were from different specialties within medicine (surgical, medical, and non-patient facing, such as research). Additionally, they were generationally diverse. Three entered medical school prior to 1980 ("Baby Boomers"), three attended medical school between 1980 and 2005 ("Generation X"), and three attended after 2005 ("Millennials"). These participants were identified as "physician-leaders" if they were responsible for managing either a department, medical institute within a university, or were in hospital administration.

Utilizing an inductive thematic approach, interviews were transcribed, and themes identified. Themes were broadly assessed into three categories: those at the individual level, those at the societal level, and those at the institutional level. Individual-level themes were factors interviewees identified as personally important to their success. Societal-level themes focus more on society's view of female physicians and their advancement. Institutional-level themes included those interventions either in place or desired by interviewees to increase female academic enhancement.

These interviews will be discussed in the following section. Given the sensitive nature of the conversations held, the high-ranking stature of many interviewees, and to encourage more forthrightness, all quotes are non-attributable. This should not affect their content or value.

INDIVIDUAL-LEVEL FACTORS

Childbearing

Childbearing was assessed by many of the participants as a significant factor affecting their career trajectories. Among the physicians interviewed, all of the physicians except our Millennial physician participants had children.

Timing of childbearing was emphasized on numerous occasions. Many women had their children during a fellowship year or prior to starting residency. One Generation-X division chief noted:

> I didn't have children until I was 37, tenured, and already had my first K grant. I couldn't let having children affect my career before I was ready.

The implicit statement is that having a child prior to a certain point in one's career could derail any advances one had made in that regard.

A director of a prominent cancer institute, and a pre-Title IX generation doctor, discussed her struggles with having children:

> I got pregnant with my first child during a research year . . . which proved to be minimally disruptive. I was pregnant with my second child at the start of my surgical fellowship. There was no maternity leave . . . there was none. There were two weeks I could take of sick leave, and I petitioned for a third week. So I was post-partum ten days and they were like "Can you come and assist on this case?" I was like "Sure, I'll just put the baby underneath and nurse while you put a surgical gown over me." And they thought I was serious.

Later she spoke about what having a child during fellowship meant:

> I was the first woman to do my fellowship at this university. My program director pulled me into his office and asked if I was planning to do *this*, in reference to my pregnancy, again. He said "This may make me think twice about taking a woman into the program again. You don't want to ruin it for everyone." This was in a time when it was common for program directors to ask female medical students what contraception they were planning on using during their training years.

These anecdotes are indicative of the difficulties surrounding motherhood for an earlier generation of female physicians. Younger female physicians who haven't had children yet express other doubts:

> I haven't had children yet because of timing. I want kids, but [my spouse] is a doctor too. Between our schedules, our debt, and our general career ambition it may still be a few more years before we have kids.

One Millennial clinic director added:

> I don't think we are likely to have children at all. Our careers are so important to us. We watch these dual-career spouses and they become absorbed with their children and do nothing else.

Interestingly, many of the participants had children in a time before the Family and Medical Leave Act (FMLA), which allows for working women in the United States to take up to twelve weeks of unpaid leave after having a child without the potential of losing their jobs. Most of these pre-FMLA women only took limited time off from work and remarked on the additional burdens related to having children. One prominent neurosurgeon notes:

> I was told early on by a female colleague that you never wanted to stand out. She made an analogy to fish—you didn't want to be too close to the bottom or you'd never get air to grow, but you didn't want to be so close to the top that the fisherman caught you. You just needed to keep your head down and do your work. My water broke in the OR and I finished my case before I checked into [Labor & Delivery] and had a baby a few hours later. There were no structured family leave policies, so I only took one week of maternity leave. I didn't want to be viewed differently from my male colleagues.

Part-time Work

Interestingly, none of the female-leaders opted for part-time work or left the workforce for any significant portion of time. Universally, they believed this decision likely contributed to their ability to become leaders over time.

A Women's Health Center director in a smaller academic community said:

> I felt very overwhelmed at one point. Yet I would have killed my husband if I had to [go part-time]. It's nice that people have that choice, but it was not a choice for me. I wanted to be a triple threat.

A few of the physician-leaders observed that while their children were young, they did pursue alternative tracks within medicine. These often came with fewer clinical hours and increased research time which allowed for less rigid scheduling. As our neurosurgeon reflected:

> It happened inadvertently. Neurosurgery is a competitive field . . . and very few physicians were referring patients to a pregnant surgeon just out of training. I applied for grants and did a lot more research during [my children's] early years. Sure my salary was less, but I also had greater flexibility.

Increased Efficiency

Overwhelmingly, participants who had children felt like they did a lot more in the same amount of time as their male colleagues. All participants without children, all the Millennial physicians interviewed, did not mention this theme at all.

This idea was best exemplified by one department chair's comments when she opted for an alternative track in medicine:

> I did opt to take Fridays off [from work] for a few years. I had a very supportive department chair and I was just grateful they let me do that and keep my salary. Only when I joined our Promotions committee did I realize I was doing so much more than some of [the others] in the department in less time.

This idea was reiterated by a prominent researcher:

> I had firm boundaries between work and my private life. I basically had no friends for a few years. I was focused on being home by 6. I would have [the nanny] prep the food and would always try to do homework with the kids . . . [and once they were in bed] I would go right back to work. I was way too sleep deprived.

Needing to Prove Oneself

There was a distinct generational difference in physician leader's responses to questions regarding discrimination. Millennial physician leaders never noted the need to be better than their male peers as a driving force behind their career decisions. This was universally espoused by pre-Title IX physicians. One pre-Title IX Gynecology leader noted:

> My first year I wrote 5 grants and 10 papers and I worked [hard] and traveled. . . . It was a very different time. . . . Now I was lucky that I had good help at home and my children were healthy. I think you proved yourself by working harder, doing better, and if they viewed you as a [threat] you would not be invited to the table where you could begin to pave a way forward [for women].

Our prominent Generation-X researcher physician reflected:

> Life is hard for smart women. I've been called overly aggressive. You can't behave the same as men. The microaggressions [I've seen] could paralyze you, but you have to dismiss them.

SOCIETY-LEVEL FACTORS

Salary Differences

Salary differences between male and female physicians featured prominently in discussions with virtually every physician. Millennial physicians did not

feel it was as pressing of an issue as Generation-X and Baby Boomer physicians. A Baby Boomer physician-leader recalls:

> I think there have been times in my life where I have been sad, frustrated, and
> mad because I knew men were getting paid more than I was. I evolved to real-
> ize that I was not going to equate my self-worth with a number on a check.
> That took a long time. I had a chairman tell me he just couldn't pay me more
> because I couldn't make more than my husband because it would affect his ego.
> . . . People very much felt that even though you were a working spouse that you
> shouldn't make more than your husband. [My husband] told me he didn't care
> if I made more then and he still holds to that now.

Among Baby Boomer female physicians, it was openly known they were
being paid less than their male colleagues. As time progressed and gender-
based pay discrimination was made a criminal offense, Generation-X female
physicians felt it more subtly and many of these salary discrepancy discover-
ies were made by accident. One prominent Women's Health leader remarked
on her experiences:

> I have felt a lot of discrimination in my medical career. I have been in four
> lawsuits with [my university] over gender-based pay equity discrimination. I
> work at a public university and salaries are publicly available. Then when you
> see how much your [male colleagues] are making, you get angry. 100% of the
> reason is because women are women. Culturally, we have salary perception
> issues. There is a conflation of gender and status in our society that plays out
> in money and power. I have turned my anger and frustration into research and
> scholarship. But it's the unfairness that gets to you. One of [my colleagues] was
> told to "budget better'" and "live in a smaller apartment" when she complained
> about her salary. It was insulting.

A Generation-X Women's Health leader built on this:

> I undervalued my work. Early on, I had male sponsors who advocated each time
> I was up for promotion to ensure I had a higher salary. But women are never
> taught to negotiate.

Another Generation-X department chair added on:

> Women are far less likely to negotiate their first contract or any subsequent
> one. They are less likely to talk to you if they feel like their salaries are
> too low. There is so much unconscious bias too. I've spoken to women in

my department and they sometimes feel not as competent, or that sense of imposter syndrome, that they're not worth as much. I have told these women when advocating for [salary increases or other opportunities] to think of it as improving the world for other women or their daughters instead of just doing it for themselves.

Childcare and Domestic Responsibilities

Childcare and domestic responsibilities, as well who were the responsible parties, were ubiquitously discussed. Disproportionately those physician-leaders with children had full-time childcare support at home in the way of nannies or family. In addition, most had paid home cleaning support as well. Only Millennial leaders noted significant spousal involvement in home maintenance, but it is important to mention that none of our Millennial leaders had children either.

Childcare was primarily carried out by women. One Generation-X department chair noted she used daycare due to having more stable clinical hours, but summed up her experiences with childcare this way:

I love my husband, and if you ask him, he always contributed 50%. But I never felt that way. It's not that he wouldn't play baseball with them, but it was the other social parts of being a parent. Thank you notes, birthday presents, these tend to fall on the women.

Later she spoke of balancing her career with her parental responsibilities:

I would be lying if I said that we didn't . . . [have strife] in our relationship . . . regarding [childcare]. If the kids were sick and home from school, he would sometimes say things like "But I have an important meeting at 10am." As if I didn't have anything important happening that day.

Another Generation-X physician-leader discussed living in a dual-physician household and raising children:

Coparenting is so important if you want to have a successful career. You need to sit down and make a list of all the household responsibilities and delegate tasks. My husband is a doctor too, so there's no "my job is more important." He has always been in charge of the trash . . . and if the trash hasn't been taken out, we know whose responsibility that was. But we make decisions . . . we never operate on the same day, and we never go out of town for conferences or meetings at the same time.

INSTITUTIONAL-LEVEL FACTORS

Mentorship and Sponsorship

The ideas of mentorship and sponsorship were spoken at in depth with all participants. Once again there were generational differences noted in participant responses. Formal structured mentorship, such as those now required in residency programs and for early career physicians, were sources of assistance for all of our Millennial physician-leaders. These opportunities did not exist for prior generations of physicians, which was a fact noted by both Generation-X and Baby Boomer physician-leaders.

For the context of this thematic section, *mentorship* was defined as a person who took a vested interest in one's career and worked with a participant to develop their interests. *Sponsorship* was defined as a person who promoted a participant's interests and either nominated or brought forth opportunities for them to develop their career.

One Millennial Chief Medical Officer focused on this formal mentorship as very important to her development:

> I got lucky that [my hospital] had a formal mentorship program where young physicians who displayed leadership capabilities were paired with older, more experienced leaders [in the hospital system]. I was paired with one of the vice presidents . . . and he gave me a lot of insight. When I doubted my capabilities to take a higher role, he recognized my feelings of being an imposter. Imposter syndrome is so real! Especially for women. Then he told me that he had those feelings too. He also told me "Every time you doubt your ability to do a job, remember how many people's [administrative] jobs you've looked at and have thought 'I could do that better.' And then you'll be just fine."

Baby Boomer physicians more than other generations noted a severe lack of mentorship throughout their careers. They often cited their gender as a source of difficulty in finding mentors as there were rarely female physicians in positions of leadership in the generations prior to theirs. There was also the perception that while mentorship existed during this time, male faculty provided mentorship only to junior male faculty members. If there was mentorship, it was noted to be indirect at best.

Sponsorship, rather than mentorship, was stated as having a bigger role in all our physician-leaders' access to leadership opportunities. One Generation-X physician-leader emphasized the importance of sponsorship:

> I will say I had a Chair who was very supportive in general. Maybe not early on, but when his daughter reached college age, he suddenly realized how hard it

was for women to succeed. He sponsored me for a female leadership course, and that's where I met a network of strong women in medicine. It taught me negotiation, problem solving . . . and introduced me to career coaching. That's the idea of hiring someone to help develop your skills. I've been using all these ever since.

Many of the female physicians noted the benefits of mentorship for others as well. Some remarked on how their own careers were stagnated due to the mentorship and sponsorship of their male peers. Our Generation-X physician researcher brought her own story to light:

When I first came [to my university], there was very little entry level funding. . . . There was a very important career funding award [that I sought]. The way that it worked was that each medical school nationally could only nominate one person . . . and [we] had nominated the same person twice who didn't get in. It was for all primary care docs and no one was even asking those departments. It wasn't just unfair for me, but an unfair process. So, my boss, when I first got here, said he was going to put the same person up a third time. And that was basically chilling out opportunity for anyone [who was interested]. I confronted him on it. "You know, I came from a place that was a meritocracy and I think we need a process. I think the dean's office should accept abstracts from anyone who is interested, and they should be deidentified, and there should be a selection committee . . . we're a big place and a lot of people could evaluate this. We could have a process, right?" It wasn't an easy conversation . . . and the body language and everything. This guy had a personal relationship and was a mentor for the man who was submitted the last two times . . . and he wasn't happy. I just felt I couldn't stand by. Long story short, [they] picked me and I got it. This made my direct boss angrier, but I did what I did. I did the best job I could.

Most of the Generation-X and Baby Boomer physicians did comment on their personal mentorship of other women. The same physician researcher above said about that:

[This hospital] was a great opportunity for me to mentor young women. We had a phenomenal fellowship program. . . . Then I was at national meetings and my fellows would present and [national leaders] were seeing how great they were. . . . This led to my meeting my greatest champions and ultimately led to me being elected into the National Academy of Medicine. People at [my own hospital] were surprised. Our Baby-boomer surgeon physician-leader remarked
     I have become the biggest female advocate. I have worked hard to promote [women]. As much as there's an old boy's club, we need an old girls club. I know when I'm looking and nominating people to positions, I look very often to women. The locker room is still very much doctors and nurses. And when [the

men] went into the "doctor's" locker room, and you did not go in with them, they did a lot of bonding and teaching [that you would never get].

Meritocracy

This idea of meritocracy being very important to career development was reiterated by many participants, including Millennial physicians. Almost all felt that it was the only way their achievements could be or were recognized. One Baby Boomer physician expanded:

> I had to seek out my own mentors. I really sought those who sought a meritocracy . . . to [increase opportunity] to build my career. I always say that if you're at a place and they don't have the culture you feel comfortable in, you either find a way to make it bearable or you leave.

A Generation-X physician-researcher added something similar:

> The chair [of my department] believed in a meritocracy. In an unlevel playing field, his playing field was level. He was a tough guy but believed in being transparent. If you were smart, put in your hours, cared about research, he would create opportunities for you. It came as a surprise for me to feel as if I were part of a group. It was extremely inclusive. That's what I tell a lot of women coming out, you're going to be in a system with a lot of implicit bias and a lot of sexism, but what really matters is who is your direct report. You can be in a heinous system, but if your direct report sees value in you and it's clear what you're supposed to do to move up, like the milestones are clear . . . as long as your direct report is treating your fairly, you can probably pull it off.

A Millennial physician-leader built on this:

> I am a first-generation college graduate and physician, as well as a woman of color. If people don't recognize me based on my accomplishments, then I don't have any other foot to stand on. My second job saw that value and offered me what I was worth. When I told my first job I was leaving, they tried to match that, but it was too late. It was telling me they didn't see my value in the first place.

Wage Gap

Salary differences were noted previously, but the persistent wage gap between female and male providers in academic settings despite attempts to standardize pay scales was separately discussed by some of the participants. One Baby Boomer physician-leader gave some thoughts as to why that is:

But also if you are dealing with being the main one who is caring for things at home, which is still the way it is, it would mean less time either for seeing patients or seeking grant funding . . . and that is the way we get paid.

A Generation-X Women's health leader had some of her own thoughts:

Look at OB/GYN or Endocrinology. These fields have become over 50% female and in the most recent ICD-10 changes, those fields are compensated even less than previously. The same surgery performed by a urologist, who are typically men, will compensate more than when it performed by a urogynecologist, who is typically a woman. This is because women participate in determining their own pay scales and every study shows they will downplay their own achievements while men will tend to up-play theirs. There's a tipping point in most medical fields, where if it becomes too female, men will stop joining and then salaries will realign to a lower level. We need to acknowledge this bias. Look at smoking as an example, there has been a clear change in cultural norms, and we need that for [women in medicine].

Not everyone thought the differences were due to outside responsibilities or inherent inequity in the field. Work, and what classifies as work, differs based on each field within academic medicine. All participants talked about which types of work were remunerated and additional duties they may have taken on which they may not have been remunerated. Our department chairman summed it up like this:

When I became department chairman, one of the first things I did was review our compensation structure. The thing that caught me was how much extra unpaid work [women] were doing. [The department's] only payment metric was RVU, but this was an academic center! We taught medical students and residents, joined committees, and spent our time in structured mentorship, and none of this was paid. So, we changed our pay structure—if you participate on a committee, it counts towards your tenure and next pay review, if you work with students or residents or as a mentor, you get paid for it. Every time a job needs to get done where someone has to take on more work, I make sure there's a title and some sort of bonus . . . and it's not just for extra clinical work. Now everyone's work is valued.

A Baby Boomer department chair commented on a different aspect of the wage gap:

I have a problem right now. We have two men in our department who have offers from other places and are asking [the department] to match their new salary. This would put their salaries at greater than others at their level, but if we want to retain talent, we have to give them some sort of raise . . . and this is how men end up making more. Women don't look for other jobs . . . and [because they don't] a wage gap exists.

One Millennial physician-leader added:

In my first job, I spent so much extra time doing things early in the morning and late at night. No one valued the extra diligence I was giving for my patients and making sure all the administrative burdens were handled. Not to mention the students and residents. Give me a medical student who didn't increase my workload. But I was told I should be glad to be in academics and so I stayed and didn't ask [for more money].

INSTITUTIONAL RECOMMENDATIONS

Participants were asked for their personal recommendations on what policies could be adopted by institutions to improve the female physician experience and increase their leadership opportunities. Many of the physician-leaders also talked in depth about what they have personally done to promote female leadership in medicine.

Flexibility

Almost every physician in every generation noted that flexibility, or lack of it, in scheduling was important to work-life balance. Interestingly, as women in both medical and surgical specialties were interviewed, each person in either specialty thought the other half had it worse. Our neurosurgeon pointed out:

Flexibility and autonomy are the two greatest ways to [avoid burnout]. You know that book *Lean In?* Well I'm like the anti-lean in . . . not that I'm anti-feminist . . . but in that sometimes we need to lean-out and as a profession we should allow [men and women] the power to decelerate and accelerate when they want.

She continued later:

We need to get rid of the word "part-time." I didn't have to declare it when I dialed back, and I think that made all the difference in my career. There should be alternative paths to be 100% employed without being 100% clinical. "Part-time" can make it sound like you're doing less or not as involved when you're not necessarily working fewer hours . . . which can lead to fewer opportunities. As for [female physicians] who leave the profession, if your job becomes less meaningful [due to few opportunities or lack of scheduling flexibility] and your family is important, why keep doing this job?

Our Generation-X Women's Health chair chimed in:

I think as a profession we need to contend with the changing gender roles and increasing number of women in medicine. Physicians who want leadership opportunities should have those available and they should have the choice to do part-time work if that's what they want as well. Being "in charge" avoids burnout. We [need to figure out] how that future looks in medicine.

Parenting

Parenting and the expectations related to this were discussed at length. While options, including live-in childcare, were discussed previously, many of the participants felt it was the responsibility of the individual and institution to create a balance between career and family.

Our prominent oncologist commented:

I did research at [an East Coast hospital] for a couple years and they were well equipped for working families . . . that way in which they would page you when it was time to breastfeed, and there were nurses who took care of sick kids away from the healthy kids so parents didn't have to miss work. [We need] more institutions to assist with childcare, especially when both parents are doctors.

A director of a Women's Health Center built on this:

We made a decision early on to allow me to work full-time. This included investing heavily in wrap-around childcare, including full-time live-in help, and having an incredibly supportive spouse who shared my career goals. I found my help by way of [another female faculty member] . . . we need ways for women to network with other working moms to [find these resources]. [Women] also need to make their lives easier. Use an app, order groceries online, pay someone to pick up the kids, do what you need to do to make life livable.

One of our Millennial participants spoke about factors that would make it easier to consider starting a family:

[The hospital] should provide on-site childcare with extended hours to help not only their physicians, but other hospital staff. People don't just get sick between 9 and 5, which means we need atypical hours for childcare as well. Not to mention, childcare is expensive, so having ways to direct pre-tax money towards childcare expenditures would go far. [Another university] started a mandatory parental leave policy this year and they found that the wage gap actually narrowed between their male and female physicians, with an unintended consequence that male physicians were opting to carry more domestic responsibilities.

Tenure and Salaries

Participants discussed ways to address the wage gap and increase women's access to opportunities. Our Generation-X department chairman had the most experience in direct implementation of policies that affect female physicians. She spoke about this as follows:

You have to have standardized salaries with periodic re-evaluation of salary differences. In addition, I realized that [women] don't advocate for themselves. I insisted that every [new] position in the department was formally announced and we invited everyone to apply. Suddenly you find out Jane is interested even though she never said anything before. I insisted every position needs a new title as well, because that's the only way you can create advancement [for everyone].

A Women's Health director spoke more to this:

[Our university] is public, so everyone's salary gets published once per year . . . and we started realizing that women were getting consistently underpaid [compared to men]. Every 3 years, the university pays an outside group to evaluate our salaries and create a plan to narrow the wage gap. You think we've addressed it, and then 3 years later there is another salary difference. Now we have implicit bias training for our promotion's committees. We have 50 years of laws against sex-based discrimination, and yet it still happens. We would like to see some change in cultural inequities.

DISCUSSION

The American College of Physicians set a goal to "eliminate the inequities that exist in compensation and career advancement opportunities and provide a more inclusive environment to realize the full potential of all physicians." Our discussions with female physician-leaders touched on those issues that create these inequities, namely limited mentorship, the prevalence of cultural stereotypes about working women which create wage and opportunity gaps, and women's ongoing and disproportionate childcare and domestic responsibilities that can not only impede career productivity but lead to burnout and career dissatisfaction.

Their responses shed light on those factors that allowed women to thrive in medicine as well. Overwhelmingly, participants proved that having supportive spouses coupled with sufficient childcare and domestic help allowed them the ability to grow in medicine. In addition, positive work environments which included sponsors who promoted a meritocratic system and places which provided access to opportunities were essential to each physician's ability to become a leader.

Recognition of the issue is important, yet large-scale problem solving can prove difficult to achieve. Fortunately, increased interest in tackling gender inequity has led to more research in how to implement institutional programs in a variety of ways to promote female growth in medicine. Trialed interventions included improving female physician access to executive coaching, having structured mentorship programs for them with older physicians as well as peers, and providing supplemental resources, such as domestic help and psychosocial support for female providers. Simultaneously, these studies have brought to light the challenges of supporting women's caregiving needs while promoting their growth and productivity (Jagsi et al., 2018).

Ongoing research also provides hope by normalizing the conversation regarding the gender-based cultural issues that pervade the medical profession. It is crucial these gender-based differences are managed soon, as women are essential to modern-day medical practice in a country with a rapidly aging population and severe healthcare provider shortages. While institutional interventions are necessary to establish equality in medical practice, true cultural shifts are essential to ensuring long-term systematic, multilevel sustainable change.

REFERENCES

Adeisoye, Taiwo. 2017. "Perceived discrimination experienced by physician mothers and desired workplace changes." *JAMA Intern Med* 177(7): 1033–36.

Association of American Medical Colleges (AAMC). 2018. *Women Majority of Medical School Applicants*. December 4. Accessed January 12, 2020. www.aamc.org/news-insights/press-releases/women-were-majority-us-medical-school-applicants-2018.

Benoit, M. F., et al. 2016. "Comparison of 2015 Medicare relative value units for gender-specific procedures: Gynecologic and gynecologic-oncologic versus urologic CPT coding. Has time healed gender-worth?" *Gynecol Oncol* 144(2): 336–42.

Bernstein, D. M. 1992. "Women in medicine: The tortuous path to professionalism." *Minn Med* 75(9): 516–23.

Brooke, E. 1997. *Medicine Women: A Pictorial History of Women Healers*. Wheaton, Ill: Quest.

Budden, A. E., et al. 2008. "Double-blind review favours increased representation by female authors." *Trends Ecol Evol* 23(1): 4–6.

Carr, P. L., et al. 1998. "Relation of family responsibilities and gender to the productivity and career satisfaction of medical faculty." *Ann Intern Med* 129(7): 532–38.

Dyrbye, L., et al. 2011. "Relationship between work-home conflicts and burnout among American surgeons." *JAMA Surg* 146(2): 211–17.

Flexner, A. 1910. *Medical Education in the United States and Canada: A Report to the Carnegie Foundation for the Advancement of Teaching*. Bulletin No. 4. Boston: Updyke.

Frank, Elena, et al. 2019. "Gender disparities in work and parental status among early career physicians." *JAMA Open Network* 2: e198340.

Han, Shasha, et al. 2019. "Estimating the attributable cost of physician burnout in the United States." *Ann Intern Med* 170(11): 784–90.

Issac, C., et al. 2009. "Interventions that affect gender bias in hiring: A systematic review." *Acad Med* 84: 1440–46.

Jagsi, R., et al. 2012. "Gender differences in salaries of physician-researchers." *JAMA* 307: 2410–17.

Jagsi, R., et al. 2016. "Work activities and compensation of male and female cardiologists." *J Am Coll Cardiol* 67(5): 529–41.

Jagsi, R., et al. 2018. "An innovative program to support gender equity and success in academic medicine: Early experiences from the Doris Duke charitable foundation's fund to retain clinical scientists." *Ann Intern Med* 169(2): 128–30.

Jena, Anupam B., et al. 2014. "Sex differences in physician salary in US public medical schools." *JAMA Intern Med* 176(9): 1294–304.

Johnson, Megan. 2018. *The Healthcare Future Is Female*. February 14. Accessed January 12, 2020. https://www.athenahealth.com/knowledge-hub/practice-management/healthcare-future-female.

Jolly, Paul. 1988. "Medical education in the US, 1960–1987." *Health Affairs* 7(Suppl 2): 144–57.

Jolly, S., et al. 2014. "Gender differences in time spent on parenting and domestic responsibilities by high-achieving young physician-researchers." *Ann Intern Med* 160(5): 344–53.

Kane, Leslie. 2019. *Medscape's National Physician Burnout, Depression, & Suicide Report 2019*. January 16. Accessed February 2, 2020. https://www.medscape.com/slideshow/2019-lifestyle-burnout-depression-6011056#1.

Kolehmainen, C., et al. 2018. "Who resembles a scientific leader—Jack or Jill? How implicit bias could influence research grant funding." *Circulation* 137: 769–70.

Ly, D., et al. 2017. "Hours worked among US dual physician couples with children, 2000 to 2015." *JAMA Intern Med* 177(10): 1524–25.

Mead, K. C. Hurd. 1938. *History of Women in Medicine from the Earliest Times to the Beginning of the Nineteenth Century*. Haddam: Haddam Press.

Rudman, L. A., et al. 2013. "Penalizing men who request a family leave: Is flexibility stigma a femininity stigma?" *J Soc Issues* 69: 322–40.

Saunders, M., et al. 2018. "Unequal pay for equal work: Where are we now?" *Ann Intern Med* 169(9): 654–55.

Walsh, M. R. 1990. "Women in medicine since Flexner." *NY State J Med* 90: 302–8.

Chapter 4

Voicing the Invisible

Women's Home-Based Work and Labor in Istanbul's Garment Industry

Saniye Dedeoglu and Asli Sahankaya Adar

INTRODUCTION

In many regions of the world, women's work in exporting industries has been at the center of major interest since the early 1970s, and this interest overlaps with the worldwide trend of "feminization of employment." Although there is a great variation in the degrees and forms of women's work from country to country, there is a strong association between women's employment and production for exports. Turkey also went through the process of export orientation of its economy and has had a growing export performance since the early 1980s. However, women's work in export manufacturing remains highly invisible in the Turkish case, where women's overall employment has been declining.

Most scholarly attention on women's home-based work is seen as a form of invisible informal activity women engaged in urban areas when they move to cities (Çınar, 1994). Home-based work was a refuge for women who could not go through the entry barriers of labor markets. These barriers are related to labor supply, including issues such as patriarchal culture, marital status, and inadequate childcare services or lack of education, as well as to low labor demand (Ilkkaracan, 2012, Toksoz et al. 2014). Though the exact size and number is not known, among women living in low-income households, women's home-based activities in urban areas are widespread (Çınar, 1994; Dedeoglu, 2012). Much of home-based work is concentrated in the garment sector, which has been an important source of employment for women not only as pieceworkers but also as formal/informal workers since the early 1980s.

The focus on home-based piecework also reveals the manifestations of "housewifization" of women (Prugl, 1999) in Turkey and of how gender ideologies played out to shape women's work and labor. Home-based workers are the main drive behind the flexibility of the industry and its success in the global competition. Having access to labor of home-based workers and keeping them within the subcontracting network requires reaching the most secluded form of labor in Turkey. Since Turkey is one of the countries with the lowest rates of female labor force participation, integrating women's labor into a labor-intensive sector such as garment has required new approaches in order to be able to tap into women living in the outskirts of the city and retain their labor. This strategy has relied heavily on the use of kin relations. Home-based work is also examined as a form of informal work of women who are in need of work but cannot work outside due to their domestic roles and responsibilities or due to patriarchal constraints keeping them at home.

This chapter examined the women's home-based piecework in the garment industry and shows gender inequalities that underlie the export success of the garment industry, in which the organization of production and workplace relations embed and reproduce gender ideology and norms. Women's engagement in garment production is ensured through the articulation of women's subordinate position with the social organization of garment production and the mobilization of kinship relations. The findings of the chapter are based on a field study of Istanbul's garment industry during the summer of 2019. The main questions driving the fieldwork are the role of women's labor in the generation of a globally competitive industry, the ways in which women became the main providers of labor for Istanbul's garment firms, and the implications of this integration into export production for gender relations. The situation and role of pieceworker women in the garment industry and the ways in which women are integrated into the garment production in Istanbul are examined through twenty interviews with home-based women workers, intermediaries, and women's family members.

HOME-BASED PIECEWORK LITERATURE IN TURKEY

Homework dates back to pre-industrial times and is not a new phenomenon. In recent years, the interest has been on the changing trends in industrial homework under the impact of global reorganization of industrial production and in global value chains. In the Turkish context, homework is most often examined in relation to women's home-based piecework activities, mostly in the garment industry. The focus on garment production is the result of the fact that it is Turkey's most global sector with a flexible organization of production and a vast employment structure. So, it offers a good vantage point to examine homework together with women's work and labor (Balaban and Sarıoğlu, 2008).

The male breadwinner model and "patriarchal contract" are the determining factors of the gendered division of labor and institutionalized gender roles establish constraints on women's labor supply in Turkey. Women use their labor to manifest their roles as "good" mothers and wives and their loyalty to their community by making their work invisible and hidden from public eyes (White, 1994; Atasü Topcuoğlu, 2010; Dedeoğlu, 2012). These studies illustrate how patriarchal dynamics restrict women's job opportunities and compel them to engage in home-based work, which is defined by low pay, long working hours, and the lack of benefits and job security (Bose, 2007; Rowbotham, 1993).

Domestic roles, responsibilities, and patriarchal constraints often relegate women to a form of informal work within the home. Therefore, home becomes a spatial meeting locus for women where their familial duties and roles are combined together with their income generation. Working at home has a contradictory effect on women's social status; it makes their life easier as their work is at home, but simultaneously has a negative effect as working from home reinforces their traditional roles of child and elderly caregiving and the performance of everyday household tasks (Aktaş, 2013).

Home-based piecework of women is examined mostly in relation to the garment production (Sarıoğlu, 2013; Tartanoğlu, 2017; Dedeoglu, 2012) and women's crucial role in the labor process of producing added value in the garment industry (Atılgan, 2007). Women workers are dependent mediators for the supply of the work and raw materials. They also have no control over the means of the production (Balaban and Sarıoğlu, 2008). It is the gendered control mechanisms that make women's obedience easy and implicit, and resistance unnecessary, as their work is constructed within familial roles and relations where women view their work within the patriarchal consensus. The gendered division of labor is inherent in the organization of home-based work. In this sense, it is very important to understand the dynamics of the organization of home-based garment work in the value chains. Control practices, in particular, are shaped by the varied patterns of gendered organization of work and labor process (Sarıoğlu, 2013).

PIECEWORKER WOMEN IN THE GARMENT INDUSTRY

In Turkey, women's employment rate is one of the lowest among OECD countries.[1] Women's labor force participation rate had a tendency to fall under the influence of urbanization which intensified after the 1980s and bottomed out with the rate of 25 percent in 2004, started slowly to increase after

2008 and reached 38 percent in 2018.[2] This seems to be a classic example of the inverted U-shaped curve of female labor force participation and economic development. Women in employment are, however, to be found mostly in precarious employment. While factually well-educated and skilled women are active participants of the formal economy, almost 70 percent of women with university degrees are in the labor market. Women with lower educational attainment and underskilled mostly concentrate on informal and marginal work such as home-based work and care work; since the 2000s, female employment is an important source of labor for the informal economy in big cities. There are three types of informal work for women in Turkey: industrial home-based work, unpaid family work, and home-based care work (Toksöz et al., 2014).

Though the exact size and number is not known, among women living in low-income households, women's home-based activities in urban areas are widespread (Cinar, 1994; Dedeoglu, 2012). In the 1990s and early 2000s, many studies pointed out that home-based work was the most common form of employment for urban women in Turkey (Dedeoglu, 2012; Toksöz et al., 2014). For example, Cinar (1994) estimates that one in every four women in Istanbul takes in homework and shows that home-based pieceworkers may outnumber the total women formally employed in the city.

The garment industry became one of Turkey's most important export industries with the neoliberal turn in economic policies in the early 1980s. The expansion of the industry is attributed to initial government support, the falling cost of labor, and the renewed capacity of the textile industry to support the rapid expansion in the manufacturing of ready-made garments (Dedeoğlu, 2012). As elsewhere, the industry in Turkey heavily draws on women's labor, although women's contribution to the export success is largely invisible in official employment statistics. Women are the main suppliers of informal labor for the industry through subcontracted and home-based piecework.

This part of the chapter examines the situation and role of pieceworker women in the garment industry and the ways in which women are integrated into the garment production in Istanbul. For this purpose, twenty interviews were conducted between June and July 2019 in Istanbul with home-based women workers, intermediaries, and women's family members. This section also includes findings of women pieceworkers of Istanbul's garment industry from a study done between 1999 and 2000 (Dedeoglu, 2012). In the report, the study findings are presented in two main sections: the first section focuses on the organizational structure of garment production in Istanbul and the second is on home-based women workers and their working conditions.

Women Pieceworkers of Istanbul's Garment Industry Piece rate home-based work as an integral part of industrial subcontracting relations in

Turkey. Sending parts of production—most of the time stitching an item on a garment, or in some cases sewing some parts of the garment with the sewing machine—to home-based women enable companies to save on labor costs and costs for space, machinery, electricity, and other required inputs such as health and safety expenses (Sarıoğlu, 2013). The home-based piecework labor process may be summarized by long and uncertain working hours, unclear employment conditions with mostly no contract, monotonous and repetitive working conditions, low wages with no social security, self-defined labor time with strict deadlines, and, because the work requires hand skills, it is defined as unskilled work in the labor markets.

Women engaged in informal production, home-based activities such as knitting, sewing, and assembly work that revolve around the demands of childcare, housework, and other obligations of a home, see their income-producing activities as a mere extension of their domestic responsibilities. The type of work in which women engage, the location of their work, and the social context and social relations of their work have tremendous implications for how they define themselves and the meaning of work in their lives.

Jenny White's study (1994) of a group of squatter settlement women in Istanbul, who engage in home-based piecework or work in family and neighborhood ateliers for export and local markets, demonstrates married women's concentration in the informal sector by its easy accommodation to women's family responsibilities. White presents a detailed analysis of why the women she studies, although intensely engaged in income-producing activities, maintain a fiction of "nonworking." Women's labor is seen as the property of the communities (i.e., their families, relatives, neighbors) they belong to, and consequently a woman's gender identity is largely defined by her labor, in the sense that her income-generating labor is conflated with her social roles and seen to be the natural extension of her domestic and communal roles. Therefore, naturally, the unpaid or poorly paid nature of women's labor is legitimized by a cultural construction of "giving" labor as a contribution to family and community and an expression of identity.

In many cases, pieceworker women do not perceive their work as proper work done outside home. Women's uneasy definitions between work and "work" and social identity in their families and communities path the way for their invisibility in the labor market. Many women engaged in different segments of garment production as pieceworkers, traditional handicraft makers, or atelier workers described their activity as a hobby or help to the family business and did not consider it as "work." Therefore, women regard their work as the extension of their traditional housewifery activities that had built upon the expression of group identity and solidarity.

PIECEWORK AND WOMEN

Home-based workers fall mainly in the age range of thirty and forty-five, have lower levels of schooling (on average they have completed five years of compulsory schooling), and are married with children. Piecework is the main work opportunity for the poor middle-aged women with few qualifications and heavy childcare and domestic responsibilities. They live in poorer households in comparison to their neighborhood's general well-being level. During the fieldwork in the summer of 2019, we conducted interview with ten women pieceworkers, most were between thirty and forty-five years old and married with children. Women over the age of forty-five are not preferred by intermediaries because the speed at work decreases with age and their eyesight deteriorates for needle and embroidery work. However, the women expect their daughters to engage in piecework during the summer holidays. During the fieldwork, we encountered two university students doing piecework with their mothers to earn some cash during the summer holidays.

In Istanbul's garment industry, workshop production and home-based work are related in terms of garment workers' life histories. It is a common practice for a mother to do de-threading work at home for the same workshop where her daughter works. Another form of mobility is for the garment worker to start work in a workshop while she is young, and become a home-based garment worker when she gets married or becomes pregnant. Workshop and home-based garment workers move in and out of employment not only because they have weak connections to the labor market but also because the fluctuating nature of the garment business creates a high turnover for workers. In this regard, a woman works in a workshop for a few months or a year or so, and then, when there is no work, she is made redundant and stays home for some time and then looks for another place to work. In some cases, women interrupt their employment due to marriage or children.

Some women were married to men who were in formal employment with social security coverage that enabled the women and children to be covered by health insurance and survivors' benefits. However, it is important to stress that not every pieceworker's husband has secure and formal employment, as many women are engaging in home-based work because their husbands are casual workers and cannot afford to support their household financially. Moreover, some women are divorcees and widows who remain without the financial support of a male provider.

The pieceworkers are portrayed as passive and vulnerable victims who occupy the last ring in the chain of global garment production. Their labor is easily substituted and their labor market vulnerability is also reinforced by their personal characteristics which are typically unskilled, poorly educated, and married with children. Usually associated with the neediest women in the community, piecework is done by women who are known to have no economic support from husbands, such as divorcees or widows; those whose husbands are not providing for them for a variety of reasons; or those who need extra cash for other reasons such as investing in home ownership. Such a woman was seen as a *fakir* (poor) woman who is usually pitied (*yazık*) in her community. This also reflects how a woman without a man's economic support is conceptualized in society (Dedeoğlu, 2012).

For garment production, home-based workers take up many different activities ranging from packing, cleaning the sewed piece from thread, sewing beads in, and embroidery as such. Working times of women change depending on the volume of work coming in and the deadline. The women stated they work longer hours particularly during periods such as holidays and New Year, stock renewal, and the beginning of the season due to the high volume of orders with tight deadlines. During these times, the working time increases to sixteen to eighteen hours per day. However, in a usual working day, women explain they work twelve hours between 9:00 and 21:00.

As discussed in the following sections, piecework is distributed to women through an intermediary, and women usually perform their tasks in their homes. However, during the fieldwork it was observed that the intermediaries sometimes rent a small shop-place (dükkan) where all pieceworker women can come together to work. These shop-places are purposefully located close to women's homes in the same neighborhood. The place where the work is done is important for women, and they either work in their homes or prefer to be in these small-workshops (if available) located close to their home, since women's piecework is the result of women's immobility due to their domestic roles and unavailability of other types of work. As Balaban and Sarıoğlu (2008) stress: "[Piecework] represents a low-paid and labor-intensive work form primarily conducted by married women, where the productive and reproductive activities of women are juxtaposed both spatially and practically" (17).

Why Home-Based Piecework?

For the home-based pieceworkers, their husbands' permission was not the only obstacle preventing their employment in a factory or atelier. Childcare, old age, and being unskilled were also cited as obstacles. A commonly encountered problem is the care of small children. Working only becomes possible when proper childcare facilities are available in the workplace; otherwise, a family needs to find alternative forms of childcare. For example, the help of other family members or private crèches, even though costly for a working-class family, are other means of sorting out childcare while the mother is at work. Using these options is viable only in the case of lucrative and stable employment. Women prefer to do home-based piecework if only marginal and temporary employment options are available to them. The testimony of one of my participants clearly singles out childcare as an obstacle to women's entrance into the labor market:

> How could I go out to work? I have two small children and my husband works all day and comes back late in the evening. I do not have anybody from my family who can look after my children while I work. My husband's family is far from where we live now. So I am doing piecework and looking after my children at the same time. We live in a one-room flat which was transformed from a kind of storage room or dükkan (shop), so it is hard for me to have a relative with us to look after my children. I wish I could work in better paid work so we could buy our own flat and live better.

Some of the women focused on other obstacles such as domestic duties and childcare responsibility that prevented their employment, rather than on the opposition of their husbands. The emphasis on those duties and responsibilities puts women in collusion with their husbands in constructing and preserving their roles as wives and mothers. The perceptions of gender roles and meanings attached to being a man or woman are internalized equally by men and women through a set of cultural practices that help to hide the unequal socioeconomic outcomes of confinement of these asymmetric gender roles.

Organization of Piecework

As indicated earlier, Istanbul's garment industry is organized in a supply chain that includes different scales of production. The top is composed of large textile companies such as LCW, INDITEX, and Trendyolmilla that determine the product design and types of fabric used in a specific design and produce a sample product. Then this sample product is passed down to the next level to an actual production workshop through a contractor specialized in finding suitable workshops or directly from the top company, where the sample design is tuned into higher volumes of products. The workshops undertake to provide all the equipment and materials required in the production process. In this process, this main workshop is also responsible for both the quality and cost of the fabric and accessories, and depends on other suppliers to produce a finished product. Therefore, this main workshop outsources different activities and tasks involved in the production process.

In the subcontracting chain, there are smaller ateliers working for the main workshop described above, specialized in sewing, yarn cleaning, ironing, and packaging operations. Among these ateliers undertaking different activities, the sewing ateliers subcontract yarn cleaning, ironing, and packaging operations to home-based women.

In the garment industry, people called *fasoncus* (outsourcers) are employed to deal with all the outsourcing activities, working with different sized workshops ranging from large to small ones. Their role is to organize the allocation of different stages of production to different ateliers. For pieceworkers, their role is to find intermediaries who could subcontract work to women. Continuing down the chain, the fasoncu brings pieces for cleaning, packaging, and ironing to intermediaries who then organize pieceworkers. Then, the role of the intermediary is to organize enough numbers of women to perform the tasks and ensure the smooth running of production. In this process, pieceworker women are responsible to the intermediary, the intermediary to the fasoncu, the fasoncu to the atelier, the atelier to workshop, and the workshop to the company. See figure 4.1 below.

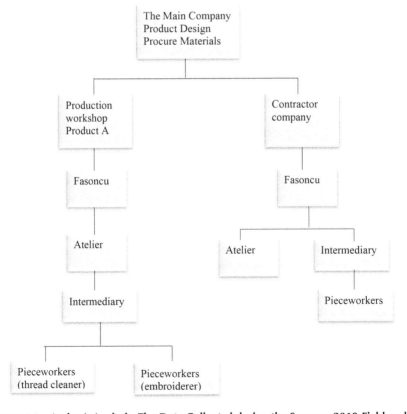

Figure 4.1 Author's Analysis: The Data Collected during the Summer 2019 Fieldwork.

During the fieldwork, we interviewed a fasoncu to better understand his role and skills in the production chain of the garment industry. A fasoncu needs to have garment production experience and connections with ateliers, suppliers, and intermediaries. The contractor we interviewed has twenty-five years of working experience in Istanbul's garment industry. He ran his own atelier for fifteen years and worked as a contractor for various companies during that time. The most difficult part of his job is that there is no fixed place of work or working hours. There is also no concept of overtime. Although he may take Saturdays and Sundays as holidays, the fasoncu can be called by the intermediaries any time of the day and every day of the week. Apart from this, he needs to move to different locations in the city and has to control the intermediaries for the distribution and supervision of the work. Therefore, he is on the move all the time. Although he stated his preferred working time is normally nine hours a day, in practice, he is working eleven to twelve hours per day.

Labor intermediaries for home-based work are usually women distributing the work to pieceworkers. Even if the intermediary is a man, he always works with his wife or another woman since their work is directly with women. The age of intermediaries ranges from thirty-five to fifty-five, and they are usually ex-garment workers with good connections to women in their close vicinity. In Istanbul's garment production, intermediaries work in two ways. The first type of intermediation is that the work coming from a fasoncu is subcontracted and distributed to pieceworkers' homes. The intermediary deals through the women and their networks for occasional and non-consistent jobs. For this type of organization, the intermediary works with one or several ateliers and deals with different fasoncus.

The second type of intermediation is based on regular business deals in which they either get regular work orders all year round or work with several different ateliers to ensure a regular inflow of work. For this, the intermediaries gather a group of eight to ten women in a workshop hired specifically to do piecework. Working with the same ateliers is an advantage for intermediaries as it ensures steady payments, and then the intermediary can pay the pieceworker women. Otherwise, if the intermediary does not receive regular payments from the ateliers, then she cannot deliver her payment to pieceworkers. This may undermine the trust relationship between the intermediary and her pieceworkers.

Intermediary women explain their work as a contribution to their household income and support for their children's education. On average, the earning of an intermediary is around 1,000 and 2,000 TL a month[3]. The intermediary we interviewed stated she makes between 1,500 and 2,000 TL depending on the volume and regularity of work. The pieceworkers working for intermediary women are often family members, relatives, and neighbors living in their vicinity, through which a trust relationship and solidarity are formed easily, thereby fostering a more flexible organization of the production process. The intermediary woman we interviewed had been working as an intermediary for the last four years and had previously worked in garment ateliers for five years. During busy times, she brought her relatives and neighbors whom she knew from her neighborhood to her already existing ten-women team. This allowed her to organize her business in a more flexible manner and respond to the changing demands and orders. Having a reliable and trustworthy team is essential for running her business, as any case of missing pieces, lost equipment, or bad quality of work can damage her reputation and may cancel her work with ateliers.

Recruitment Strategies

The case of women's home-based work in Istanbul's garment industry illustrates that the organization of women's piecework and atelier production is based on gender and social relations as well as kinship relations, in which women's work is embedded. This in turn causes both men and women to devalue women's home-based work. These relations and ideologies also provide a mechanism whereby women produce cheaply for international and national markets. Thus, women's labor, both paid and unpaid, is conflated with their social and gender identity and membership of social groups such as the family. Women's informal work in home-based piecework or in garment ateliers tends to reproduce the patriarchal character of social relations without any public recognition of the work. In this regard, the recruitment strategies of women pieceworkers reflect a gendered integration into garment work. There are three different strategies utilized in Istanbul's garment production to integrate women into piecework.

Unpaid Family Workers

In this group, there are family members who work as pieceworkers for their own atelier to reduce cost and provide flexibility and reliable labor. Istanbul's garment workshops rely heavily on close family members and relatives, whose labor is a reliable, flexible source. They are available for work as long as their fathers, husbands, or uncles run the workshop. The mothers or wives of workshop owners are the invisible heart of this core labor force, akin to the workshop owners' wives in Hsiung's study (1996). Their roles in family business are quite diverse and range from direct contribution to production to cooking for garment workers and cleaning the workplace. These women are not only burdened with trimming and cleaning garments at home, but they also organize their neighbors and relatives to engage in piecework when extra labor is needed. Mothers of workshop owners look after the family's young children, while the wives are at work in the workshop. Although they remain housewives, these women extend their domestic tasks beyond meeting the physical needs of household members to providing and maintaining particular ties with relatives, neighbors, and friends, who are in turn a source of aid and reserve labor. Their involvement creates an environment in which the workshop is viewed as a family setting for women's work that further attracts more women into production. While this group of women is not usually paid for their activities, they are clearly contributing to garment production in many diverse ways. Not only do they support garment workshops with their labor, they also provide family care labor and manage relations in the neighborhood—activities that are key to the survival of the family business.

The roles of this group of women can vary over the course of their life. Some young girls, by gaining garment-making skills and experience and establishing networks of new friends and contacts, manage to find better working conditions and may even move into formal factory employment if their family gives consent. For married women, workshop jobs have a different trajectory from those of young girls, as their labor is often more closely tied to household needs and family business cycles. If a family business closes down, women go back to their homes and children, or if the business expands through partnerships with other workshops and increases the number of nonfamily employees, the married women are excluded from the work and stay home.

Recruiting through an Intermediary

In Istanbul's garment industry, some tasks are subcontracted directly from a workshop to women and others are allocated by middle-women, who are sometimes relatives of the workshop owner. There was a distinctive difference between how larger-scale factories managed their subcontracting, and how garment ateliers organized their relations with home-based pieceworkers. Garment ateliers are the mediators for large-scale factories in distributing garment pieces to home-based workers. As it is a time-consuming and costly activity to deal with home-based work, large-scale factories preferred to subcontract the work to garment ateliers. Despite some factories subcontracting piecework to ateliers, the ones that specialized in designer and high fashion production had direct relations with home-based workers, as the tasks required highly delicate and skilled handicraft, such as embroidery or making ornaments on garments. In order to find the right women for the work, factories establish an efficient network of subcontracting.

Here is an example of how a large-scale factory directly managed its subcontracting relations with home-based pieceworkers. Two workers were allocated to distribute garments to pieceworkers, who were all women and lived in neighborhoods close to the garment factory. One of these workers was the driver of the van, and he was also in charge of carrying the garments. The other worker was a woman who was in control of the women pieceworkers. She demonstrated to the women what should be done to the new pieces and kept records of the garments distributed and the payments each worker should receive. She could decide independently how many pieces to be subcontracted and to whom. This woman, Serpil, who was thirty-five years old and the mother of two children, told her story of how she became the middlewoman of the factory.

> I am good at maths and also a high school graduate. Most of my colleagues are primary school graduates and I was quick to learn every job at the factory. So, our manager (müdür) asked me to do this job when they decided to subcontract some tasks to women instead of doing them in the factory. Now, we have 50 women in different mahalles around here and some of these women have been working for more than 8 years. What I do is very difficult because if a piece is missing or something is wrong with the quality of the work I am responsible. I try to work with women whom I trust and have known for a long time. In the beginning, there were just a few women whom I reached through my own personal contacts and mostly from my own family and neighborhood. We need to make sure that women have skills to do the job. Even though most women have skills of sewing and embroidery it is more important to follow the designs and be precise, clean and on time.

Although Serpil was an ordinary worker in the factory, her role as a middlewoman of the factory gave her decision-making power over the pieceworkers. Serpil was like a manager with pieceworkers and demanded information about the process of their work. She often reminded the women that the timing of task completion was very important and if the work was not completed on time payment would have to wait until the following month. She was certainly the boss of the pieceworkers, for whom having a good relationship with Serpil was the channel for getting access to regular piecework.

Networks of Pieceworker Women

The irregular nature of piecework and the strict rules of work completion have resulted in the composition of a complex alliance between women pieceworkers and middle-women, which shows the extra-economic relations underlying the social organization of piecework in Istanbul's garment industry. This irregular structure of work has developed a network of women in which a pieceworker, for example, is the main subcontractor of the factory but also shares her quota with other women in her household or neighborhood. In cases of surplus work and under time pressure, a pieceworker uses the help of her neighbors and pays them later. This practice of collaboration among women generates further flexibility in the organization of piecework, and shifts the responsibility of middle-women, in terms of finding new subcontractors, to pieceworkers.

In one of Serpil's visit to her pieceworkers where she distributed some work and collected the finished pieces, there were two women pieceworkers whom Serpil had known for a long time. These two women were working together and making their garment pieces. Serpil gave them the new garments and explained what was required, and then a third woman suddenly appeared and carefully listened to what Serpil had to say. Later, it became clear that the other two women shared some of their work with her. When there was too much work and too little time to finish all the pieces, Serpil herself gave work to the third woman. This was one of the ways that the factory's circle of subcontracted women enlarged over time.

Garment ateliers establish their network of pieceworkers through using the personal connections of the women in their families. Extended families always have some untapped labor of women that can be drawn into production whenever necessary. For example, the grandmother of the family usually stays in charge of childcare during the day, while other family members are working in the atelier. Sometimes she also does the finishing of garment pieces by cleaning stitched edges, or, in some cases, she acts as the middle-woman in their immediate environment by distributing garments to other women. Ateliers that are unable to utilize their own family labor usually have a number of pieceworkers who have worked for them for a long time. These women establish a small network of pieceworkers in which they have the leading role as distributor. Their networks can be as small as four or five women.

While piecework is an individual activity and each woman is paid individually for her work, it is common in the literature to argue that women work collectively in their homes (White, 1994; Cinar, 1994). Often a neighbor would come in and join in the work for an hour or so and leave. There was a clear sense among all the women interviewed in this research that piecework is low paying and extremely tedious, and all subcontracted tasks are repetitive, time-consuming, and require very little skill. That is why pieceworkers are those who are in extreme economic difficulty with few other available sources of work.

Home-based garment work is usually done in a network of reciprocity among women. When there is a need to finish the work quickly, other women help out with their piecework by getting together for tea gatherings. The women in the community volunteer their labor and maintain the relations of cooperation based on such mutual help, in anticipation of receiving the same kind of help from others, in case they should ever be in similar need.

Income from Piecework: Charity or Survival?

Although pieceworkers make a substantial contribution to the global garment manufacturing in Istanbul, their income is conceptualized as *pazar parası* (bazaar money), which is seen as charity to poor women. This conceptualization was made clear in one atelier owner's statement, where he explained how and why he subcontracted to women:

> We subcontract only to women and they sometimes come and ask us whether there is any work. Most women are regulars and all are from this area. In the past, we hired women to do hand-work of the pieces as full-time workers but the garment business is irregular. Sometimes these women had nothing to do for weeks and we had to pay their salaries. Later on, we decided to subcontract women at home so that we delivered pieces to them when there is work and pay them on a piece basis. For women, it is better to do piecework than sitting idle at home so they earn their pazar parası. I think that this work is good for women because fakir kadın (poor women) need to feed their children and at the same time they can watch over their children. Times are hard for families, so people are trying hard to make ends meet and everyone has to do something in order to survive (hayatta kalmak için). Piecework gives the opportunity to live without depending on anybody (el açmadan yaşama).

The women involved in home-based piecework are usually pitied in their community. They are divorcees or widows, those whose husbands are not providing any money for them for a variety of reasons, or those who need cash to acquire an asset, for example. Such a woman was seen as a *fakir* (poor) woman, who is usually pitied (*yazık*) in her community. Workshop owners represent piecework as a kind of social charity to those women in need, even though it is entirely a business matter for them.

CONCLUSION

The current research on home-based work in Turkey is examined in relation to Istanbul's garment production (Sarıoğlu, 2013; Tartanoğlu, 2017; Dedeoğlu, 2012) and women's crucial role in the labor process of value chains in the garment industry (Atılgan, 2007). Women workers are dependent mediators for the supply of the work and raw materials. They also have no control over the means of production (Balaban and Sarıoğlu, 2008). It is the gendered control mechanisms which make women's obedience easy and implicit, and resistance unnecessary, as they see their relations with the mediator as part of the patriarchal consensus. The gendered division of labor is inherent in the organization of home-based work. In this sense, it is very important to understand the dynamics of the organization of home-based garment work in the value chains. Control practices, in particular, are shaped by the varied patterns of gendered organization of work and labor process (Sarıoğlu, 2013).

It is true that the garment industry has been the top exporting sector in Turkey since the early 1980s when Turkey started to adopt economic liberalization policies. Since then, the garment industry heavily draws on women as the main suppliers of informal labor through subcontracted and home-based piecework. This chapter discussed in detail that gender inequalities underlie the export success of the garment industry in which the organization of production and workplace relations embed and reproduce gender ideology and norms. Women's engagement in garment production is ensured through the articulation of women's subordinate position with the social organization of garment production and the mobilization of kinship relations. While piecework is an individual activity and each woman is paid individually for her work, the collectivity of women working in their homes is common in the literature (White, 1994; Çınar, 1994).

The piecework in Istanbul's garment industry is defined as women's work because of the assumed characteristics of patience, endurance, lack of mobility, and dexterity associated with women, and also because of the low amount of money paid for each piece. The networks of collaboration created among women are the main element of recruitment of pieceworkers and a further aspect of flexibility in garment production in Istanbul. These studies illustrate how patriarchal dynamics restrict women's job opportunities and compel them to engage in home-based work, which is defined by low pay, long working hours, and the lack of benefits and job security.

NOTES

1. In 2018, women's employment rate was 32.9 percent in Turkey while the OECD average is 61 percent for the same year (OECD Data Centre, https://stats.oecd.org/viewhtml.aspx?datasetcode=LFS_SEXAGE_I_R&lang=en#).

2. OECD Data Centre, https://stats.oecd.org/viewhtml.aspx?datasetcode=LFS_SEXAGE_I_R&lang=en#.

3. In July 2019, the minimum wage in Turkey is 2,020 TL a month, which is around 380 USD.

REFERENCES

Aktaş, Gül. "Üretiyorum Öyleyse Varım: Buldan'da Ev Eksenli Çalışan Kadınların Aile ve Toplumsal Yaşamda Görünmeyen Emeği," *Sosyal ve Beşeri Bilimler Dergisi 5* (2013): 258–267.

Atasü-Topçuoğlu, Reyhan. "Home-Based Work and Informal Sector in the Period of Globalization: An Analysis Through Capitalism and Patriarchy: The Case of Turkey" (Master's Thesis, The Graduate School of Social Sciences, Middle East Technical University, 2005).

Atılgan, Saniye. "Evden İçeri Bir Ev: Ev Eksenli Üretim ve Kadın Emeği," *Birikim Dergisi 217* (2007): 134–140.

Balaban, Utku, and Esra Sarıoğlu. "Home-Based Work in İstanbul: Varieties of Organization and Patriarchy" (Working Paper, *Social Policy Forum*, Boğaziçi University, 2008).

Bose, Mallika. "Women's Home-Centered Work in India: The Gendered Politics of Space," *International Development Planning Review 29* (2007): 271–298.

Çınar, Emine Mine. "Unskilled Urban Migrant Women and Disguised Employment: Homeworking Women in İstanbul, Turkey," *World Development 22* (1994): 369–380.

Dedeoğlu, Saniye. *Women Workers in Turkey-Global Industrial Production in İstanbul.* New York: I.B. Taurus, 2012.

Hsiung, Ping-Chun. *Living Rooms as Factories: Class, Gender, and the Satellite Factory System in Taiwan.* Philadelphia: Temple University Press, 1996.

Ilkkaracan, Ipek, "Why So Few Women in the Labor Market in Turkey?," *Feminist Economies 18* (2012): 1–37.

Prugl, Elisabeth. "What Is a Worker? Gender, Global Restructuring and the ILO Convention on Homework." In *Gender Politics in Global Governance*, edited by Mary K. Meye and Elisabeth Prugl, 197–209. Rowman & Littlefield Publishers, 1999.

Rowbotham, Sheila. *Homeworkers Worldwide.* London: Merlin, 1993.

Sarıoğlu, Esra. "Gendering the Organization of Home-Based Work in Turkey: Classical Versus Familial Patriarchy," *Gender, Work & Organization 20* (2013): 479–497.

Tartanoğlu, Şafak. "The Voluntary Precariat in the Value Chain: The Hidden Patterns of Home-Based Garment Production in Turkey," *Competition & Change 22* (2017): 1–18.

Toksöz, Gülay. "Gender Based Discrimination at Work in Turkey: A Cross Sectoral Overview," *Ankara Üniversitesi SBF Journal 59* (2014).

TurkStat (2016) *Labor Force Statistics.* Available at: http://www.turkstat.gov.tr/Start .do;jsessionid2nmMY8qfFfL8cLl8JX9NtvpZfhNyVTVQplGHp5xHSLmn8d5NJ WkV.

White, Jenny. *Money Makes Us Relatives: Women's Labor in Urban Turkey.* Austin: University of Texas Press, 1994.

Part II

THE USE OF LANGUAGE TO DEVALUE WOMEN IN THE WORKPLACE

Chapter 5

How Students Think about Women Professors

Enforcement of Hegemonic Femininity in Students' End-of-Term Evaluations

Elizabeth Hoffmann and Chris Sahley

Universities' science, technology, engineering, and math departments continue to employ fewer women faculty than other disciplines, reflecting the gender disparities both within academia, generally, and specifically within these disciplines. Qualitative analysis of students' comments in professors' end-of-term evaluations shows that students enforce hegemonic gender roles with both criticism for women professors' violation of gender norms and praise for their performance of hegemonic femininity. These additional demands for women professors may account for women faculty's lower numerical scores: quantitative analysis found that women faculty received on average almost half a point lower than men faculty. This study suggests that, in addition to the abilities students require of both women and men professors (e.g., fair tests), they also want their women professors to conform to norms of hegemonic femininity by being friendly, encouraging, expressing care, and appearing conventionally attractive. These student comments illustrate how gender hierarchy mediates professional status.

INTRODUCTION

Women continue to be underrepresented as faculty in many academic departments, especially the Science, Technology, Engineering, and Mathematics (STEM) disciplines (Berdousis and Kordaki, 2016; Li and Koedel, 2017; Nadler, Berry, and Stockdale, 2013). Villablanca, Beckett, Nettiksimmons, and Howell found that even though "women receive nearly half of all doctoral degrees and show a high interest in academic careers, the pipeline is leaky" and far fewer women PhDs enter post-secondary teaching than their men counterparts (Villablanca et al., 2011: 1485). Additionally, many studies have documented a continuing wage gap for women academics despite efforts to close this gap (e.g., Nadler, Berry, and Stockdale, 2013; Renzulli et al., 2013).

The difficulties women professors face in achieving tenure and promotion through the ranks have been attributed to a range of factors, including fewer support networks and women role models (Todd et al., 2008), competing family demands (Morrison, Rudd, and Nerad, 2011), differences in doctoral education and organizational features of academic work (Fox, 2006), fewer collaborators and industry connections for research (Bozeman and Gaughan, 2011), measurement against a male standard (Brink and Benschop, 2012), lack of knowledge regarding resources (Turner et al., 2011), and fewer patents (Whittington and Smith-Doerr, 2008).

Women professors' lower social status means that they may be "less protected from affronts to their authority, even when in the same occupational position as men" (Bellas, 1999: 104). Students question the authority and knowledge base of women professors more than men (Basow, Phelan, and Capotosto, 2006; Moore 1997). Perhaps as a result, some research indicates that students demand greater lecture preparation from women professors (Monroe, 2013) and expect them to share more personal illustrations and experiences as part of the lectures (Kierstead, D'Agostino, and Dill, 1988).

Students' end-of-term evaluations of their courses' professors are often the primary measures of faculty efficacy used in tenure and promotion decisions, directly affecting faculty members' career trajectories, promotions, and pay raises (Park, Sine, and Tolbert, 2011; Todd et al., 2008). However, such evaluations can be very subjective (Brink and Benschop, 2012) and may be unfortunately mediated by students' gendered expectations of faculty (Nadler, Berry, and Stockdale, 2013; West, 1995).

This chapter explores student evaluations of their men and women professors in STEM disciplines in a large public university in the central United States. In particular, this chapter examines the additional demands students make of their women professors. Gendered expectations are demonstrated in student comments and reference the compliance, or noncompliance, of women faculty with norms of hegemonic femininity. These expectations are consistent with the additional demands for performance of gendered behavior often placed on women employees in other employment contexts (Eagly and Carli, 2007; Gorman, 2005; Gwen Daverth, 2016; Ridgeway, 2011).

These different demands may have affected students' quantitative assessments of their women and men professors, with women professors averaging a half-point lower score than their men colleagues at this university. Since most evaluations were between three and five, this half-point distinction is actually a difference of 25 percent. In understanding this difference in evaluation, we raise the possibility that women professors' violations of norms of hegemonic femininity may negatively affect these women faculty's student evaluations. Negative evaluation subsequently could affect promotions and pay. We suggest that this particular manifestation of social structure in the lenses of individual students should be considered in how and to what extent students' end-of-semester faculty evaluations are used in teaching evaluations.

GENDER HIERARCHY, STUDENT ASSESSMENT, AND THE STEM CLASSROOM

Despite efforts toward increasing the numbers of women in the STEM fields, women continue to be underrepresented (Bilimoria, Joy, and Liang, 2008; Cech et al., 2011; Coutinho-Sledge, 2015). The small number of women STEM faculty both reflects the gender disparities in these disciplines, generally, and illustrates how academia struggles with gender equity in the STEM areas in particular. In turn, the paucity of women STEM faculty might contribute to the lower numbers of undergraduate women majoring in STEM disciplines, with few women role models and mentors (Berdousis and Kordaki, 2016; Ehrenberg et al., 2012). Some research suggests that women's evaluations rank them lower and make them less likely to be promoted into higher levels of academia (Galbraith, Merrill, and Kline, 2012; Goos and Salomons, 2017). Evaluation of professors' teaching often exclusively relies on students' end-of-term faculty assessments. These student assessments may be substantially biased by expectations of gender norms (Nadler, Berry, and Stockdale, 2013; West, 1995).

Gender Hierarchy in Academia

Hochschild and coauthors refer to the "stalled revolution" in achieving gender equality (Blair-Loy et al., 2015; Hochschild and Machung, 2012). As has been noted in a variety of professions and occupations (Acker, 1990; Albiston, 2009; Berrey, Hoffman, and Nielsen, 2012; Bobbitt-Zeher, 2011; Coutinho-Sledge, 2015; Eagly and Carli, 2007; Gorman, 2005; Haveman and Beresford, 2012; Hoffmann, 2004; Ridgeway, 2011; Roth, 2004), academia also continues to employ women in smaller numbers, in lesser-status positions, and at lower salaries than men. For example, 44 percent of full-time faculty (including tenured, tenure-track, adjuncts, and interim) in 2015 were women (Education and Statistics, 2017) and 31 percent of senior positions

(Winchester and Browning, 2015). Similarly, in their study of forty selective public universities, Li and Koedel found that only 35 percent of the faculty were women (2017: 344).

The positions and conditions of women's employment in academia also vary from that of men professors. Women faculty are particularly under-represented in advanced- and higher-level positions and overrepresented in nontenure-track positions (Nadler, Berry, and Stockdale, 2013). Within the variations between universities, women faculty are often underrepresented at research universities and elite colleges (Li and Koedel, 2017; Nadler, Berry, and Stockdale, 2013; Rivera, 2017).

This clustering may contribute to the finding that women faculty earn sub-stantially less than similar men faculty (Nadler, Berry, and Stockdale, 2013). Particularly in predominantly white universities and elite black universities, men professors earn more pay than women professors (Renzulli, Grant, and Kathuria, 2006). For example, West found that full professor women faculty earned 88 percent of what similar men earned (West, 1995). Much pay inequality may be caused by "the allocation of men and women into niches defined by the intersection of institution, division, and rank . . . [with] [w]omen more likely than men to be located in niches that pay less well." (Renzulli et al., 2013: 69)

Ehrenberg and coauthors found that colleges and universities with women presidents, provosts, and more than a token number of trustees grow their proportions of women faculty more quickly than peer institutions with more men in leadership (Ehrenberg et al., 2012). Higher educational institutions also developed mentoring programs and equity workshops, and worked to foster supportive and collegial climates (Stepan-Norris and Kerriessey, 2016: 228). However, Nielson reports that university-level initiatives at gender equity "often lack consistent coordination and support at the faculty and department levels." (Nielsen 2017: 297)

Colleges and universities have made efforts toward increasing the numbers of women faculty in STEM, both out of concern for equity among professors but also to encourage more women STEM students (Berdousis and Kordaki, 2016; Ehrenberg et al., 2012). Nevertheless, women professors' numbers remain particularly low in STEM departments (Berdousis and Kordaki, 2016; Li and Koedel, 2017). Li and Koedel, for example, found that women faculty constituted 18 percent to 31 percent of STEM departments, in contrast to a range of 47 percent to 53 percent in non-STEM areas (2017).

Student Assessment of Instructors

Student assessment of instructors has become an established part of pro-fessors' evaluations. In many colleges and universities, these evaluations "remain the most common method of evaluating faculty performance in the classroom." (Winkler 2000: 739) Frequently they are "used to measure teaching quality in higher education and compare it across different courses, teachers, departments and institutions." (Angervall, 2018; Goos and Salomons, 2017: 341) In addition to demonstrating institutional performance broadly, they are often used to demonstrate teaching quality in promotion decisions for individual faculty members (Galbraith, Merrill, and Kline, 2012; Kherfi, 2011).

However, some research suggests that students' assessments are not consistently sound evaluations of teaching skill and "tend to partially reflect student, course, and teacher characteristics which may not be related to teaching quality" (Goos and Salomons, 2017: 343; Spooren, Brockx, and Mortelmans, 2013). In evaluating faculty, students often are substantially influenced by their first impressions and draw on stereotypes in forming their official opinions (Nadler, Berry, and Stockdale, 2013).

Students often have preconceived ideas about what college and university professors should be like; most often these stereotypes are around race (white) and sex (male) (Ford, 2011). For example, West explains that students are so strongly swayed by gender norms that these beliefs will override contrary data (1995). Dasgupta and Asgari (2004) found that greater exposure to women faculty produced less likelihood among students to express stereotypical beliefs about women and women faculty, while minimal exposure to women faculty increased stereotypic beliefs. This latter situation was most pronounced in the male-dominated disciplines of the STEM courses (Dasgupta and Asgari, 2004).

Hegemonic Femininity

The enforcement of gender norms erodes a professional woman's power. That is, while her professional status, demonstrated ability, and acquired knowledge elevate her power, her female gender decreases her power. West and Zimmerman provide the example of a woman physician to illustrate how even when women are in positions of some power, hegemonic femininity is enforced to maintain the gender hierarchy: "A woman physician may be accorded respect for her skill. . . . Nevertheless, she is subject to evaluation in terms of normative conceptions of" compliance with hegemonic femininity (West and Zimmerman 1987: 139).

Hegemonic norms of femininity and masculinity as social structure dictate "[w]hat a society considers 'men's work' and 'women's work' result[ing] in gender segregation in many occupations" (Hechavarria and Ingram 2016: 246). Hegemonic femininity demands behavioral, emotional, and physical conformity by women to certain female stereotypes. Violations of these gender expectations can be "swift and severe social sanctions for women who take on or enact hegemonic masculinity" (Bilimoria, Joy, and Liang 2008: 246).

Just as "[h]hegemonic masculinity refers to the idealized standards for men and male bodies, [hegemonic] femininity refers to the idealized standard for women and female bodies . . . [creating a] bipolarization . . . where men are the ideal norm and women are the marginalized 'other'" (Hechavarria and Ingram 2016: 246). Because hegemonic masculinity equates manhood with being in control, able, dependable, and successful, some scholars assert that women being in control and fully capable is, itself, a violation of hegemonic femininity (Bilimoria, Joy, and Liang, 2008).

Gender stereotyping affects how workers are perceived and evaluated. Even seemingly positive gender stereotypes can diminish perceptions of those workers' competence, commitment, and appropriateness at work (Bobbitt-Zeher, 2011). For example, the image of the ideal worker is often a male worker, so that a female worker who might be quite competent and committed to her job might be seen as not as fit for her position as a similar male worker if she is seen as conforming to stereotypes of women (Acker, 1990; Heilman, 2001).

Stereotypes can affect work evaluations, hiring decisions, and promotion deliberations (Eagly and Carli, 2007; Gorman, 2005; Gwen Daverth, 2016; Ridgeway, 2011). As Haveman and Beresford wrote, "Widely held cultural expectations about what men and women can and should do—gender stereotypes about [e.g.,] who can do mathematics . . . and who should lead—are the basic cause of observed gender differences in educational attainment, job preferences, and work experience" (Haveman and Beresford 2012: 125).

Gender Norms and STEM Classrooms

The social sciences have long established that gender is something that is performed. In their classic work, "Doing Gender," West and Zimmerman explained that "[o]nce the [gender] differences have been constructed, they are used to reinforce the 'essentialness' of gender" (West and Zimmerman 1987: 137). This allegedly essential nature of women—stereotypic gender traits—is increasingly referred to as *hegemonic masculinity* and *hegemonic femininity* (Connell and Messerschmidt, 2005; Schippers, 2007; Stone and Gorga, 2014; Strong, 2017; Velding, 2017). In other words, the norms of femininity are so widespread and consistent that they are deemed hegemonic. Hegemonic femininity and masculinity are constituted in interactional contexts—the college classroom is one such interactional context.

Hegemonic femininity places men more naturally in the workplace in general and in STEM fields in particular, and has therefore impeded women's advancement in STEM-related jobs as well as in academic positions in STEM departments (Haveman and Beresford, 2012; Schippers, 2007). For example, although research shows "only weak evidence of actual gender differences in mathematical skills . . . most college students believe men are better at mathematics than women" (Haveman and Beresford 2012: 121).

Beliefs about gender norms can critique professors' personal affect also. For example, Winkler explains that, "although students expect more caring and warm behaviour from women, they may interpret such behaviour as being 'too feminine' for that of a professor; but if a woman faculty member acts in a strong and assertive manner she may be viewed as 'too masculine'" for a woman (2000: 740).

In addition to demanding certain behaviors, such as caring, hegemonic femininity demands the display of normative emotions, either be genuinely felt or performed through requisite emotional labor. When the performance of certain emotions is part of one's job, scholars refer to it as "emotional labor" (Hochschild, 1983). Performance of emotional labor may include vocal tone, posture, and facial expressions, as well as actions and words, often specific to one's gender, such as wanting men to act angry or women to act nurturing (Sallaz, 2010; Wharton, 2011).

Occupations that have traditionally been held by women (e.g., nurses), often require stereotypic "feminine emotional displays" (e.g., nurturing, soothing). Emotional labor can be as essential to some jobs as mental or physical labor. Noncompliance by not displaying the correct emotion, such as a waitress who is grouchy, would be as much an infraction as not executing the correct mental labor, such as forgetting customers' orders, or physical labor, such as dropping dishes. Required emotional labor is often a display of gender-specific emotions in reaction to certain situations (Grandey, 2000; Hochschild, 1983; Hoffmann, 2007; Pierce, 1996; Polletta and Tufail, 2016). Employers have long realized that how their employees display emotions can affect the success of the business, especially when the employees have a great deal of customer contact (Lopez, 2011). In a university setting, the professors' "customers" are their students, in that this is the population that consumes what the professors are producing.

Hegemonic femininity also includes physical appearance that conforms to gendered expectations of beauty. While hegemonic masculinity may include aspects of physical appearance, it is attractiveness that is central to hegemonic femininity (Schippers, 2007). Women's physical attractiveness is often characterized by a woman who is "thin, young, White, upper-class, and heterosexual" with accenting make-up and hairless body (Velding, 2017: 508).

Students' minimal exposure to women faculty (such as in predominately male disciplines like STEM) increases students' confidence in gender stereotypes (Dasgupta and Asgari, 2004). Some studies have found that students—individuals or small numbers—may be overtly combative and hostile to women faculty. Enforcement of gender norms may result in students aggressively challenging the women professors' authority (Nast and Pulido, 2000; Winkler, 2000). For example, a study of 158 college students found that approximately one-third had sexually harassed a professor at least once, with men students being more likely to do so than women students (DeSouza and Fansler, 2003). Other studies have found that students are more likely to request additional help and special favors from women professors than from men professors (Basow, Phelan, and Capotosto, 2006; El-Alayli, Hansen-Brown, and Ceynar, 2018).

METHODS AND SAMPLING

To better understand how students perceived and evaluated their professors, this study examined students' end-of-term assessments administered to each course by their university. The university studied is located in the north-central United States ("The Midwest"). The university, over 100 years old, has well-established graduate and undergraduate programs in many disciplines. However, it is particularly known for having strong STEM departments.

These student assessments were drawn from online student course evaluations for 100–400 level courses in STEM departments at a large, public university. Only those evaluations for faculty who would go up for tenure were included, excluding evaluations for already tenured professors. Evaluations excluded courses that enrolled fewer than ten students. Additionally, due to concern that new professors' first year of teaching might include a teaching learning curve or unusually poor teaching as they adapt to college-level teaching, this chapter includes only professors with at least five course ratings. This ensured that everyone in this study has had adequate teaching experience.

To address the main question of this chapter—What do students want from their professors?—the qualitative portion of the study examines the open-ended, write-in comments for the Spring, 2011, the end-of-the-semester evaluations. The two open-ended questions were: "What is something/are some things that the instructor does well?" and "Make a suggestion(s) for improving the course." Student responses that had no write-in comments or had only one-word comments were eliminated from the qualitative analysis. This reduced the number of evaluations analyzed to 12,949.

The student responses were coded for area of concern: (1) lecturing/teaching; (2) tests, exams, and homework; (3) knowledge/expertise; and (4) personal attributes. This final category, personal attributes, was more closely coded for content: (a) being friendly and accessible, (b) encouraging and enabling students, (c) expressing care and understanding, and (d) physical appearance. The student responses that are included in this chapter are followed by the course in which the evaluation was made.

Quantitative analysis provides an insight into numerical ratings of faculty. This portion examined 178,313 evaluations from six semesters, 2008–2011, for STEM courses to investigate differences in instructor rating across genders for the response variable: "Overall, I would rate this instructor as;" Students select from a scale of 5 for "excellent," 4 for "good," 3 for "fair," 2 for "poor," and 1 for "very poor." The linear mixed model was used to account for the possible correlation among responses from the same instructor and to adjust for other possible explanatory variables and their interactions with gender. These other explanatory variables include the semester the course was taught, the college offering the course, the level of the course, and the log-number of students in the course who provided evaluations. The log-number was chosen to reduce the influence of very large courses (i.e., the distribution of the number of responses was strongly skewed to the right).

RESULTS AND DISCUSSION

While quantitative analysis of numeric scores begins to sketch the picture of students' different assessments of their men and women professors, qualitative analysis of what students wrote in the comments sections of the evaluations provides deeper insight into how students are perceiving and assessing their professors. Students' comments demonstrate that they demand that their women professors comply with norms of femininity, rewarding compliance with, and criticizing deviance from, those norms. Hegemonic femininity includes both physical appearance and behavior (Schippers, 2007), and these are reflected in students' comments regarding women professors' kindness, helpfulness, cheerful attitudes, and attractiveness.

The numeric portion of the evaluations shows that women faculty scored −0.467 lower than men faculty.

Figure 5.1 displays the distribution of average ratings for each gender. In general, the women professors' ratings appear shifted to the left relative to the men's ratings (unadjusted mean gender difference is 0.23). To adjust for other possible explanatory variables, we fit our linear mixed model. Only gender and the log-size of the course were found to be significant. For class size, the bigger the course, the lower the average rating (−0.15, P=0.001). Difference in students' scores of women faculty was found to be almost half a point lower than their assessments of men faculty (0.4670, P=0.0003). However, it

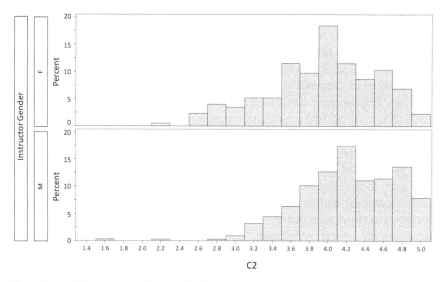

Figure 5.1   Histograms of Course C2 Ratings by Gender.

should be noted that most evaluations were between three and five, meaning that this half-point difference is, in reality, a difference of 25 percent.

However, we were even more curious to understand *how* the students were evaluating their faculty. While content analysis of students' responses to open-ended questions showed many similarities regarding students' expectations and demands for their women and men professors, importantly, the data also showed that students have additional demands for women faculty. In particular, these data demonstrate how the students reinforce hegemonic femininity and how gender hierarchy might be played out in the university classroom.

Gender-Neutral Standards

Some student comments were common for both men and women professors. These assessments covered various topics. Students wrote about the lectures, exams, laboratory sections, and course requirements.

Sometimes these comments were positive, as the examples below illustrate.
I liked the way that he paused after every step to make sure everyone was on board with the process [College of science: Mathematics].
She discusses key points that we should know and that will appear on the quiz.
I enjoy having the opportunity to have information on the quiz posed before to further understand the concept [College of Science: Biological Sciences].

I really enjoy the structure of how the class is set up. [He] makes you stay on top of the topic [College of Technology: Building Construction and Management]. He goes through the lab thoroughly step-by-step so that you understand what exactly it is you're doing and why you are doing it [College of Science: Biological Sciences].

I learned a lot from his lectures, explained things well [College of Veterinary Medicine: Surgery].

Other times the comments were negative:

Often times when we ask a question in class the answers are too vague. He could give more detailed answers during the labs when students ask for help. He speaks in very general terms so as not to give anything away, which does not help my understanding of the problem [College of Technology: Building Construction and Management].

It is often difficult to understand what Dr. __ is talking about. . . . He asks questions . . . and then a student answers [and yet] we can't hear what they said. Therefore I usually don't know what is going on [College of Technology: Computer Graphics Technology].

He was a fair grader and all but I thought some things in this class weren't good. I thought [his] exams were very hard and comparing it to the others I wasn't expecting it [College of Science: Department of Computer Science].

She was very, very difficult to understand. It made listening to and paying attention in lecture difficult [College of Science: Chemistry].

He is not very good at explaining basic concepts [College of Science: Physics and Astronomy].

Comments like those above were made to both men and women professors. These comments are not surprising. Indeed, the extant literature establishes that college students are increasingly embracing a consumer mentality in which they enter the classroom with expectations of standards and service (Galbraith, Merrill, and Kline, 2012; Spooren, Brockx, and Mortelmans, 2013).

HEGEMONIC FEMININITY

However, in addition to the above standards that students had for both men and women professors, students also assessed their women professors on their compliance with, or deviance from, conventional gender norms. Students wrote positive comments for women professors who conformed to the gender norms of being kind and caring, helping students, displaying positive emotions, and appearing physically attractive. With only a few exceptions, men professors did not receive this scrutiny.

Praise for Compliance

One key area in which women professors were evaluated was the extent to which they accomplished the norm of "kindness and caring." Students would comment on whether their women professors were interested in the welfare of their students. This seemed to be a requirement to care about the students themselves, rather than simply about the students' learning or skills, as the following quotations illustrate.

> Makes each student feel important. Knows our names and shows genuine concern [College of Technology: Organizational Leadership and Supervision].
> She is very kind and wants us to do well [College of Veterinary Medicine].
> Friendly, kind and smart. Is incredibly knowledgeable about the topic. Cares about her students [College of Science: Biological Sciences].
> [Name] makes everyone feel valued and important. She is extremely kind and wants everyone to do well [College of Technology: Electrical and Computer Engineering Technology].
> [She's a] very loving and understanding teacher! [College of Technology: Computer Graphics and Technology].

In many ways, these comments are placing the woman professor into the hegemonic "mother role": a nurturing woman who cherishes each charge (see Kanter, 1977). Beyond merely enabling her students' learning, this requires a level of affectionate caring. This appreciation for classroom mothering is a good example of the "persistent feminine ethic of care" that has been documented in a variety of work contexts (Lu 2018: 74; Nielsen, 2017).

Other positive comments praised the woman professor for enabling and encouraging students. These comments reflect the image of the "helper" who lifts up her students to reach their potential, such as those below.

> She walks us through anything that we want her help with. She was very friendly and very understanding. A great teacher overall [College of Technology: Computer Graphics].
> She was friendly and very supportive of my special needs, and was very willing to help me [College of Science: Mathematics].
> [Name] is very helpful and patient to all. She adapted well to all of the students [College of Science: Mathematics].

Very helpful and a good personality [she] is easily approachable [College of Science: Biological Sciences].

These comments situate the woman professor as one who enables students by adapting to the different needs of each student so that each one can achieve in her or his own way. Hegemonic femininity's conception of the woman as helper, underlines that she is less a primary actor in her own right, but more important for what she can enable others to do. The extant literature has commented that this valuation of women primarily for how they can increase others' worth results in diminishing the efforts of the woman working, and also makes her labor less visible and seem less important (Hechavarria and Ingram, 2016; Schippers, 2007).

Additionally, students praised women professors who present themselves as happy. The performance of this sort of emotional labor is a key component of hegemonic femininity. For example:

She always seems happy and makes a positive environment [College of Science: Chemistry].

She was a very wonderful person. She taught the class what they needed to know with a good attitude. She was upbeat and open to any question [College of science: Physics & Astronomy].

Dr. [name] is very approachable and personable. She is a very accomplished lady [College of Veterinary Medicine].

I love how she makes the learning more fun than other professors [College of Science: Chemistry].

She is very friendly [College of Science: Physics].

An important part of these women professors' jobs was not simply to convey knowledge and information, but to depict themselves as happy teachers who create fun classrooms. These comments were rarely included in men professors' student evaluations, yet are prominent in evaluations of women professors.

Emotional labor, that is, presentation of positive emotions as part of one's job performance regardless of how sincerely held those emotions might be, has been identified in a variety of occupations and professions (Bulan, Erickson, and Wharton, 1997; Grandey, 2000; Hoffmann, 2016; Polletta and Tufail, 2016). Women workers, in particular, often have to perform specific emotions, regardless of authenticity, such as airline stewardesses (Hochschild, 1983), paralegals (Pierce, 1996), museum performers (Tyson, 2013), and sales people (Martin, Knopoff, and Beckman, 1998).

However, much emotional labor performed by women professors is somewhat unusual in that professors' emotional labor is largely performed alone, in front of the classroom, or lecture hall, without the benefit of nearby coworkers who can provide support, buffers, and assistance in performing the necessary emotional labor. For example, Lively's (2000) study of paralegals showed how these lower-status workers were able to help each other perform emotional labor for the attorneys. "By turning to similar others in reciprocal if not simultaneous support, paralegals are better able to manage their own and each others' negative emotional reactions to the emotional and task-related demands of their jobs" (Lively 2000: 58).

Occasionally, women professors were also assessed on their physical conformity to gender norms. Below are illustrative quotations.

> Be less beautiful so I can focus [College of Science: Biological Sciences].
>
> You are a beautiful woman and I can see that you get flustered in class. If nothing else, I loved having you lecture the class and would enjoy being a personal friend of yours outside the class [College of Science: Mathematics].
>
> She had some really long legs that she flaunted a lot, it was nice [College of Technology: Building Construction and Management].

The positioning of the woman professors, not only as attractive, but as objects of heterosexual desire, conforms to key norms of hegemonic femininity. As Schippers wrote, "Compulsory heterosexuality and hegemonic constructions of sexuality as natural" reinforce the gender hierarchy (Schippers 2007: 90–91).

Regardless of their real or perceived attractiveness, men professors' bodies were not noteworthy. This may be because men as professors conform to the gender norm in students' view. As Acker asserted about employees generally, "the worker is actually a man; men's bodies, sexuality" and physical presence is assumed, while the woman's body is out of place and worthy of comment (Acker 1990: 139).

Criticism for Noncompliance

Women professors not only received praise for their compliance with gendered norms, but they also received criticism when they deviated from hegemonic femininity. For example, one evaluation criticized the woman professor for inadequately caring for her students:

> Also, I only ever asked Prof [Name] one question and with this she was quite short and did not understand what I was saying. I was left to figure it out on my own [College of Science: Chemistry].

This evaluation complains that the student had to "figure it out" independently (the "mother" having abandoned her children [see Kanter, 1977]).

Additionally, the professor was "quite short," rather than being warm and nurturing.

Similarly, women professors received criticism for when they were seen as not reaching out to help students, such as in this evaluation: "Doesn't interact with class at all, just reads off powerpoints—not helpful; felt bored during lecture." [Chemistry] This student found this professor aloof, unhelpful, and boring. These are the opposite of the encouraging, helpful "cheerleader" (see Kanter, 1977) gender norm. Indeed, positive emotional labor was also monitored by students in their faculty evaluations. For example:

> It seemed like the only time you were making actual eye contact with anyone was when you were telling someone to be quiet. otherwise, you were staring at the screen with your back to the students and that is a difficult atmosphere to learn in [College of Science: Chemistry].
> [In contrast to most days] you were friendly and smiling during the [specific instrument] lab and I think it made a difference in how people saw you [College of Veterinary Medicine].

The performance of the gender-appropriate emotions is a key part of hegemonic femininity (see Schippers, 2007). These women professors did not consistently display happy, welcoming emotions while teaching. One student even asserted that this lack of welcoming emotions by the professor was sufficiently damaging to learning that the classroom became "a difficult atmosphere to learn in," emphasizing how the performance of gender is a necessary component of her professional performance of teaching.

Finally, a few evaluations criticized women professors for being insufficiently physical attractive, such as the evaluation: "Looks count, right? You could try to be pretty. It's your job." [Organizational Leadership and Supervision] This student characterized the professor's job as requiring "be[ing] pretty"—ostensibly, in addition to her other job requirements of lecturing, grading, research, and service.

Students were aware of the norms of hegemonic femininity, gender hierarchy, and gender norms. They had definite standards to which they held their women professors, but rarely their men professors. Students' enforcement of hegemonic femininity demonstrates how gender hierarchy can overlay the women professors' professional status.

SUMMARY

Student evaluations of professors are a measure of faculty efficacy used in tenure and promotion decisions and may be mediated by students' gendered expectations of faculty. This chapter's findings resonate with those by earlier researchers of other occupations who found that women, particularly in mostly men work situations, were evaluated with additional requirements, in comparison to their men coworkers. This chapter suggests that unexamined expectations of faculty based on gender could undermine academe's efforts at gender equality.

This study contributes to the understanding of gender disparity in the university setting and the challenging situations that women professors face, particularly in STEM programs. The analyses suggest that gendered expectations are evident in student evaluations of their women and men professors. While the quantitative examination of students' evaluation showed the magnitude of the gender differences in student evaluations, the qualitative analysis explained how gendered expectation may work to depress faculty ratings. Difference between women and men faculty members' end-of-term evaluation scores was almost half a point; however, since most evaluations were between three and five, this half-point difference plays out as a difference of 25 percent.

The qualitative portion of this study sought to understand how the students understood the work of their women and men professors and what they were considering as they evaluated them and scoring the women professors substantially lower. Student expectations of women professors' conformity with hegemonic norms of femininity constitute an additional demand on these women professors. Men professors in this study did not need to worry about, nor allot any special effort to, satisfying such student demands. Indeed, since hegemonic masculinity (a topic worthy of discussion, but beyond the reach of this chapter) includes men being in positions of authority, demonstrating knowledge and expertise, and working in the STEM areas, the men professors were conforming already. By fulfilling the basic requirements of the jobs, as knowledgeable experts in STEM disciplines, these men professors were inherently satisfying the "masculinized ideal worker norm," documented in other types of organizations (Kelly et al., 2010).

Thus, in addition to conducting high-quality research, service work, and teaching, women must also conform to hegemonic norms of femininity in the classroom. These results build on earlier findings that students criticize women professors more than men professors when they do not adequately perform gender roles (Kierstead, D'Agostino, and Dill, 1988) and often make more requests for help from women professors (El-Alayli, Hansen-Brown, and Ceynar, 2018). These classroom findings echo what Bulan, Erickson, and Wharton found in other occupations: that women's success at work often involves "speech, action and emotion that symbolize a willingness to 'do for' the customer or client" (1997).

In this case, the "customer or client" to satisfy is the student. Since students' end-of-term evaluations are often the only measure of teaching ability, these evaluations could impact women professors' careers. Both pay raises and promotion through the ranks officially consider teaching effectiveness (Winkler, 2000). By depressing women's teaching scores, women are less likely to thrive in academia, a current situation already well documented by other studies (e.g., Bozeman and Gaughan 2011; Feldman, 1993; Morrison, Rudd, and Nerad, 2011; Turner et al., 2011).

Sociological gender theory addresses differential evaluations of women and men. In explaining enforcement of gender norms, West and Zimmerman provided the example of the woman physician who receives respect for her skill, but still is evaluated "in terms of normative conceptions of appropriate attitudes and activities for her sex category" (West and Zimmerman 1987: 139). Similarly, the women faculty in this chapter are given respect for their position as professors, but the students' comments attempt to maintain the gender hierarchy. The students' critiques of women professors' kindness, supportiveness, positive emotions, and physical beauty assert the gender hierarchy over these women's professional status. Similar demands for conformity to the norms of hegemonic femininity have been identified in a variety of occupations: wait staff (Hall, 1993), clerical work (Gwartney-Gibbs and Lach, 1994), finance (Blair-Loy and Wharton, 2004), taxicab driving (Hoffmann, 2005), and forestry (Coutinho-Sledge, 2015).

However, this chapter's data underline how women in academia may be uniquely situated compared to women in other fields. For the teaching component of their job duties, women professors' evaluations come from those subordinate to them in the organizational hierarchy. Yet, the enforcement of gender roles in these evaluations reinforces the subordinate position of these women professors in the societal hierarchy.

Thus, this chapter demonstrates the tensions between different sources of power—gender norms versus professional status. By drawing on hegemonic norms of femininity, the students enforce additional demands for gender conformity on women professors. Criticism of women faculty for violating gender norms, such as being insufficiently nurturing, as well as praise for compliance with norms, such as positive emotional labor, underline the importance, in the students' minds, of normative gender performance by the women faculty. As comparisons against key standards of hegemonic femininity permeate students' evaluations of women faculty, these results raise serious concerns about how reliance on student evaluations and their use in promotion decisions could impede equality in the academic workplace.

A key strength of this chapter is that it examined student evaluations across several STEM disciplines. In addition to this diversity in academic disciplines, the university studied here has better-than-average racial diversity (and average gender diversity) in its student body. This diversity provides a substantial robustness of the data and findings.

A limitation of this chapter is that it draws on data from only one university. While this university may be typical, future research should draw on data from many different institutions, sampling both small colleges and large universities from beyond the Midwestern United States. Additionally, in this chapter, the students' qualitative answers to the open-ended questions on the student evaluations were not paired with their numeric scorings of their professors. Future research might seek similar but matched data.

Future research also might explore student evaluations of faculty in non-STEM courses. Since women are underrepresented in the STEM areas, this chapter deliberately focused on these disciplines in order to provide research that might shed light on and ameliorate gender disparities found there. However, the dearth of women in the STEM fields—both within and outside academia—could affect students' assessments of their professors. Indeed, some research asserts that students will enforce fewer gender norms and subscribe to fewer stereotypes if they are exposed to more women in positions of authority (e.g., Dasgupta and Asgari, 2004). Future work should explore whether this chapter's findings are limited only to STEM disciplines or also are found elsewhere.

REFERENCES

Acker, Joan. 1990. "Hierarchies, Jobs, and Bodies: A Theory of Gendered Organizations." *Gender & Society* 4(2):139–58.

Albiston, Catherine. 2009. "Institutional Inequality." *Wisconsin Law Review* 2009(5):1093–167.

Angervall, Petra. 2018. "The Academic Career: A Study of Subjectivity, Gender and Movement among Women University Lecturers." *Gender and Education* 30(1):105–18.

Basow, Susan A., Julie E. Phelan and Laura Capotosto. 2006. "Gendered Patterns in College Students' Choices of Their Best and Worst Professors." *Psychology of Women Quarterly* 30:25–35.

Bellas, Marcia L. 1999. "Emotional Labour in Academia, the Case of Professors." *The Annals of the American Academy of Political and Social Science* 561:96–110.

Berdousis, Ioannis and Maria Kordaki. 2016. "Computing and Stem in Greek Tertiary Education: Gender Representation of Faculty Members During the Decade 2003–2013." *Gender and Education* 30(1):1–21.

Berrey, Ellen, Steve G. Hoffman and Laura Beth Nielsen. 2012. "Situated Justice: A Contextual Analysis of Fairness and Inequality in Employment Discrimination Litigation." *Law & Society Review* 46(1):1–36.

Bilimoria, Diana, Simy Joy and Xiangfen Liang. 2008. "Breaking Barriers and Creating Inclusiveness: Lessons of Organizational Transformation to Advance Women Faculty in Academic Science and Engineering." *Human Resource Management* 47(3):423–41.

Blair-Loy, Mary and Amy S. Wharton. 2004. "Mothers in Finance: Surviving and Thriving." *Annals of the American Academy of Political and Social Science* 596:151–71. doi: 10.1177/0002716204268820.

Blair-Loy, Mary, Arlie Hochschild, Allison J. Pugh, Joan C. Williams and Heidi Hartmann. 2015. "Stability and Transformation in Gender, Work, and Family: Insights from the Second Shift for the Next Quarter Century." *Community, Work & Family* 18(4):435–54.

Bobbitt-Zeher, Donna. 2011. "Gender Discrimination at Work: Connecting Gender Stereotypes, Institutional Policies, and Gender Composition of Workplace." *Gender & Society* 25(6):764–86.

Bozeman, Barry and Monica Gaughan. 2011. "How Do Men and Women Differ in Research Collaboration? An Analysis of the Collaborative Motives and Strategies of Academic Researchers." *Research Policy* 40:1393–402.

Brink, Marieke Van den and Yvonne Benschop. 2012. "Slaying the Seven-Headed Dragon: The Quest for Gender Change in Academia." *Gender, Work, and Organization* 19(1):71–92.

Bulan, Heather Ferguson, Rebecca J. Erickson and Amy S. Wharton. 1997. "Doing for Others on the Job: The Affective Requirements of Service Work, Gender, and Emotional Well-Being." *Social Problems* 44(2):235–56.

Cech, Erin, Brian Rubineau, Susan Silbey and Caroll Seron. 2011. "Professional Role Confidence and Gendered Persistence in Engineering." *American Sociological Review* 76(5):641–66.

Connell, R. W. and James W. Messerschmidt. 2005. "Hegemonic Masculinity: Rethinking the Concept." *Gender & Society* 19(6):829–59.

Coutinho-Sledge, Piper. 2015. "Feminized Forestry: The Promises and Pitfalls of Change in a Masculine Organization." *Gender, Work and Organization* 22(4):375–89.

Dasgupta, N. and S. Asgari. 2004. "Seeing Is Believing: Exposure to Counterstereotypic Women Leaders and Its Effect on the Malleability of Automatic Gender Stereotyping." *Journal of Experimental Social Psychology* 40(5):642–58.

Daverth, Gwen, Catherine Cassell and Paula Hyde. 2016. "The Subjectivity of Fairness: Managerial Discretion and Work–Life Balance." *Gender, Work and Organization* 23(2):89–107.

DeSouza, Eros and A. Gigi Fansler. 2003. "Contrapower Sexual Harassment: A Survey of Students and Faculty Members." *Sex Roles* 48(11–12):529–42.

Eagly, Alice H. and Linda L. Carli. 2007. *Through the Labyrinth: The Truth About How Women Become Leaders*. Boston: Harvard Business School Press.

Ehrenberg, Ronald G., George H. Jakubson, Mirinda L. Martin, Joyce B. Main and Thomas Eisenberg. 2012. "Diversifying the Faculty Across Gender Lines: Do Trustees and Administrators Matter?" *Economics of Education Review* 31(1):9–18.

El-Alayli, Amani, Ashley A. Hansen-Brown and Michelle Ceynar. 2018. "Dancing Backwards in High Heels: Female Professors Experience More Work Demands and Special Favor Requests, Particularly from Academically Entitled Students." *Sex Roles* 78(7–8):542–60.

Feldman, Kenneth A. 1993. "College Students' Views of Male and Females College Teachers." *Research in Higher Education* 34:151–211.

Ford, Kristie A. 2011. "Race, Gender, and Bodily (Mis)Recognitions: Women of Colour Faculty Experiences with White Students in the College Classroom." *Research Policy* 40:853–63.

Fox, Mary Frank. 2006. "Women and Academic Science: Gender, Status, and Careers." Pp. 17–28 in *Are Women Achieving Equity in Chemistry: Dissolving Disparity and Catalysing Change*, edited by C. H. Marzabadi, V. Kuck, S. Nolan and J. Buckner. New York: American Chemical Society.

Galbraith, Craig S., Gregory B. Merrill and Douglas Kline. 2012. "Are Student Evaluations of Teaching Effectiveness Valid for Measuring Student Learning Outcomes in Business Related Classes? A Neural Network and Bayesian Analyses." *Research in Higher Education* 53(3):353–74.

Goos, Maarten and Anna Salomons. 2017. "Measuring Teaching Quality in Higher Education: Assessing Selection Bias in Course Evaluations." *Research in Higher Education* 58(4):341–64.

Gorman, Elizabeth H. 2005. "Gender Stereotypes, Same-Gender Preferences, and Organizational Variation in the Hiring of Women: Evidence from Law Firms." *American Sociological Review* 70(4):702–28.

Grandey, Alicia A. 2000. "Emotional Regulation in the Workplace: A New Way to Conceptualize Emotional Labor." *Journal of Occupational Health Psychology* 5(1):95–110.

Gwartney-Gibbs, Patricia A. and Denise H. Lach. 1994. "Gender Differences in Clerical Workers' Disputes Over Tasks, Interpersonal Treatment, and Emotion." *Human Relations* 47(6):611–39.

Hall, Elaine J. 1993. "Waitering/Waitressing: Engendering the Work of Table Servers." *Gender & Society* 7(3):329–46.

Haveman, Heather A. and Lauren S. Beresford. 2012. "If You're So Smart, Why Aren't You the Boss? Explaining the Persistent Vertical Gender Gap in Management." *The Annals of the American Academy of Political and Social Science* 639(1):114–30.

Hechavarria, Diana M. and Amy E. Ingram. 2016. "The Entrepreneurial Gender Divide: Hegemonic Masculinity, Emphasized Femininity and Organizational Forms." *International Journal of Gender and Entrepreneurship* 8(3):242–81.

Heilman, Madeline E. 2001. "Description and Prescription: How Gender Stereotypes Prevent Women's Ascent Up the Organizational Ladder." *Journal of Social Issues* 57(4):657–74.

Hochschld, Arlie and Anne Machung. 2012. *The Second Shift: Working Families and the Revolution at Home*. New York: Penguin Books.

Hochschild, Arlie Russell. 1983. *The Managed Heart: Commercialization of Human Feeling*. Berkeley: University of California Press.

Hoffmann, Elizabeth A. 2004. "Selective Sexual Harassment: How the Labeling of Token Workers Can Produce Different Workplace Environments for Similar Groups of Women." *Law and Human Behavior* 28(1):29–45.

Hoffmann, Elizabeth A. 2005. "Dispute Resolution in a Worker Cooperative: Formal Procedures and Procedural Justice." *Law & Society Review* 39(1):51–82.

Hoffmann, Elizabeth A. 2007. "Open-Ended Interviews, Power, and Emotional Labor." *Journal of Contemporary Ethnography* 36(3):318–46.

Hoffmann, Elizabeth A. 2016. "Emotions and Emotional Labor at Worker-Owned Businesses: Deep Acting, Surface Acting, and Genuine Emotions." *The Sociological Quarterly* 57(1):152–73.

Kanter, Rosabeth Moss. 1977. "Some Effects of Proportions on Group Life: Skewed Sex Ratios and Responses to Token Women." *American Journal of Sociology* 82(5):965–90.

Kelly, Erin L., Samantha K. Ammons, Kelly Chermack and Phyllis Moen. 2010. "Gendered Challenge, Gendered Response: Confronting the Ideal Worker Norm in a White-Collar Organization." *Gender & Society* 24(3):281–303.

Kherfi, S. 2011. "Whose Opinion Is It Anyway? Determinants of Participation in Student Evaluation of Teaching." *The Journal of Economic Education* 42(1):19–30.

Kierstead, Diane, Patti D'Agostino and Heidi Dill. 1988. "Sex Role Stereotyping of College Professors: Bias in Students' Ratings of Instructors." *Journal of Educational Psychology* 80(3):342–44.

Li, Diyi and Cory Koedel. 2017. "Representation and Salary Gaps by Race-Ethnicity and Gender at Selective Public Universities." *Educational Researcher* 46(7):343–54.

Lively, Kathryn J. 2000. "Reciprocal Emotion Management: Working Together to Maintain Stratification in Private Law Firms." *Work and Occupations* 27(1):32–63.

Lu, Hangyan. 2018. "Caring Teacher and Sensitive Student: Is It a Gender Issue in the University Context?" *Gender and Education* 30(1):74–91.

Martin, J., K. Knopoff and C. Beckman. 1998. "An Alternative to Bureaucratic Impersonality and Emotional Labor: Bounded Emotionality at the Body Shop." *Administrative Science Quarterly* 43(2):429–69.

Monroe, Kristen. 2013. "Tougher Standards for Female Scholars? The Psychology Behind Them and Policies to Eliminate Them." *International Studies Perspectives* 14(4):476–84.

Moore, Melanie. 1997. "Student Resistance to Course Content: Reactions to the Gender of the Messenger." *Teaching Sociology* 25:128–33.

Morrison, Emory, Elizabeth Rudd and Maresi Nerad. 2011. "Onto, up, Off the Academic Faculty Ladder: The Gendered Effects of Family on Career Transitions for a Cohort of Social Science Ph.D.S." *Review of Higher Education* 34:525–53.

Nadler, Joel T., Seth A. Berry and Margaret S. Stockdale. 2013. "Familiarity and Sex Based Stereotypes on Instant Impressions of Male and Female Faculty." *Social Psychology of Education* 16(3):517–39.

Nast, Heidi J. and L. Pulido. 2000. "Resisting Corporate Multiculturalism: Mapping Faculty Initiatives and Institutional-Student Harassment in the Classroom." *Professional Geographer* 52(3):722–37.

Nielsen, Mathias Wullum. 2017. "Scandinavian Approaches to Gender Equality in Academia: A Comparative Study." *Scandinavian Journal of Educational Research* 61(3):295–318.

Park, Sangchan, Wesley D. Sine and Pamela S. Tolbert. 2011. "Professions, Organizations, and Institutions: Tenure Systems in Colleges and Universities." *Work and Occupations* 38(3):340–71.

Pierce, Jennifer L. 1996. *Gender Trials: Emotional Lives in Contemporary Law Firms*. California: University of California Press.

Polletta, Francesca and Zaibu Tufail. 2016. "Helping Without Caring: Role Definition and the Gender-Stratified Effects of Emotional Labor in Debt Settlement Firms." *Work and Occupation* 43(4):401–33.

Renzulli, Linda, Linda Grant and Sheetija Kathuria. 2006. "Race, Gender, and the Wage Gap: Comparing Faculty Salaries in Predominately White and Historically Black Colleges and Universities." *Gender & Society* 20(4):491–510.

Renzulli, Linda A., Jeremy Reynolds, Kimberly Kelly and Linda Grant. 2013. "Pathways to Gender Inequality in Faculty Pay: The Impact of Institution, Academic Division, and Rank." *Research in Social Stratification and Mobility* 34(2013):58–72.

Ridgeway, Cecilia L. 2011. *Framed by Gender: How Gender Inequality Persists in the Modern World*. New York: Oxford University Press.

Rivera, Lauren A. 2017. "When Two Bodies Are (Not) a Problem: Gender and Relationship Status Discrimination in Academic Hiring." *American Sociological Review* 82(6):1111–38.

Roth, Louise Marie. 2004. "Engendering Inequality: Processes of Sex-Segregation on Wall Street." *Sociological Forum* 19(2):203–28.

Schippers, Mimi. 2007. "Recovering the Feminine Other: Masculinity, Femininity, and Gender Hegemony." *Theory and Society* 36(1):85–102.

Spooren, Pieter, Bert Brockx and Dimitri Mortelmans. 2013. "On the Validity of Student Evaluation of Teaching: The State of the Art." *Review of Educational Research* 83(4):598–642.

Stepan-Norris, Judith and Jasmine Kerriessey. 2016. "Enhancing Gender Equity in Academia: Lessons from the Advance Program." *Sociological Perspectives* 59(2):225–45.

Stone, Amy L. and Allison Gorga. 2014. "Containing Pariah Femininities: Lesbians in the Sorority Rush Process." *Sexualities* 17(3):348–64.

Strong, Melissa J. 2017. "'The Finest Kind of Lady': Hegemonic Femininity in American Women's Civil War Narratives." *Women's Studies* 46(1):1–21.

Todd, Zazie, Anna Madill, Nicky Shaw and Nicola Bown. 2008. "Faculty Members' Perceptions of How Academic Work Is Evaluated: Similarities and Differences by Gender." *Sex Roles* 59(11–12):765–75.

Turner, Caroline, Sotello Viernes, Juan Carlos Gonzalez and Kathleen Wong. 2011. "Faculty Women of Colour: The Critical Nexus of Race and Gender." *Journal of Diversity in Higher Education* 4:199–211.

Tyson, Amy. 2013. *The Wages of History: Emotional Labor on Public History's Front Lines*. Boston, MA: University of Massachusetts Press.

U.S. Department of and National Center for Education Statistics. 2017. *The Condition of Education 2017 Congress*, NCES 2017-144.

Velding, Victoria. 2017. "Depicting Femininity: Conflicting Messages in a 'Tween' Magazine." *Youth and Society* 49(4):505–27.

Villablanca, Amparop C., Laurel Beckett, Jasmine Nettiksimmons and Lydia P. Howell. 2011. "Career Flexibility and Family-Friendly Policies: An NIH-Funded

Study to Enhance Women's Careers in Biomedical Sciences." *Journal of Women's Health* 20(10):1485–96.

West, Candace and Don H. Zimmerman. 1987. "Doing Gender." *Gender & Society* 1(2):152–51.

West, Martha S. 1995. "Women Faculty: Frozen in Time." *Academe* 81(4):26–29.

Whittington, Kjersten Bunker and Laurel Smith-Doerr. 2008. "Women Inventors in Context: Disparities in Patenting Across Academia and Industry." *Gender & Society* 22:194–218.

Winchester, Hilary P. M. and Lynette Browning. 2015. "Gender Equality in Academia: A Critical Reflection." *Journal of Higher Education Policy and Management* 37(3):269–81.

Winkler, Julie A. 2000. "Faculty Reappointment, Tenure, and Promotion: Barriers for Women." *The Professional Geographer* 52(4):737–50.

Chapter 6

Explicit and Implicit Career Impediments for Women

The Case of Turkish Engineering Academia

Fatma Fulya Tepe and Per Bauhn

When I began this research on career impediments of Turkish women academics in engineering in 2009, I searched for research participants to interview and asked professors I knew if they could put me in touch with women academics in engineering. The results of these efforts were not very fruitful. A male professor I knew very well even told me: "Come on Fulya, can a woman be an engineer?" as a response to my request. This reply brought to my mind some lines from a 1935 novel by a Turkish woman writer, Rebia Arif. In this novel, called *Kadın Tipleri* (Woman Types), the daughter of the family, Bilen, declares to her parents that she intends to be a mechanical engineer and she wants to build and fly her own plane. The parents were shocked by their daughter's wish. The mother felt as if she had seen her daughter's exploded head and broken body next to a plane wreck. But the father is the one who breaks the silence. He says:

> OK, Bilen, let's assume you had this education and became successful. What would happen next? What is this education for? At every moment, there is a probability that you will smash your head, or break a leg or an arm, isn't there? . . . To leave a man's job to a man, and not to waste a woman's strength, that is to know how to be a woman. . . . Yes, a woman should have a profession, an art suitable for herself. There are many other professions or lines of work, such as being a lawyer, a teacher, a chemist. But you should give up on the plane thing. (Arif 1935, 18–19)

Remembering these lines from Rebia Arif's novel and juxtaposing them with what the male professor told me, I came to think that perhaps not much has changed since the 1930s regarding the approach to women's presence in engineering. Now, as one explores the literature, one becomes more puzzled. Certainly, the barriers faced by women in science in the Western world have been documented extensively, at least for the last five decades (Lewin and Duchan, 1971; Jones and Lovejoy, 1980; Tripp-Knowles, 1995). However, although only 19.1 percent of the professors in Turkish engineering and technology faculties are women (European Commission 2013), the discrimination of women in Turkish academia is not perceived as a major problem, at least according to a large part of the existing research (Acar 1983; Köker, 1988; Acar, 1991; Özkanlı and Korkmaz 2000a, 2000b; Öztan and Doğan, 2015; Özkanlı et al., 2008). On the other hand, this view has been challenged by more recent research (Poyraz 2013; Yenilmez 2016; Adak 2018; Ergöl et al., 2012; Gönenç et al., 2013; Tepe 2019a, 2019b, 2019c). We conducted, analyzed, and conceptualized the present phenomenological study based on interviews made with sixteen women academics from engineering faculties in Turkey to provide support for this more recent research. Moreover, the chapter aims to outline a distinction between explicit and implicit career impediments for women and to show how these different types of impediments operate in engineering academia.

According to our study, career impediments are *explicit* when a university management openly states that it will not hire or promote women academics, or when women are in fact not hired although they are better qualified than male applicants. The concept of *implicit* career impediments, on the other hand, aims to capture obstacles to women's academic careers that relate to beliefs about women's inferior abilities or to values that place women in a position inferior to that of men. These beliefs and values may manifest themselves in diminishing or deprecatory remarks about women or in actions that suggest that women should know their place and not presume to be equal to men.

Relevant to the explicit and implicit career impediment categories used in this chapter is Benokraitis and Feagin's distinction between overt, subtle, and covert discrimination. According to their study, "overt sex discrimination refers to an unequal and harmful treatment of women that is readily apparent, visibile [sic], and observable and can be easily documented" (Benokraitis and Feagin 1986, 30). While "(s)ubtle sex discrimination refers to the unequal and harmful treatment of women that is visible but often not noticed because we have internalized sexist behaviour as 'normal,' 'natural,' 'acceptable,' or 'customary,'" covert discrimination refers to "hidden, clandestine, maliciously motivated" unequal and harmful treatment of women that is "very difficult to document" (Benokraitis and Feagin 1986, 31).

In this chapter, we prefer to focus on the contents of two career impediments rather than on their being visible or invisible. The impediment we call implicit is neither invisible, nor hidden; it is there for anyone to observe, provided that one pays careful attention to the attitudes, beliefs, norms, and values that are being implied in what is being said and done to women in Turkish academic workplaces.

Moreover, by distinguishing between explicit and implicit impediments, it is also possible to explain why discrimination against women has not been fully recognized in previous research. Only looking for explicit impediments makes it all too easy to conclude that there is no discrimination, given that there is no formal ban on hiring women, and given that a substantive number of women academics is in fact being hired. However, if one also looks for implicit career impediments, it is possible to reveal the attitudes that obstruct women in their careers after their being hired.

METHOD

This chapter relies on a qualitative research design focusing on the experiences and perceptions of the informants. In qualitative research:

> [r]ather than determining cause and effect, predicting, or describing the distribution of some attribute among a population, we might be interested in uncovering the meaning of a phenomenon for those involved. Qualitative researchers are interested in understanding how people interpret their experiences, how they construct their worlds, and what meaning they attribute to their experiences. (Merriam 2009, 5)

Hence, we approach the career impediments of women academics in engineering from the perspective of the informants and their perceptions of such impediments.

More specifically, the phenomenological design of this research explores the experiences of individuals to clarify phenomena of which they might be aware but of which we do not have a detailed or deep understanding. Interviews play a prominent part in data collection. As is the case with oral history studies (McCracken, 1988), the point is not to provide statistically valid generalizations but rather to establish the existence of a particular way of thinking or acting and to suggest new research directions (Reinharz, 1992). The analysis of the data collected in these interviews focuses on conceptualization and on uncovering thematic structures. Phenomenologically designed studies, like other qualitative research, do not lend themselves to generalizations or representative quantification; however, they help us recognize and understand the phenomena studied, aided by the testimony and lived experience of the informants (Yıldırım and Şimşek 2008, 72–75).

The data gathering instrument used in this research is the semi-structured interview, which

> is in the middle, between structured and unstructured. In this type of interview, either all of the questions are more flexibly-worded or the interview is a mix of more or less structured questions. Usually, specific information is desired from all respondents, in which case there is a more structured section to the interview. (Merriam 2009, 90)

In the interviews in this chapter, three main questions were posed to the research subjects: *(1) Have you ever felt being treated differently (positively or negatively) at the university because of your gender? (2) What are the difficulties you experienced in your academic career due to your gender? (3) What kind of difficulties might young women academics encounter at the universities due to their gender?* The answers given to these questions were then further explored by the researcher, and the research subjects were encouraged to talk about their experiences.

A mix of snowballing sampling and convenience sampling was used to reach the research subjects. The snowballing method is often used in qualitative research and involves the researcher's being led from one research participant to another by benefiting from the first participant's personal network. This method is especially useful if the research topic is a sensitive one (Biernacki and Waldorf 1981, 141).

The sixteen interviews were made between 2009 and 2017. They took place in the offices or laboratories of the academics at the universities. All academics in this research come from various engineering departments or faculties. All of them have international publications. Interviews were recorded with a digital voice recorder and then selectively transcribed. The analysis carried out in this research can be best described as descriptive. The present chapter does not make any claim as to generalizability.

WOMEN REPORTING EXPLICIT CAREER IMPEDIMENTS IN ENGINEERING ACADEMIA

When university management openly states they do not hire women or when they refuse to hire a woman and instead hire a man, although the woman is better qualified for the position in question, then women are exposed to explicit career impediments or gender discrimination. However, according to the literature, this kind of explicit obstruction to women's career does not exist any more in the Western world (MIT 1999, 3; Roos and Gatta, 2009). Although the situation in Turkey in this regard is not that straightforward, most of the data about explicit career impediments in engineering in this research are about events that took place fifteen to twenty years ago. However, some of the data refer to contemporary events as well.

A woman professor described how she received a conditional acceptance by a male professor in a context where women were explicitly rejected for employment. She was explicitly told that her position depended on the male professor's good will. Such a conditional acceptance gets its meaning from a background of explicit career impediments for women academics. Against such a background, in which women cannot expect to be hired at all, a conditional offer of employment might appear as an act of benevolence, and this is also how this woman viewed it:

> In those days I had it in my mind to become an academic, but as girls we didn't have any hope about being successful in this. Back then, scientific fields were organized in chairs. I don't want to name them since I don't want it to be on record. They could tell us, "Sorry, we don't hire girls." In the field that I wanted to enter, there was a similar rumour. . . . A professor, God bless him, who really helped me a lot later on, told me: "OK, you may join us. But you will leave when I tell you to go." I said "OK, of course." . . . They could say: "You will not make me have any problems with you. You will go when I say so." Years later, I talked to some male friends. I heard that none of them was told anything like that. I was probably a bit naïve at the time, too. I thought that these things just happen. . . . But back then it also felt heavy on me. Still, as I said, I cannot deny that this professor later worked on my behalf. He gave me full support later. (Interviewee #1)

This woman professor agreed to being quoted in the present chapter only on condition that the passage about the male professor later on becoming supportive of her was also included. Her story tells of explicit career impediments, both when a university openly declares it does not hire women, and when a professor makes it clear to a woman applicant that she should not expect anything beyond a conditional employment, and that she should be ready to leave her job when he tells her to do so. The woman professor's determination to emphasize that this male professor was later supportive of her also testifies to how explicit career impediments can operate without making their victim feel conflicted about her loyalties to the very persons who subjected her to such an impediment. Instead, the very fact that the male professor offered this woman only a conditional employment makes her feel even more grateful to him when he later supports her. Instead of feeling discriminated against by him, she feels loyal to him. Still, she was subjected to an explicit career impediment, since she was accepted on conditions that a male applicant would never have had to deal with.

The same woman professor reports another case of what she perceives to be an explicit career impediment, in which a woman academic was denied a position as associate professor simply because she was a woman:

> Two persons, one man and one woman, both good friends of mine, went on parallel career tracks from the beginning. Both were given the title of associate professor. And then there was a position of associate professor available to the division, and it was given to the male. According to what people said, this was done because he was a male. I and my friends even made this issue public, telling the management that "Your decision is based on the gender identity of the applicants and this is nonsense." I was married at the time, and my woman friend was divorced. So she was in a worse position than the male—she needed housing. We told the management "Base your selection on a more objective criterion, don't make it on the basis of gender." But nobody took us seriously. This was seen as a natural selection, an exact natural selection. I also think that behind all this there was a thought: If a man is appointed, he will be more useful. . . . If a woman and a man apply to the same position, the woman can get this position only if she is twice as qualified, academically speaking . . . especially in a male dominated field like ours. (Interviewee #1)

The next case stems from problems at the assistant professorship level:

> As I was going to be appointed to assistant professorship, sad things happened. My appointment was delayed with one year. . . . They matched me against another person, a male. There were two positions. Neither of us was appointed. Me, having three positive reports and he having three negative reports. . . . Older people at the university told me to take the issue to court. Unlike now, I found it very inappropriate to sue the institution where I worked. I didn't do it. . . . Later another position was opened. This time I was immediately appointed. But for six or seven months or perhaps even for a year, I could not become an assistant professor. With three positive reports, I still wasn't appointed. . . . At the time, the dean told me not to take this personally. How could I not take this personally? If this was not personal, then what was it? He didn't say anything. He just said that he would certainly take care of this in the next period. And so he did. He could have fixed this already then. I was the same then as I was later, when I was appointed. Three positive reports. Then what was it for, the jury of professors who wrote these positive reports? (Interviewee #2)

In the above example, a woman's promotion was delayed, and she was not made an assistant professor although she had three positive reports from the reviewers. The university could have promoted both of the applicants or just the woman applicant, but they could not promote only the male applicant, given the woman applicant's better qualifications. So they chose to promote none of the applicants. Hence, this constitutes an explicit career impediment for the woman applicant. This would also be consistent with the dean's advice to the woman applicant not to take this personally: The university had nothing against her as a person—they just did not want to promote a woman.

In another case, a woman academic suffered an explicit career impediment because she was the mother of two children. She reports how she was explicitly told she was not fit to become an assistant professor because she was a mother: "I had finished my Ph.D. and was working to become an assistant professor. The head of my department called me only because he was concerned about me, and told me 'You have two children, and a woman with two children could not do this job, so let's make you an instructor instead'" (Interviewee #3). Here motherhood is turned into a reason for obstructing a woman academic's career opportunities.

Likewise, a woman associate professor reported that when she was seeking a position in an institute, the answer of the director of the institute was a "no" to her while it was "yes" to male candidates:

> I talked with the director of the institute. He behaved in a very loving way, but told me there is no position. It is very interesting that after I had been told this, in the following several years many new positions were created and only men were hired. After many years, there was a woman faculty member as well. After I had become an associate professor I called on him many times and asked for a position, and he said "no." But for all the other ones who applied there, there was a position. (Inteviewee #4)

These illustrations of explicit career impediments for women in engineering academia taking place many years ago might suggest this is perhaps a thing of the past. However, the next case indicates something else. Here a woman full professor reports how women may still face explicit career impediments in male-dominated engineering departments:

> In laboratories they may pay attention to gender when hiring research assistants. For instance, they would consider it difficult for women to work in a laboratory, and for this reason they would say, "We should hire a male research assistant." It is like this especially in our profession. In the industry, there is a similar problem. And because the field of engineering is thought of as a male profession, they will directly tell you when they want to hire someone that they are looking for a man. . . . But the reason for this is the male management mentality. If it had been a woman making the decision, she would not think in this way. Instead she would think like this: "If I as a woman can do this, then so can she." That's why

a woman decision-maker would not feel the gender dilemma. But otherwise it happens like this. (Interviewee #5)

The above quoted woman professor believes that a woman decision-maker would not be gender biased against women applicants. However the findings of Moss-Racusin et al. (2012), as well as the findings by Reuben, Sapienza, and Zingales (2014), seem to suggest that both male and female employers may discriminate against women.

It is safe to assume women still face explicit career impediments due to their gender in Turkish engineering academia. Still, the above interviews, besides illustrating various demoralizing explicit career impediments, testify to the strength, resilience, and adaptive power of academic women.

WOMEN REPORTING IMPLICIT CAREER IMPEDIMENTS IN ENGINEERING ACADEMIA

In Western countries, many studies on gender equality in the last fifty years (Lewin and Duchan, 1971; Jones and Lovejoy, 1980; Tripp-Knowles, 1995) suggest there are laws to protect and secure gender equality in all spheres of life. In these countries, according to the recent literature, there is no overt gender discrimination in the academia anymore (Roos and Gatta, 2009). Instead, since the 1990s, the difficulties women face in academia are expressed in terms of hidden or subtle discrimination (MIT 1999, 3; Morley, 2006; Roos and Gatta, 2009).

More recent studies have discussed implicit discrimination in the form of employers' negative associations regarding women in math or science. For instance, in 2012 Moss-Racusin et al. designed a laboratory experiment in which subjects were "hired" to perform an arithmetic task. The employer did not have any information about the candidates other than their physical appearance. According to the findings, "Women were only half as likely to be hired as men, because they were (erroneously) perceived as less talented for the arithmetic task: Both men and women expected women to perform worse" (Moss-Racusin et al., 2012, 4403). In 2014 Reuben, Sapienza, and Zingales designed another experiment which "examined whether, given an equally qualified male and female student, science faculty members would show preferential evaluation and treatment of the male student to work in their laboratory" (Reuben, Sapienza, and Zingales 2014, 16474). The results of this stud "revealed that both male and female faculty judged a female student to be less competent and less worthy of being hired than an identical male student, and also offered her a smaller starting salary and less career mentoring" (Reuben, Sapienza, and Zingales 2014, 16475). The results of this study suggest that the reported gender bias is implicit or unintended and stems from being repeatedly exposed "to pervasive cultural stereotypes that portray women as less competent" (Reuben, Sapienza, and Zingales 2014, 16474).

The situation in Turkey regarding this matter is worse in some respects. It is a well-known social fact there are large and overt gender inequalities in Turkey (Toprak 1982, 1999; Kağıtçıbaşı, 1986). When it comes to academia, there are only a few studies on sexism and gender discrimination, and most of them have found no evidence of such practices. Still, only 19.1 percent of all engineering professors are women.

Régner et al. (2019) might provide an explanation for the Turkish conundrum. The findings suggest that "committees might be more likely to act on their implicit gender biases when, at an explicit level, they do not strongly believe that systemic biases are a problem that need[s] to be addressed. Under these conditions, committees are less likely to select accomplished women for elite research positions" (Régner et al., 2019, 1175). Hence, simply because they are convinced there is no discrimination against women (which is the prevailing view in Turkish academia), members of various selection committees may be unguarded against their biases against women.

On the other hand, even studies that underline positive facts, such as there is a higher percentage of women at engineering departments in Turkey than in the United States, also reveal that female students in these departments "perceive lesser opportunities than their male peers" (Smith and Dengiz 2010, 52). Likewise, it has been noted discrimination against women in engineering departments may often come in subtle and covert forms, such as "the tendency to guide female graduate students into those fields of engineering which are viewed as more convenient for women, jokes made by the professors about women's incompetence in engineering and the marginalizing attitudes of male classmates towards female students" (Zengin-Arslan 2002, 407).

Sometimes negative assumptions about women academics' qualifications may be so ingrained in a person's belief system that they operate without them being fully conscious of them. Reskin (2003) points to such unconscious forces that work against women in organizations. Likewise, Roos and Gatta (2009) examine "the various mechanisms that continue to produce gender inequity, through nonconscious beliefs and attitudes that operate through workplace interactions, and through the use of subjective policies and procedures institutionalized in the academic workplace" (177).

A woman professor testifies to the often unconscious nature of these beliefs and attitudes: "There is this thing in our profession: 'A woman cannot do it.' . . . In the Turkish male structure, there is such a belief, even if he would not admit it, there is at least an unconscious belief that a man would solve a problem in a better way" (Interviewee #5).

Sometimes the reluctance to hire a woman academic is obscured by a rhetoric that appears woman friendly. A woman assistant professor tells about trying to apply for a university position:

> My family lives in an Anatolian town and I thought about transferring to the university there because there is nothing that connects me to the big city here. I tried to get an appointment with the rector. Although I tried very hard, it did not happen. I talked to the vice rector. He told me that the rector was a very modern man and the fact that I am a woman wouldn't be a problem, either. (Interviewee #6)

Here the very statement that being a woman "wouldn't be a problem" suggests the opposite. Why would the vice rector even mention this, if it was not on the list of possible obstacles? And this woman did not get her interview with the rector either.

The reluctance to hire a woman is often based on various essentialist assumptions about womanhood, which are revealed in the next quotation from a woman professor:

> Our engineering faculties have more male-dominated departments compared to the social science faculties. Therefore, at the time of hiring, you can hear people asking: "Hmm, is it a woman?" Even the departmental management and the people who work close to them talk like this. How do they think? They think that she will get married, that she will have a child. But this should be a natural thing and to make it a problem like this is negative discrimination. I still believe that women academics in our country are victims of discrimination. (Interviewee #7)

A woman academic, who was a full professor at the time this interview was made, reports about how her professional capacity was diminished in the beginning of her career by a gatekeeper professor. After getting her PhD degree, she searched for a university position and went to meet with a professor to whom she had written earlier, when she was a student:

> When I went to meet the professor, the situation there was like this: They had a huge staff, there, but the professor was on his own. He had two doctoral students and he was looking for someone who could do his secretarial work.

"These people are all men" he said, "I am looking for a new faculty member who could do the secretarial work." Later, I met with this professor in the associate professorship exams. He is a very nice person. But that expression "I am looking for a new faculty member who could do the secretarial work" made me angry, it hurt some part of me. I doubt if he would tell this to a male candidate. (Interviewee #4)

This is also a case of implicit career impediment, as the male professor's offer implies that he considers the qualifications of a woman academic as suitable only for secretarial work.

In another interview, a women professor close to retirement age mentioned an old professor who expressed a suspicion regarding women's capacity to work in their department when she first applied for a technician's job that might lead to a future academic position:

We had an old professor who once said "How would a woman be able to do this job?" He said one or two things more, but it never went beyond words. I am not paying any attention to it. . . . After all, he did not prevent me from having a job as a technician in the department. And the last signature of approval belonged to him. (Interviewee #8)

The negative comment of the old professor regarding women's capacity to work in an engineering department is important since he was in a power position, and the final signature of approval belonged to him. The fact that he, in the end, did not prevent the woman applicant from being hired should not allow us to ignore the fact his comment is evidence of gender discriminatory views that could support actions to demoralize women and discourage them from applying for a job (although this did not happen in this particular case). As such, it is an illustration of an implicit career impediment, revealing a negative view of women's academic capability in general.

The belittling or dismissive attitudes toward women academics associated with implicit career impediments can sometimes take on a physical expression. Here is an account of a slap on the face:

When I was hired by this university as a research assistant, I had graduated as a valedictorian and I was hired to work in labs where only men work. The professor who decided on my hiring was the person at the top of the group hierarchy. He was our most experienced professor. I think he decided about my employment without discussing it with the ones who worked under him. . . . But, of course, in the beginning there was an objection. An elder 'brother' in that group gave me a 'tough greeting': He softly slapped me on my cheek. And this "tough greeting" . . . I asked my friends to see whether I had misunderstood it. They said "Never mind, his style is like that." (Interviewee #9)

As we can see from above quote, the woman research assistant wants to make sense of the light slap with the help of her male colleagues, but their answer does not make it any easier to understand. They advise her to "never mind" and suggest that this attitude has not anything to do with structures but is only a matter of personal style. However, there is something diminishing in this light slap on the face—this is how one might treat a pet animal or a child. It is not the way to treat a colleague whom you respect as your equal. Instead it might be a way for a male academic to tell a woman colleague that she should know her place.

A woman academic supports the view that even if women are hired by engineering faculties, they are not accepted on the same conditions as male colleagues, and that the gender inequality of the organization shows itself in implicit and indirect ways such as women having to take on extra work: "After hiring they will probably have to work more than their male friends. Until they have managed to move up to a certain level, until they have proven themselves, they have to work more in order for them to succeed. This is very important" (Interviewee #7).

The view that women academics in engineering have to work more than their male colleagues has been repeated by different respondents in the course of this research. This is also an indication of an implicit career impediment, as it is based on an assumption that women are not really as good as men, and hence, they will have to prove themselves in a way that men are not expected to do.

To be made to feel that they are inferior to men is obviously damaging to women's confidence and ability to promote themselves within academia, and, as such, is an implicit career impediment. Here a woman professor tells about how women research assistants were belittled by a head of department:

I do not know if it was a coincidence but the other research assistants were male, and the head of the department used to work with male research assistants. They would be one step ahead of us in everything. For instance, they were the first to gain the master[s] degrees and to become senior engineers. . . . They were the first to become doctors. We received these degrees later than them. The approach of the head of the department to women was important in these matters. . . . He thought that women do not understand much. He could tell a woman something and then ask her "Did you understand?" as if she was slow in catching up. He had such a style. . . . I felt this in a few conversations that I had with him when he asked me if I understood that[,] it was as if he thought I had difficulties in getting his point. Several times I felt there was also a warning in his question [that she did not deserve her academic position]. (Interviewee #10)

Another woman professor tells about how she, as a new assistant professor trying to benefit from the subsidized housing service of the university, was repeatedly told that her applications had been lost. Later she found that the senior academics informally rejected her application because of her gender:

> When I returned to Turkey after almost 15 years abroad and wanted an apartment for myself, the rent would cost me about 60–80 percent of my salary. . . . I was desperate. At the age of 30, I was living with my family, being treated as a child, my comings and goings constantly observed, and so on. I had no time for myself, and I was disturbed by all this. To find housing for myself subsidized by the university seemed the best solution for me. I was applying for this repeatedly but somehow my application forms always disappeared. Now, we had a coffee/ tea room and there, after having their meal, came our senior professors. One of them . . . was a professor of whom I had a high opinion. . . . But when I told him "Professor, whatever I do, this subsidized housing is not happening, it does not work," out of the mouth of this man came these words: "There are many single male assistant professors in the subsidized apartments of the university. If you make arrangements with one of them, you will both have a subsidized apartment and a husband." . . . Present at the time was also another professor who had earlier told me that "Being an academic here is very easy. You can look after your child as well." She now turned to me and said: "It is true. This is not a bad solution," and then they began to laugh. How disappointed, how angry I was. I replied: "Then you give me a list of them and I will start visiting them." (Interviewee #4)

Here the academic woman is being diminished and belittled. She is not treated as a person with rights equal to those of her male colleagues, but rather as inferior to them. Instead of having herself and her application treated seriously and with respect, she is advised to go and find herself a man that already enjoys subsidized accommodation. Implicit in all this is that only men are taken seriously as academics, while women are expected to focus on marriage and family rather than on having an academic career. This kind of disrespectful attitude to a woman academic can obviously be a discouragement and an impediment to her career.

Likewise, academic women can be exposed to diminishing and belittling attitudes masquerading as friendly warnings and pieces of advice. A woman PhD gives an example:

> Another difference which I felt in relation to gender occurred when I told the dean about my wish to do post-doc studies abroad. As he was informing about his views on this, he also took the opportunity to tell me that "They might deceive you abroad." Moreover, he asked me whether my husband would give

me permission to go abroad. This was another instance which made me freeze. (Interviewee #11)

This woman academic was treated by her dean as someone who was not able to look after her own interests—as someone who was likely to be the victim of deceit and fraud when being far away from her home environment. Moreover, she was asked about whether she would get her husband's permission to go abroad. Regardless of having a doctorate, she was treated as a child, as a minor in need of a mature person's permission. This also exemplifies an implicit career impediment, as it reveals an utter distrust in women's capabilities and a rejection of their right to freedom.

Academic women might experience implicit obstructions even late in their careers. Here a woman professor reports how her male colleagues reacted when she started to prove herself in research after having quit the position of head of department:

> Here what I love to do is to engage in projects, publish and go to conferences. But I could do these kinds of things only after I resigned from the position of head of department. I took on projects from the science council. We established a very nice group. We published. Then I started to feel it. Until that day there was no problem. No one stood against me. But when I implied with my academic activities that "I exist, too, look at me," . . . there something happened. . . . There were reactions. Reactions that I don't understand the reasons for. But now if you ask me what happened, I can't give you a concrete example. But I encountered one thing. A very concrete thing. I had an assistant, very successful, and now an assistant professor in another university. This person fulfilled all the conditions of the university and the department for assistant professorship, but he was rejected by our department. This was the first thing. This was not an objection only to him but it was a rejection of me, too. . . . There I felt it . . . as if they could not accept that I could be successful academically, too. (Interviewee #8)

This example illustrates an implicit career impediment in the sense it suggests women, when they cannot be stopped in their career, still can be subjected to vindictive and spiteful reactions. If they themselves can no longer be touched, their protégées might instead be exposed to the vindictive feelings of resentful male colleagues.

Sexist attitudes are an important factor in implicit career impediments. Even when sexism seems to work in women academics' favour, it also damages their careers. One woman professor told that women proceed swiftly up the career ladder if they are beautiful. However, to the extent that this is the case, this is not an advantage for academic women but actually a diminishing of them, since they are valued in accordance with their looks, not in terms of their academic achievement. The same woman professor also complained that the marital status of women is a criterion for approval or disapproval in engineering academia:

> Being single is difficult. You belong to the most dangerous category of people if you are single. In their eyes, if you are childless, you are cruel. For instance, I am in a meeting with the board of directors. They tell me "You don't understand this, you don't have a child." Sometimes I think of getting married just to get a divorce, so that I can have some charisma. Being single is the worst position, the most dangerous one. Being divorced is better. The best is to be married and to have children. (Interviewee #12)

According to this professor, in addition to being exposed to male sexist diminishing, women academics subject themselves to a sexist self-dimin-ishing, suggesting that they have internalized the male perspective of them-selves: "Women generally talk about issues like putting on or losing weight, or about dying the new grey part of the hair, or about children's day care. There is no discussion on academic matters. Instead they might ask you why you had your hair made like that, telling you that you look like a child, and so on" (Interviewee #12).

Attitudes like these discourage women from thinking of themselves in terms of academic achievement and instead reinforce a sexist perception of themselves as being around for the sake of pleasing men. A sexualist concep-tion of women at an academic workplace undermines their academic agency by reducing them to bodies and biology. One woman professor interviewed in this chapter claims that on the whole she gets along well with her male colleagues. Then she tells about the jokes they exchange: "Sometimes, if a woman is nervous, a man can ask her: 'Are you having your bleeding?' And at another time, when he is nervous, I can tell him 'I think you have your bleeding.' Even if they are men, we can talk like this. This is a joking matter between us" (Inteviewee #9).

Even if this woman professor thinks that her being able to imitate her male colleague's disrespectful joke makes them equals, this does not really capture what is going on between them. The joke in question is made at the expense of a female bodily function, and to introduce that kind of joke in an academic setting is also to contribute to a sexualized stereotypization of women, reduc-ing them to their biology.

The sexualization of the workplace also forces women academics to assume responsibility for how they appear. A woman PhD reports:

> I try not to impose my gender on others. For instance, I don't wear skirts or dresses very often. I really do want to wear them, but at the same time I am

reluctant to do it. . . . When I attempted to dress up like this many years ago, friends asked me if I had "converted." It is a silly joke suggesting that I used to be a man and had converted to become a woman by wearing feminine clothes. There and then I stopped wearing a skirt. (Interviewee #13)

This joke, however, is not just silly. It also suggests that dressing as a male, and implicitly being a male, is the norm of the academic workplace.

CONCLUSION

We have here distinguished between two kinds of career impediments facing academic women in Turkish engineering faculties. Explicit impediments involve universities openly refusing to hire and promote women, while implicit impediments involve beliefs and attitudes that diminish women and undermine their status and perception of themselves as competent agents. Implicit impediments can only be revealed by the kind of research undertaken in this chapter, that is, a kind of research which is qualitative and which focuses on the lived experiences of women academics rather than on statistics regarding the number of women employed in academica. Our introduction of the concept of implicit career impediments has also enabled us to explain how gender discrimination can exist at Turkish universities, although many previous studies, relying on quantitative data about the number of women academics employed, have disputed this. In this way, by combining conceptual innovation with a qualitative empirical approach, we have tried to contribute an informed perspective on the obstacles faced by women academics at Turkish universities.

REFERENCES

Acar, Feride. 1983. "Turkish Women in Academia: Roles and Careers." *ODTÜ Gelişme Dergisi* 10(4): 409–446.

Acar, Feride. 1991. "Women in Academic Science Careers in Turkey." In *Women in Science, Token Women or Gender Equality*, edited by Veronica Stolte-Heiskanen, Feride Acar, Nora Ananieva, and Dorothea Gaudart, 147–173. Oxford and New York: Berg.

Adak-Özçelik, Nurşen, and Necmiye Cömertler. 2005. "Türkiye'de Akademide ve Akademik Yönetimde Kadınlar." *Sosyoloji Araştırmaları Dergisi* 8(2): 5–22.

Arif, Rebia. 1935. *Kadın Tipleri*. İstanbul: Semih Lütfi Bitik ve Basım Evi.

Benokraitis, Nijole V., and Joe R. Feagin. 1986. *Modern Sexism, Blatant, Subtle and Covert Discrimination*. Englewood Cliffs, NJ: Prentice-Hall.

Biernacki, Patrick, and Dan Waldorf. 1981. "Snowball Sampling: Problems and Techniques of Chain Referral Sampling." *Sociological Methods & Research* 10(2): 141–163.

Ergöl, Şule, Gülten Koç, Kafiye Eroğlu, and Lale Taşkın. 2012. "Türkiye'de Kadın Araştırma Görevlilerinin Ev ve İş Yaşamlarında Karşılaştıkları Güçlükler." *Yükseköğretim ve Bilim Dergisi* 2(1): 43–49.

European Commission. 2013. *She Figures 2012: Gender Research and Innovation.* Luxembourg: Publications Office of the European Union. Accessed 8 February 2020, http://ec.europa.eu/research/science-society/document_library/pdf_06/she-figures-2012_en.pdf.

Gönenç, İlknur M., Şenay Akgün, Şevkat Bahar Özvarış, and Tanfer Emin Tunç. 2013. "An Analysis of the Relationship Between Academic Career and Sex at Hacettepe University." *Education and Science* 38(170): 166–178.

Jones, Jennifer M., and Frances H. Lovejoy. 1980. "Discrimination Against Women Academics in Australian Universities." *Signs* 5(3): 518–526.

Kağıtçıbaşı, Çiğdem. 1986. "Status of Women in Turkey: Cross-Cultural Perspectives." *International Journal of Middle East Studies* 18(4): 485–499.

Köker, Eser D. 1988. "Türkiye'de Kadın, Eğitim ve Siyaset, Yüksek Öğrenim Kurumlarında Kadının Durumu Üzerine Bir İnceleme." PhD diss., Ankara University.

Lewin, Arie Y., and Linda Duchan. 1971. "Women in Academia." *Science* 173(4000): 892–895.

Massachusetts Institute of Technology. 1999. "A Study on the Status of Women Faculty in Science at MIT." *The MIT Faculty Newsletter* 11(4). Accessed 8 February 2020, http://web.mit.edu/fnl/women/women.html.

McCracken, Grant. 1988. *The Long Interview.* Newbury Park, CA: Sage.

Merriam, Sharan B. 2009. *Qualitative Research: A Guide to Design and Implementation.* San Francisco, CA: Jossey-Bass.

Morley, Louise. 2006. "Hidden Transcripts: The Micropolitics of Gender in Commonwealth Universities." *Women's Studies International Forum* 29(6): 543–551.

Moss-Racusin, Corinne A., John F. Dovidio, Victoria L. Brescoll, Mark J. Graham, and Jo Handelsman. 2012. "Science Faculty's Subtle Gender Biases Favor Male Students." *PNAS* 109(41): 16474–16479.

Özkanlı, Özlem, and Adil Korkmaz. 2000a. "Turkish Women in Academic Life: Attitude Measurement Towards Gender Discrimination in Academic Promotion and Administration." In *Emerging Economies: Academy of Business Administrative Sciences 2000 International Conference Proceedings* 1(1), 56–65. Prague: St. Bonaventure University.

Özkanlı, Özlem, and Adil Korkmaz. 2000b. *Kadın Akademisyenler.* Ankara: Ankara University.

Özkanlı, Özlem, Maureen Bickley, Sue Fyfe, and Linley Lord. 2008. "Attitudes and Experiences of University Academic Leaders." *Journal of Global Strategic Management* 2(1): 105–113.

Öztan, Ece, and Setenay N. Doğan. 2015. "Akademinin Cinsiyeti: Yıldız Teknik Üniversitesi Örneği Üzerinden Üniversite ve Toplumsal Cinsiyet." *Çalışma ve Toplum* 46(3): 191–221.

Poyraz, Bedriye. 2013. "Akademi Kadınların Cenneti mi?: Ankara Üniversitesi Örneği." *Ankara Üniversitesi Sosyal Bilimler Enstitüsü Dergisi* 4(2): 1–18.

Régner, Isabelle, Catherine Thinus-Blanc, Agnès Netter, Toni Schmader, and Pascal Huguet. 2019. "Committees with Implicit Biases Promote Fewer Women When They Do Not Believe Gender Bias Exists." *Nature Human Behavior* 3: 1171–1179.

Reinharz, Shulamit. 1992. *Feminist Methods in Social Research*. New York: Oxford University Press.

Reskin, Barbara F. 2003. "Including Mechanisms in Our Models of Ascriptive Inequality." *American Sociological Review* 68: 1–21.

Reuben, Ernesto, Paola Sapienza, and Luigi Zingales. 2014. "How Stereotypes Impair Women's Careers in Science." *PNAS* 111(12): 4403–4408.

Roos, Patricia A., and Mary L. Gatta. 2009. "Gender (In)equity in the Academy: Subtle Mechanisms and the Production of Inequality." *Research in Social Stratification and Mobility* 27(3): 177–200.

Smith, Alice E., and Berna Dengiz. 2010. "Women in Engineering in Turkey—A Large Scale Quantitative and Qualitative Examination." *European Journal of Engineering Education* 35(1): 45–57.

Tepe, Fatma Fulya. 2019a. "Essentialist Views on Women and Men in Engineering Academia in Turkey." *Journal of Social Sciences of Mus Alparslan University* 7(4): 71–81.

Tepe, Fatma Fulya. 2019b. "Women's Discrimination in Engineering Faculties: A View from Turkey." *Journal of Social Sciences of Mus Alparslan University* 7(3): 199–209.

Tepe, Fatma Fulya. 2020. "Researching Sensitive Topics: The Case of Sexism and Gender Discrimination at Turkish Universities." In *Macro and Micro-Level Issues Surrounding Women in the Workforce: Emerging Research and Opportunities*, edited by Başak Uçanok Tan, 236–261. Hershey, PA: IGI Global.

Toprak, Binnaz. 1982. "Türk Kadını ve Din." In *Türk Toplumunda Kadın*, edited by Nermin Abadan-Unat, 361–374. Genişletilmiş 2. Basım. İstanbul: Türk Sosyal Bilimler Derneği.

Toprak, Binnaz. 1999. "Emancipated but Unliberated Women in Turkey, the Impact of Islam." In *Women Family and Social Change in Turkey*, edited by Ferhunde Özbay, 39–50. Bangkok: UNESCO.

Tripp-Knowles, Peggy. 1995. "A Review of the Literature on Barriers Encountered by Women in Science Academia." *Resources for Feminist Research* 24(1/2): 28–34.

Yenilmez-İnce, Meltem. 2016. "Women in Academia in Turkey: Challenges and Opportunities." *Journal of Administrative Sciences* 14(28): 289–311.

Yıldırım, Ali, and Hasan Şimşek. 2008. *Sosyal Bilimlerde Nitel Araştırma Yöntemleri*. Ankara: Seçkin Yayınları.

Zengin-Arslan, Berna. 2002. "Women in Engineering Education in Turkey: Understanding the Gendered Distribution." *International Journal of Engineering Education* 18(4): 400–408.

Part III

INSTITUTIONAL STRUCTURES WHICH REINFORCE WOMEN'S SECONDARY STATUS

Chapter 7

A Feminist Perspective on the 2017 Labor Reform in Brazil

Impacts on Higher Education Faculty

Lygia Sabbag Fares and
Ana Luíza Matos de Oliveria

INTRODUCTION

This chapter aims to understand the 2017 labor reform in Brazil and how it affects women, specially faculty. To understand this process, we must go back to the period between 2006 and 2014, in which Brazil experienced economic growth and reduction of inequality in access to social rights (Oliveira 2019) accompanied with premature deindustrialization (Castillo and Martins 2020). In addition to the increase in commodities prices that support the first phase of growth, the Workers' Party government, under Luis Inácio Lula da Silva (2003–2010) and Dilma Rousseff (2011–2014) implemented social economic policies such as credit expansion, increase in public investments, and income redistribution which served as pillars to foster economic growth and social development (Carvalho 2018).

The optimism changed around 2013. During the preparation for the 2014 FIFA World Cup, protests demanding better social services occurred and were taken over by new right-wing movements, which became important political actors. Nonetheless, Dilma was reelected in 2014 (Guerra et al., 2017) for a turbulent second term. In early 2015, in order to compromise with the right wing and the Congress, she announced Joaquim Levy, a mainstream economist, as finance minister. The austerity shock applied by the minister was abrupt and profound and 2015 is considered a turning point (Fagnani, Biancarelli, and Rossi 2015). The government rapidly increased gas and energy prices as well as interest rates and made deep cuts to public pending/investment. At the same time, a 50 percent devaluation of the Brazilian Real vis-à-vis U.S. dollars occurred (Rossi and Mello 2017). Fueled by political uncertainty and the effects of the *Operação Lava-jato* (car wash operation)—a task force to combat corruption inspired by the Italian *Mani Pulite*—Brazilian Gross Domestic Product (GDP) decreased in 2015 and 2016.

The abrupt changes in economic policy impacted the labor market. The stock of formal jobs, measured by *Cadastro Geral de Empregados e Desempregados*, declined from 49.6 million in 2014 to 48.1 million in 2015 and 46.1 million in 2016.

In this context, Rousseff, Brazil's first female president, was impeached in 2016 and Michel Temer, her vice president, took power. The answer to the crisis was to implement more austerity measures and reduce labor rights. Temer implemented two important reforms, a labor reform via Law 13.467/2017 and the Constitutional Amendment 95/2016, and pushed for the implementation of a pension reform, which was only implemented in 2019 during Jair Bolsonaro's term. These reforms followed the austerity paradigm (Blyth 2017), advocating that a fiscal contraction would have an expansionary effect over economic activity and that excessive labor regulation was hampering the creation of jobs.

The 2017 labor reform affected workers negatively, impacting men and women, black and white. In order to introduce the debate, the first part of this chapter discusses gender inequalities in the Brazilian labor market under a historical perspective. The second part focuses on the drivers and objectives of the 2017 labor reform and its analytical framework in order to understand how it affects Brazilian labor. Finally, the third part offers a gendered analysis of its early outcomes (two years after its implementation) regarding faculty workers and explores possible impacts of the reform regarding productive and reproductive labor. The availability of macro data on labor flexibilization remains limited, as post-reform data is not available yet and, additionally, the current government is cutting spending on census and other household surveys, risking a data blackout in the country. Given these challenges and in order to grasp how the 2017 labor reform impact women, faculty members are heard as a way to understand and exemplify how labor reform impacts this group of workers focusing on faculty experiences and on how they perceive the impacts of the reform.

The case of faculty workers is an interesting case study due to the variety of work schemes for higher faculty jobs in Brazil. Working conditions depend on the type of institution (public or private), on size (university or college), on the ratio of faculty/students, on academic qualification, on the work regimen (lecturer, part time, full time), on the existence or not of a career plan (small institutions usually do not have one), and on the multiple and sometimes contradictory demands of activities of different natures (teaching undergraduate, graduate, or distance learning, management), among other aspects.

A FEMINIST PERSPECTIVE ON THE
BRAZILIAN LABOR MARKET

There is not only one reality for women, and the challenges faced by them vary immensely regarding race, social status, and region of the country. Black women usually have lower educational and income levels (due to Brazil's history with slavery), are frequently at the bottom of the labor force, presenting higher unemployment rates, and are the majority in rural work or domestic work. White women remained largely excluded from the productive workforce until the 1970s (Saffioti 2013). Poor white women engaged in "typically female" activities such as early childhood education, health care, and administrative services as a receptionist or secretary (generally related to organizing a man's life). Black women face strong discrimination in jobs which demand "good looking" women, and black women are not regarded as such (IPEA 2014). Black women are the majority in domestic and precarious work.

The participation of Brazilian women in the labor market expanded greatly from the 1970s onward. Changes in the family structure, such as the decrease in fertility ratio, facilitated their entrance in the labor market. Another substantial change is the increase in households headed by women and single-parent families, while extended families and even couples with children families decreased, impacting unpaid domestic work (IPEA 2011).

Today, while a small proportion of women succeed in paid work, the vast majority remain in low-paid jobs related to the services and care economy, engage in less socially valued activities, and have lower income than men. This is a reality even if women have higher educational levels than men. Artes and Ricoldi (2016) posit women are more present in higher education careers of lesser social prestige and, consequently, will likely have lower-paid jobs in institutions of lesser prestige. Also, the higher the schooling levels, the bigger the wage gap between men and women (Teixeira 2013).

Male-dominated sectors such as manufacturing, construction, and engineering have better working conditions and stronger trade union representation but also more socially unfriendly working hours such as shift, night, and weekend work, difficult arrangements to reconcile with the rigid schedule of childcare, making these jobs awkward for married women and mothers in a context of a still rigid sexual division of labor.

This brings us to another important feature regarding gender inequalities and labor market segregation: unpaid reproductive labor. In Brazil, as in most countries, the unpaid reproductive labor is mostly conducted by women. Being the person responsible for household chores and caring for children and the elderly has numerous implications for women, such as increased chances of being in poverty, lower economic independence, and as mentioned before, less availability to perform paid labor. The particularity of Brazil in this sense is that public social services, which would allow payments for social services such as child and elder care or laundry or restaurant services, are less available than in European countries, and income is lower than in developed countries.

Nevertheless, many women combine paid with unpaid labor, having a double burden (Gibb and Oliveira 2015). The domestic responsibilities have further implications on women's insertion in the labor market. Typical female branches (teaching, health care, and administrative services) historically have a shorter workday to allow reconciling productive and reproductive work. Also, according to Gibb (2017) some women opt for informal work as a strategy to reconcile productive and reproductive work. This partially explains why in 2015, 42.9 percent of the women employed did not have a formal contract (CLT). Among them, 17.4 percent were self-employed, working from home (outsourced to some company, producing homemade goods to sell, or worked as autonomous resellers), 14.3 percent were domestic workers, and 11.2 percent had other jobs without a contract (Gibb 2017). It is worth mentioning that the husbands of women employed in the formal sector, on average, perform one hour more of domestic work per week than those whose wives work in the informal sector; the better the insertion of women in the labor market and the higher their educational level, the less disadvantageous will be their position in the domestic labor division (Alvarenga 2008).

The unemployment rate is significantly unequal in terms of sex and race; in 2015, the female unemployment rate was 11.6 percent, the male unemployment rate was 7.8 percent, for black women 13.3 percent and for black men, 8.5 percent (IPEA 2015). Table 7.1 reflects unemployment numbers in Brazil by sex.

The economic crisis in Brazil, since 2015, has impacted workers independently of sex. However, women's positions in the labor market are more fragile and precarious. Table 7.1 shows that reduction on unemployment from 2012 to 2014 was accompanied by a more equal distribution in terms of sex. In the most critical years of the crisis, 2015 to 2017, men's and women's share on unemployment drew closer, which could be explained by the decrease in investment on industry and construction, as men's participation in these sectors is high. Also, as unemployment slightly decreased in 2018 and 2019, the gap between women and men unemployment rose.

Table 7.1   Unemployed Workers by Sex (Brazil, 2012–2019)

Year	Total	Men (%)	Women (%)
2012	7,057,500	45.97	54.03
2013	6,923,750	46.07	53.93
2014	6,698,750	47.55	52.45
2015	8,531,000	48.17	51.83
2016	11,695,500	49.47	50.53
2017	13,176,000	49.27	50.73
2018	12,789,750	48.72	51.28
2019	12,575,000	46.87	53.13

Source: PNADC 2020.

DISCOURSE AND SCOPE OF THE 2017 LABOR REFORM

In 1943, under Getúlio Vargas's dictatorship, the *Consolidação das Leis do Trabalho* (CLT, meaning Consolidation of Labor Laws) was established, creating a set of labor relations rules. CLT was greatly transformed since then, suffering many changes in the 1990s, under the Washington Consensus (Fornazier and Oliveira 2011).

From 2015 onward, as discussed before, there was growing pressure from various economic sectors to once again reform regulation in Brazil. This context culminated in the Bill 6787/2016 presented by Temer to the House of Representatives on December 23, 2016. The bill was called by Brazil's Order of Lawyers as a "new CLT" due to the substantial number of labor regulation changes presented by the reform.

The main justification for this labor reform was the diagnosis that the cause of high unemployment in Brazil from 2015 was the so-called high level of social protection (Martins-Filho 2017). This explanation disregards that during the beginning of the twenty-first century, Brazil increased the level of formal jobs in the economy under the same labor regulation.

Another important justification for the reform was an alleged need to allow for workers and employers to negotiate working conditions "freely," rather than having them set by the law or the labor justice. This was known as "negotiation over legislation" and ignored the asymmetrical power relations between labor and capital (Marx 1957), especially in times of crisis and high unemployment.

General strikes against the reform were organized throughout the country. However, on July 11, 2017, the reform was approved by the Brazilian Senate; two days later Temer signed it under Law 13.467/2017 (Brasil 2017), and the law was enforced on November 11, 2017. The main changes brought by the reform are explained in table 7.2.

Table 7.2 shows how the reform reduces labor rights and workers' stability and welfare. From a gender perspective, reducing labor standards in

Table 7.2   Selected Changes Derived from Labor Reform (Law 13.467/2017)

	Before the Reform	*After the Reform*
Vacation	Thirty days a year, divided into maximum two periods of time; one of them must comprise ten days or more; 1/3 of the working time could be "bought" by the employer.	Thirty days a year, divided into maximum three periods of time; one of the must comprise fifteen days or more.
Working Time	Up to 8 hours a day, 44 hours a week, 220 hours a month, up to 2 hours overtime a day; defined as time in which the employee is available, either working or waiting for instructions. Women intitled to a 15 minutes break before starting overtime.	Up to 12 hours a day with 36 hours rest, respecting the limit of 44 hours a week (or 48 hours, counting overtime) and 220 hours a week; defines that resting, studying, eating, interacting with colleagues, personal hygiene and change of uniform is not working time. 15-minute break before overtime for women is not mandatory.
Payment	Payment per productivity cannot be lower than the daily rate of the minimum wage or the wage defined by the professional category. Gratifications and tips must be added to wages.	Payment per productivity can be lower than the daily rate of the minimum wage or the wage defined by the professional category. How gratifications and tips are paid for is subject to negotiation between employer and employee.
Career Plan and Wages	Career plan and wages must be approved by the Labor Ministry and be explicit on the contract.	Career plan and wages can be negotiated between employees and employers freely and does not need to be in the contract; It can be changed during the contract.
Intermittent Job / Zero Hour	Not permitted	Worker can be paid by time worked (hours or days), entitled to proportional rights and benefits like vacation, *Fundo de Garantia do Tempo de Serviço*, social security and 13th salary; contract must establish the hourly wage, which cannot be lower than the hourly minimum wage or wage of other employees in the same function; employee must be summoned at least 3 days before the work and can work for other employers during inactivity.
Home Office	Not regulated	Equipment, energy and internet expenditures must be agreed upon on contract and work is controlled by task.
Part-Time	Maximum 25 hours a week, overtime prohibited. Worker is allowed proportional paid vacation of maximum 18 days and is not allowed to sell vacation time to employer.	Maximum 30 hours a week, overtime prohibited; or maximum 26 hours a week, up to 6h overtime, paid with an increase of 50%. A third of vacation time can be sold.

	Before the Reform	After the Reform
Negotiation	Conventions and collective agreements can establish different working conditions than regulated by law only if promoting superior standards.	Conventions and collective agreements can lower working conditions regulated by law. Individual agreements prevail over collective ones in case the worker has a higher education degree and has a monthly wage of over R$11062,62.
Collective Agreement	Collective agreement regulates individual working contracts and can only be modified by new collective bargaining. An expired collective agreement remains valid until a new one is reached.	What is negotiated might not be incorporated into the individual contract.
Representation	In companies of over 200 employees, one unionized representative must be elected.	In companies of over 200 employees, three representatives are elected, unionized or not.
Dismissal	When worker resigns or is dismissed with cause, s/he is entitled to 40% fine over *Fundo de Garantia do Tempo de Serviço*.	If employer and employee agree, contract can be extinct, and worker would be entitled to 20% fine over *Fundo de Garantia do Tempo de Serviço*
Moral Damages and Harassment	Compensation decided on the labor court, case by case.	Severe offenses can reach maximum fifty times the last wage of the worker in question.
Union Fee	Obligatory; payment made once a year, equivalent to a day's wage.	Optional.
Pregnancy/ Breastfeeding	Pregnant and lactating women are forbidden to work in unsanitary conditions. Breastfeeding breaks guaranteed twice a day.	Pregnant and lactating women are allowed to work in unsanitary conditions if a medical certificate guaranteeing no risk for mother and fetus is presented. Breastfeeding breaks must be agreed upon directly with employer via individual contract.
Termination	Must take place at the trade union.	Can take place at the firm, with legal assistance for both parties; trade union assistance is not obligatory.
Legal Action	Fees regarding legal action started by employees are paid by the government.	Regulations for seeking legal action are tightened. In case worker loses legal action, s/he must pay respective fees.

Sources: Adapted from Varella (2017), Brasil (2017), and Medeiros (2018).

a country where women, especially black women, have a more vulnerable insertion can be detrimental (Medeiros 2018). The reform also created new vulnerable categories in the labor market such as "zero hour" contracts. And if individual negotiation is preferred over collective agreements or to the law, women might be even more vulnerable, more subjected to being pressured into signing a false contract termination and end up not receiving fees due by employers (Imenes 2020). Women are also more exposed to harassment (Rodrigues 2019), and the reform has linked indemnity to wages (the higher the wage, the higher the indemnity), therefore, as women present lower wages, their suffering is valued as less important.

Specifically, regarding the permission for pregnant and lactating women to work under unsanitary conditions if a medical certificate is issued, some argue that reducing labor regulations regarding pregnant and lactating women would increase their chance of employment but, in reality, would decrease levels of welfare in Brazilian society by pressuring women to accept substandard working conditions. This measure, with obvious impacts for women and fetuses, was overturned by the Brazilian Supreme Court in April 2019, while analyzing the Direct Action of Unconstitutionality 5938. Also, having to discuss breast-feeding breaks individually might also expose women (and babies) to vulnerability. Another change was the suppression a woman's right to a fifteen-minute break before starting overtime, when it would be better if both men and women acquire this right (Medeiros 2018). Lastly, another modification more heavily weighted against women is to transfer the obligations of uniform hygiene to the worker, as it adds to reproductive working time which is mostly done by women (Gibb and Oliveira 2015). In general, the specificities of women in the labor market were disregarded by the reform and as a result gender inequality might increase.

It is also worth mentioning that outsourcing, which was not permitted in core activities, now is allowed in any kind of activity, under law 13.429/2017 (Brasil 2017b), also approved during Temer government in addition to the reform being analyzed.

Neither the reform nor increased formalization fulfilled the promises of creating six million jobs. Unemployment decreased in 2017 and 2018 due to an increase in informality and in the number of discouraged workers. As delivery companies such as Ifood, Uber, and Rappi become the biggest "employers" in Brazil (Putti 2019), the promises of increasing formal employment due to the reduction of labor rights remain unfulfilled.

LABOR REFORM AND IMPACTS
FOR WOMEN FACULTY

Faculty faced a dizzying intensification of work in private and public higher education institutions in Brazil due to growth in the number of graduate students until 2015 (Oliveira 2019). Also, these workers face staggering demands for academic productivity, which contrast with increased unemployment, precarious retirement, and low wages (Mancebo et al., 2020). In this scenario, the literature points to a naturalization of work overload, with recurring assessments and internalization of pressures, the interpolation of work and private life, the weakening of labor relations due to competition and, very often, pathogenic management. In this environment faculty increasingly report illnesses related to the nonrecognition of/at work, to the limitations to resist to managerialist pressure, which sometimes euphemistically preaches the collectiveness, and to the quality in a system that demands competitiveness, individualism, and quantitative assessments. Even though workers are exhausted and sick, they maintain a discourse of identity with their activity which facilitates and justifies suffering (Elias and Navarro 2019).

It is important to highlight the type of contract as a factor of instability and insecurity generated by the fear of dismissal or reduction of working time at each semester (Gibb 2017). Precarious contracts are more frequent in the private sector but are also present in the public sector. In the private sector, the movements described are combined with an enhanced education commodification. Since 1990, but more intensely from 2007 onward, higher education industry in Brazil is changing from a rather relative competitive market structure in an oligopsony as large educational conglomerates are consolidated with the growth of publicly traded education companies (such as *Kroton, Estácio, Ânima,* and *Ser Educacional*), local institutes are bought by international groups, and already large groups such as *Universidade Paulista* and *Universidade Nove de Julho* grow even more (Vale 2020). This process led to a general cutback in wages, as well as a reduction in working hours.

In the public sector, faculty also face cuts in government spending and investment to a critical point where overtime and other rights, electricity bills, and security personnel (as well as other outsourced services) are not being paid. Also, work is intensified due to the non-replacement of retiring faculty, scholarships being cut, and moral harassment been perpetrated by the government (Oliveira 2019). In addition, Decree No. 9741, of March 29, 2019, cut 42.27 percent of investment expenses from the budget of the Ministry of Science, Technology, Innovations and Communications. In public institutions, there is a strong wage contention and a structural paralysis, which obviously affect working conditions (Mancebo et al., 2020).

According to the National Institute for Educational Research Anísio Teixeira (INEP), in 2018 3.4 million students began an undergraduation program and 83.1 percent of them in private institutions. In 2017, there were 380,673 faculty positions (one professional may be counted in more than one institution). The average number of courses per faculty is 2.7 per semester. Unlike other educational levels such as basic education in which female teachers are the majority, in higher education most teaching functions are male (54.2%) (Brasil INEP 2018).

In 2018, in the public sector, 86.3 percent of the faculty had a full-time contract, 10.8 percent part time, and 2.6 percent were lecturers (hourly contract). While in the private sector, 27.5 percent of faculty had a full-time contract, 42.4 percent part-time, and 30.1 percent were lecturers (Brasil INEP 2019). Brasil INEP (2019) also shows that more than 70 percent universities' faculty have a full-time contract, while 28.2 percent university centers' (intermediate-size) faculty, and only 22.0 percent of those employed by smaller institutions worked full time (Brasil INEP 2019).

Despite being a more masculine sector, since 1996 women's participation in the sector has grown five percentage points above the male index every year. This coincides with the increase in precarization of faculty work (i.e., fewer full-time jobs, more hourly contracts, lower wage levels, new forms of flexibility such as distance learning, reduction of time in class, as 20 percent of the required "in class" hours can now be done through distance learning[1], transference of administrative work to faculty supported by technology, among others), especially in private institutions, as a consequence of the sector restructuring with the entry of large groups.

Even before the reform, the hourly contract was reported as the main element of flexibilization and extension of the working day since a considerable number of hours are used to prepare classes and to correct exams and those hours are not remunerated in this kind of contract (Gibb 2017). Also, the low hourly wage and the uncertainty regarding the working schedule (and remuneration) from one semester to the next were pointed out as reasons to look for various jobs as a strategy to guarantee enough working hours (Gibb 2017).

For women, in addition to the high demands in terms of time and availability, the remuneration is lowering and the entry in the job market is postponed as more education time is required. Lack of incentives from the employer, family, and society, prejudice in the selection of candidates for postgraduate courses, negative perspectives in the job market, the preference for men or women without children for certain jobs, moral and sexual harassment, and a lack of women as role models act as obstacles for women in this sector. Also, many must manage caring for young children and sick parents while completing a master, doctorate, post doctorate, or public exam to be hired at a public University. In sum, the long path to becoming a professor may explain why women comprise the majority at the base of the pyramid in academia, but their trajectory funnels toward the top (Gibb 2017).

The 2017 reform adds even more complexity to this context for female faculty workers. In order to grasp the impacts of the reform in an already fragmented labor market with gender inequalities, this chapter focuses on listening to female workers in academia. This assisted the authors in understanding the effects of the reform beyond the official statistics. An online questionnaire with thirty-five questions, including multiple choice, select box (allows for multiple or no selection), and open-ended, was built on Google Forms in Portuguese and, after tests, was made available on February 28 until March 2, 2020. Through a snowball technique, the researchers used their personal network to distribute the link and asked participants to share it with faculty colleagues.

The questions covered general information such as sex, career time, the nature of the institution (public or private), working time arrangement, type of contract, remuneration, labor reform implementation, reproductive work, and trade union.

From the 194 respondents, 81 were men and 113 women; 154 respondents started teaching before the labor reform and 32 after the labor reform. Sixty-nine declared they worked in public universities while 125 worked in private institutions; regarding gender, in private institutions women were 60 percent while 55 percent in public. Concerning working time, 103 people declared either to have an hourly work contract or a part-time job, and 91 were full-time workers (this division is much better that the average for the sector, as mentioned in part one). From this universe, 62 percent of women work either as hourly or part-time worker while 53.85 percent had a full-time job. Also, 45 respondents affirmed that their work time was reduced after the labor reform and 73.33 percent of those were women. Female faculty reported reduction of classes from four to three hours, (and pay) 67.31 percent against 32.69 percent of men. In terms of contract, the majority (111) are still on permanent contract but nine reported to be either in temporary or individual intrapreneurship contracts, from those six are women.

Concerning respondents' control over increasing or reducing working hours and remuneration, seventy-two workers in private institutions declared having no control, and forty-eight respondents reported partial control over the issue. Women felt like they have less control than men, as an average 60 percent of them reported having partial or no control of it. Both men and women (36) reported to have noticed gender, race, and religion discrimination, and the majority reported to have felt discriminated against or harassed because of their ideology. Thirty workers were fired, and ten have filled a lawsuit after the reform. Only eighty-four workers still contribute to the trade union after it was made optional and sixty workers feel the performance of the trade unions worsened after the reform. It also calls to attention that workers expect institutions will apply more of the new labor reform laws.

Respondents were also encouraged to offer testimonies. Regarding how changes in working time affect their finances and personal/family life, it was possible to observe a clear distinction from the respondents' in the public and private sector. "I have the instability of a freelancer with the risk of dismissal every semester" (private sector male). Another male worker mentions

Table 7.3   Faculty Member Survey—Selected Female Responses

Type of Institution	How does the reduction/increase of working time between one semester and the other affect your finances and personal/family organization?
Private Institution	In impacts on my financial support to my children.
	Completely. I can only make plans for four months.
	It impacts a lot, right now I want to work less yours to finish my PhD, but the institution implicitly threatens me with dismissal
	Instability, affliction, anguish, uncertainty.
Public Institution	It doesn't influence anything, because my salary is fixed, regardless of the number of class hours.
	There is no change in remuneration due to the public contract.

Source: Questionnaire conducted by authors.

"Everything can work out ok, but you can also end up driving an uber." Some testimonials from female workers are included in table 7.3.

In terms of working life balance and reproductive working time, 62.12 percent of women reported having difficulty to reconcile personal and professional life after the labor reform and 64.18 percent of women reported to find it difficult to reconcile reproductive and productive work.

Regarding the question who does reproductive care work in your family, from those respondents (11) that affirm that the partner performs reproductive care alone, 81.82 percent of them were men, also 64 percent of women and 36 percent of men declared to do reproductive care alone. "I help my partner in caring out reproductive duties, but s/he does more" was the answer of 62.5 percent of men and only 37.5 percent of women.

The last question asked was meant for respondents to freely express themselves and add new information. While a minority described satisfaction with working conditions and workload, many described an atmosphere of coercion, pressure, and uncertainty, as seen in table 7.4.

Thus, the atmosphere of uncertainty, persecution, and pressure in recent years described by the literature is apparent from the respondents' answers.

CONCLUSION

The 2017 labor reform was approved with little dialogue from Brazilian society, disregarding dissonant voices. The reform treats unequal workers as equals and increases already existent inequalities, being highly detrimental to workers, especially women (Medeiros 2018), downgrading social rights, disrespecting international labor standards, and increasing labor inequality (Silva 2018). All workers are impacted (men and women; black and white).

Table 7.4 Faculty Member Survey: "Is there anything you want to add regarding your working conditions and regulations?"

Type of Institution	Gender	Is there anything you want to add regarding your working conditions and regulations?
Private Employment Institution	F	The reform legitimized precarious hiring processes that were underway.
	M	I feel that the future is bleak for private universities. Reduction of workload, distance education advancing, contract flexibility, among others. The work is exhausting, poorly paid and gives no chance, for example, for teachers to supplement their salaries with other activities (schedules organized in such a way that teachers cannot get two jobs or receive benefits).
	F	Remuneration is very low compared to the demand for work. Today we work harder to earn the same amount as before the reform due to the reduction in workload.
	M	The working conditions at the Faculty [name suppressed], where I teach, are terrible. The teacher has no autonomy regarding the content taught in the classroom (lesson plans are made collectively with the supervision of the course coordinator). Students who do not adapt to their teaching method go directly to the director of the institution, creating a bad atmosphere in the work environment. Several teachers were fired without having a chance to explain their position in relation to students' complaints about grades, content, and teaching methods.
	F	I work for a longer period of time than I am paid to.
	F	The institution where I work, at the beginning of the school year, informed a reduction of classes from 4 to 3 hours a day and coerced many teachers to request a reduction in the number of hours, when in fact it was imposed.
	M	There is always a risk of dismissal each semester depending on your performance and assessment of the student-client.
	M	The process is uberization. Although I have not yet suffered directly, I think I will soon be hit. We all will be.
	F	There is constant coercion to reduce weekly working hours
	M	So far, I have had no problems with the institution in labor terms. Sometimes I think they push me to teach more and that ends up making my research worse—and worse paid. But it is within 30h.
	M	The main problems I face are related to the excessive size of some classes, the disorganization of the curricular friar and the lack of pedagogical autonomy.
	F	My master's degree diploma was not incorporated for the additional remuneration.

(Continued)

Table 7.4 Faculty Member Survey: "Is there anything you want to add regarding your working conditions and regulations?" (Continued)

Type of Institution	Gender	Is there anything you want to add regarding your working conditions and regulations?
Public Employment Institution	M	We at Public Universities work much more than 40 hours because many of our activities are unpaid (extension, management and research). Unlike the University sector (where I worked for 10 years) the hour in class is not our most intense work. I feel that our work is getting heavier, with hours operating management systems, management of pedagogical actions, etc. in addition to undergraduate and graduate supervisions, which have become virtual and constant.
	F	I am a temporary worker at a federal university. I noticed an increase in this form of hiring due to cuts in education spending, since the spending cap law (Constitutional Amendment 95/2016).
	F	The working conditions are good.
	F	I think we are frightened with the persecution suffered by left-wing professors. We think more about what we are going to talk about, and we are intimidated if students want to film or record classes.
	F	The demand for increased academic productivity
	F	The academic area is being scrapped every day. Respect for our class is deteriorating. The psychological is being harmed. Many illnesses caused by stress in the academic community.
	M	In a general sense, it has visibly worsened.
	M	Since 2016, after the Coup, but especially after 2019, with the current government, professors are suffering moral harassment, given the constant threats to universities, salaries, budget cuts, graduate school, the full-time regime, in short, a set of attacks that has clearly caused the illness of professors committed to the Brazilian public university.
	F	Contract of substitute teachers 20 hours with class load in the classroom sometimes greater than the effective 40 hours full-time
	F	Precariousness. Constant threats in the classroom.
	F	There was a significant increase in the hiring of temporary teachers, which has an impact on the administrative workload for permanent teachers, overloading them. Since 2016 we have not had wage restitution. More recently, the government increased the social security contribution rate by 3 percent due to the pension reform.

Source: Questionnaire conducted by authors.

However, as women have a more vulnerable insertion in the labor market, they are even worse off.

Faculty are also highly impacted by the reform and women especially, as our respondents show. The reform's impacts are more visible for faculty working in the private sector, until now. However, it will affect public sector faculty as well as public sector jobs in general. Higher education workers face constant demand for academic productivity increase, a naturalization of work overload, with recurring assessments and internalization of pressures, the interpolation of work and private life, the weakening of labor relations due to competition etc. Brazil's specificity, especially in the last years, is the mix of this highly pressured atmosphere with unemployment, financialization of the sector, cuts on government spending on higher education and research as well as attacks on academic freedom (Oliveira 2019).

From our respondents, it was more frequent for women to have their work time reduced after the labor reform. Women also expressed less control than men regarding changes in their working time. This generates "instability, affliction, anguish, uncertainty," as one female faculty added. Their responses also made clear that reproductive work was the responsibility of women, either female faculty or male faculty's partners, showing that even among highly educated workers the sexual division of labor continues unequal. That also explains why more women pointed out that the difficulties to reconcile productive and reproductive work before the reform and even more after it.

The reform has been implemented only two years ago and its results are already impacting workers lives negatively. Moreover, the combination among the commodification of the faculty career and education in general together with the new permissive laws allowed by the reform are being implemented by the institutions. And it is the perception of workers that the institutions will use the permission given by the law even more in the near future in order to raise profits and exploit workers. This was summarized by one of the female workers: "Precariousness. Constant threats in the classroom."

Therefore, the 2017 labor reform must be understood as a strategy of capital toward productive restructuring, attacking working-class organizations, especially trade unions and reordering the State order to reduce social and labor rights, and expanding discretionary use of work, which affects and overloads women even more.

NOTE

1. Institutions have reduced their class time from four to three hours. The fourth hour now is supposedly performed at home. The hourly faculty member is not remunerated for this fourth hour.

REFERENCES

Alvarenga, C. F. (2008). *Relações de gênero e trabalho docente: jornadas e ritmos no cotidiano de professoras e professores*. São Paulo: Dissertação de mestrado.

Artes, A., & Ricoldi, A. M. (2016). Mulheres e as carreiras de prestigio no ensino superior brasileiro: o não lugar feminino. In N. R. Itaboraí, & A. M. (Org.), *Até onde caminhou a revolução de gênero no Brasil?: implicações demográficas e questões sociais* (pp. 81–94). ABEP.

Blyth, M. (2017). *Austeridade: a história de uma ideia perigosa*. São Paulo: Autonomia Literária.

Brasil. (2017a). *LEI Nº 13.467, DE 13 DE JULHO DE 2017*.

Brasil. (2017b). LEI Nº 13.429, DE 31 DE MARÇO DE 2017.

Brasil, I. N. (2018). Censo da educação superior 2017.

Brasil, I. N. (2019). Censo da Educação Superior 2018: Notas estatísticas.

Carvalho, L. (2018). *Valsa Brasileira: do boom ao caos econômico*. São Paulo: Todavia.

Castillo, M., & Martins, A. (2020, 02 28). *Cepal*. Retrieved from https://repositorio. cepal.org/handle/11362/40241.

Elias, M. A., & Navarro, V. L. (2019). Profissão docente no ensino superior privado: o difícilequilíbrio de quem vive na corda bamba. *Cadernos de Psicologia Social do Trabalho*, pp. 49–63.

Fagnani, E., Biancarelli, A., & Rossi, P. (2015). *Apresentação. Revista Política Social e Desenvolvimento*.

Fornazier, A., & Oliveira, A. L. (2011). O ideário neoliberal no Brasil na década de 1990 e suas implicações no trabalho e nos setores produtivos. *Oikos*.

Gibb, L. S. (2017). The dissolution of working time patterns: Implementation in Brazil and impacts on women. *UNICAMP*.

Gibb, L. S., & Oliveira, A. L. (2015). A desigualdade na distribuição do trabalho total no Brasil: a quem favorece? *Pesquisa & Debate*, 26(2(48)), pp. 87–104. Retrieved from https://revistas.pucsp.br/rpe/article/view/22683.

Guerra, A., Oliveira, A. L., Carvalho, A. C., Jakobsen, K., Vitagliano, L. F., Manzano, M., Toledo, M. T., Ribeiro, P., Silva, R., Silva, R., Bokany, V., & Nozaki, W. (2017). *2016: Recessão e golpe*. São Paulo: Editora Fundação Perseu Abramo.

Imenes, M. (2020). Lei atual abre brecha para empresas aplicarem golpe em trabalhadores, entenda. *IG*.

IPEA. (2011). *Retrato das desigualdades de gênero e raça - 4ª ed*. Brasilia: Instituto de Pesquisa Econômica Aplicada, Ipea.

IPEA. (2014). *Políticas sociais: acompanhamento e análise, n. 22*. Brasília: Intituto de Política Economica Aplicada, Ipea.

IPEA. (2015). *Retrato das Desigualdades de Gênero e Raça – 1995 a 2015*.

IPEA. (2016). Mulheres e trabalho: breve análise do período 2004–2014. *Instituto de Pesquisa Econômica Aplicada*.

Mancebo, D., Santorum, K. M., Ribeiro, C. V., & Léda, D. B. (2020, January). The Work in Higher Education. *Education Policy Analysis Archives*.

Martins-Filho, I. G. (2017). É preciso flexibilizar direitos sociais para haver emprego, diz chefe do TST. (L. Alegretti, Interviewer) Retrieved from shorturl.at/jtw25.

Marx, K. (1957). *Das Kapital: Kritik der politischen Ökonomie.* Stuttgart: Alfred Kröner.

Medeiros, C. M. (2018). Impactos da lei 13.467/2017 sobre o trabalho da mulher.

Mello, G., Welle, A., & Oliveira, A. L. (2018). *Nota de Conjuntura: Baixo crescimento e alta desigualdade: a letargia brasileira pós-recessão.* Retrieved from Cecon: https://goo.gl/qTJpWq.

Oliveira, A. L. (2019). Educação superior brasileira no início do século XXI: inclusão interrompida?

Putti, A. (2019). Apps são os maiores empregadores, mas precarização dá o tom nos trabalhos. *Carta Capital.*

Rodrigues, T. S. (2019). A precarização do trabalho feminino reforçada pela reforma trabalhista: uma análise sobre as alterações trazidas pela lei n 13.467 sob o ponto de vista do direito da mulher no trabalho.

Rossi, P., & Mello, G. (2017, 05 04). *Choque recessivo e a maior crise da história: A economia brasileira em marcha ré.* Retrieved from CECON: https://goo.gl/mQHuWd.

Saffioti, H. I. (2013). *A mulher na sociedade de classe: mito e realidade.* São Paulo: Expressão Popular.

Silva, P. L. (2018). O feminismo popular na resistência pelo direito à igualdade de gênero e ao trabalho decente: um olhar das Amélias sobre a lei 13.467/2017.

Teixeira, M. (2013). O mercado de trabalho reitera relações desiguais que se constoem no âmbito das relações econômicas e sociais. In F. P. Abramo & F. F. Ebert, *Classes? Que classes?* São Paulo: Editora Fundação Perseu Abramo e Editora Fundação Friedrich Ebert.

Vale, A. A. (2020). Trabalho Docente no Setor Privado da Educação Superior e a Reforma Trabalhista: Destruição de Direitos e Precarização da Vida. *Arquivos analíticos de políticas educativas - Dossiê Especial O Trabalho no Ensino Superior*, Volume 28 Número 10.

Varella, I. (2017). *Os 22 pontos da Reforma Trabalhista.* Retrieved from JusBrasil: shorturl.at/enHV3.

Chapter 8

The Effect of Indirect Bias on Gender Equality in the Building Trades

Marquita R. Walker and Armand Chevalier

INTRODUCTION

This chapter specifically focuses on indirect bias as the root cause of histori-cally generated gendered oppression which leads to the marginalization and underrepresentation of women in the building trades. Covert and gatekeep-ing institutional and social bias leads to discrimination from governments, markets, employers, and unions even though anti-discrimination policies are structurally embedded in the policies/customs/rules which regulate these institutions' behaviors. Situated in political economy theory which posits past influences contribute to the oppression of equity-seeking groups in the absence of collective action, implicit bias fosters gender discrimination, the historic marginalization of women, and has a deleterious effect on the hir-ing and retention of women in trades. It is important for all stakeholders to address these deficiencies through strategies which encourage the inclusion of women in construction, strengthen legislative and workplace policies promot-ing women, and decrease masculine dominance in the workplace.

Skill shortages and a weakened labor supply in the construction industry necessitate serious consideration of reasons why women's participation in construction remains below legal and necessary limits. The consequences of delay in addressing these concerns result in a continued mismatch between labor and management, an inadequate workforce to fill future construction jobs, a diminished capacity to compete in a globalized marketplace, and a weakened ability to maintain a position of dominance within world markets.

Implicit bias is an unconscious mental process. According to Greenwald and Kreiger (2006), implicit bias functions "outside conscious attentional focus" (p. 947) and prominently figures in the determination of discrimina-tion against women and minorities through implicit attitudes and implicit stereotypes. Implicit attitudes, unconscious and predicated on favorable/ unfavorable impressions, color human tendencies to take actions for/against something or someone. The stark differences between implicit and explicit attitudes, known as dissociations, are commonly observed toward stigmatized groups, including groups defined by race, age, ethnicity, disability, and sexual orientation (Greenwald 2006, 949). Implicit stereotypes are socially constructed beliefs associated with a group's characteristics and attributes. Stereotypes "represent a set of qualities perceived to reflect the essence of a group . . . and affect how people perceive, process information about, and respond to, group members" (Dovidio 2013, 6). Individuals in a stereotyped group behave in expected ways because they self-fulfill expectations of stereotypical traits transmitted through socialization, the media, and language and discourse.

Implicit bias is problematic because the behavior it produces can differ from an individual's espoused beliefs, values, and principles, and makes identifying discrimination, which by law must be intentional against a protected group, difficult to expose. Much research documenting implicit bias as unintentional comes from the Implicit Association Test (IAT), a social psychological measure which detects an individual's automatic association between two target concepts in a two-choice task (Greenwald, 1995). The IAT reflects a preference for white and male subjects whether participants are white or black, male or female. These findings predict actual biased behavior (Greenwald, 2006). Within an employment context, implicit bias affects the way policies relating to outreach, hiring, and retention are fashioned and the way employees are treated. The effect of implicit bias on policies relating to gender discrimination should be exposed and mediated because of its propensity to negatively affect workers' job opportunities, earning ability, job security, and job satisfaction.

Implicit bias is not new. Dovidio et al. (2013) provide a comprehensive understanding of how "specific emotions, nonconscious processes, and fundamental neural processes contribute to biases" and "how social structure creates and justifies biases, which permeate social institutions" (p. 2). Individuals and institutions often hold stereotypical and objective views as "cognitive schemas used by social perceivers to process information about others" (Hilton and von Hippel (1996) in Dovidio 2013, 5) and imply that information about qualities or expectations not readily apparent to the viewer can be constraining or enriching (associating positive or negative behavior with a group).

This chapter, situated in political economy theory of discrimination, suggests the past's influence on the present and the unequal power relations and unequal access to resources between and among social groups/organizations as a component of a system of racial and gender oppression which historically marginalizes and disenfranchises equity-seeking groups and persists in institutional discrimination in the absence of collective action (Albelda 2001, 184). Implicit bias plays a significant role in the gender oppression and discrimination advanced by political economy theory and contends the environment within which present-day institutional and social bias occurs is the result of past influences on women's place in society and women's roles in institutional and cultural environments.

Political economy theory uses groups as a basic unit of analysis and assumes that external influences (religions, economic systems, and social institutions) shape contextual relationships such as social experiences, situations, and circumstances which drive group behavior. *Groups*, defined as some set of individuals who share some interest, have a social relationship to other groups with which they share commonalities or compete for scarce resources. The nature of the group then is explored through "context, collective behavior, conflicting interest, and change" (Albelda 2013, 106). Political economy theory posits social and institutional discrimination, embedded in the institutional practices/polices which guide decision making concerning labor and management and reflect external social environments, can be reduced through collective action's "impact on social attitudes, market dynamics, organizational behavior, and government policies" (Albelda 2013, 159). Recommendations for addressing these barriers include enforcing government policies which mandate more women in the trades, changing the masculine culture of union/employer construction workplaces through the promotion of mentoring components in apprenticeship programs which provide to women one-on-one support, and making concerted efforts within the firm toward implementation of more gender-neutral, family-friendly, and work-life balance policy.

Individuals self-select into groups predicated on their economic and social status, educational and political experiences, and traditional and hereditary mores within the social categories of race, class, and gender. Group power lies in the collective ability to affect change and incur group rewards or punishments. Individual decision making is subsumed by the group and predicts the chances of success or failure. Political economy theory requires concerted action by groups. Within the political economy there will always be winners and losers and successes and failures.

Societies' social construction of biological differences into distinct racial, class, and gendered social categories provides context for shifting power dynamics between groups at home and at work. We see this in the domination of whites over blacks, rich over the poor, and men over women. The constant struggle for domination leads to forms of oppression through exploitation and exclusion: whites exclude and exploit blacks, the rich exclude and exploit the poor, and men exclude and exploit women in order to protect their turf and remain the dominant power. Exploring the broad-based and extensive oppression of equity-seeking groups resulting from the domination of race, class, and gender provides the foundation for more specific research into the gendered division of labor.

BACKGROUND

Evidence as to why significant numbers of women fail to enter and remain in the building trades (Tomlinson, 2005; Dainity, 2004; Denissen, 2010) includes family and caregiving duties, inflexible and/or long hours of work, masculine workplace cultures, employer's stereotypical attitudes, and few work-life balance initiatives. We argue these outcomes are an extension of implicit biases' effect on social and institutional factors which historically relegate women to secondary power positions resulting in discriminatory racial and gendered beliefs, injustices, and policies against women and other equity-seeking groups. Prior to 1960, this gendered division of labor was less a problem because men and women conformed to societal roles based on economic and cultural systems which considered men as breadwinners and women as secondary or subservient. This taken-for-granted approach was not questioned until working women mobilized across the nation and agitated for change via women's caucuses, moved on to organizing for clerical jobs, and then turned toward affirmative action to address the number of women in poverty. Enlisting women to fight for their right to enter more nontraditional jobs continues especially in the field of construction (Maclean, 1999).

LEGISLATIVE ACTION AND WOMEN'S PUSH BACK AGAINST GENDER INEQUALITY

The push for female equality owns a great deal to the Black civil rights organizations of earlier generations who fought against employment discrimination and secured some reforms. For instance, the Negro American Labor Congress (NALC) was formed in 1961 to end "male-female differentials" for black women in wage-earning positions (Maclean 1999, 50). The concept of affirmative action, which addressed past racial and gendered injustices and established a barrier against future racial and gendered harm, became policy in the 1960s. Supporters and detractors of affirmative action sought a balance between equality for all and individual freedom; consequently current affirmative action rulings have been weakened by the conservative courts (Wagner, 2015).

The Civil Rights Act of 1964, Title VII embedded into law anti-discrimination prohibitions which made it illegal for employers to discriminate against protected classes or "adversely affect the status of anyone because of race, color, religion, sex, or national origin" (SEC 2000e2 [Section 703a] (Tomaskovic-Devey 2007, 50). The law is interpreted to depend on the ability of an individual in a protected class to "prove" an employer has blatantly and intentionally discriminated against him or her. Providing evidence of intentional proof to discriminate is very difficult, so many discrimination cases simply can't be proven and call into question the intent and interpretation of the law.

The Equal Employment Opportunity Commission (EEOC), formed in 1965 as an agency to enforce Title 7 of the Civil Rights Act of 1964 (1964a) and charged with monitoring and ending workplace discrimination was never effective in seeking redress for working women who constituted about one-fourth of all complaints concerning unequal wages, sex-segregated seniority, unequal health and pension coverage, and male-biased job recruitment and promotion policies (Modesitt 2010). The EEOC lacked enforcement power and staff to investigate and resolve discrimination claims and still maintains a huge backlog of cases.

As a result of the lethargic response of the EEOC to adjudicate cases, The National Organization for Women (NOW) was formed in 1966. NOW's goal, then and currently, is to promote grassroots activism to eliminate discrimination and gain equal rights for all women (2017). The Federal Women's Program (FEW) was created in 1967 by Executive Order #11375 during the Johnson administration and "added sex as a prohibited form of discrimination" (2016). Under the auspices of the EEOC, FEW has a presence in every federal agency with responsibilities to identify hiring, advancement, and enhancement barriers to opportunities for women in federal jobs.

In 1965, the Office of Federal Contract Compliance (OFCC) was created to advance hiring people of color for private firms with more than fifty employees and federal government contracts of more than $50,000. Non-compliance meant firms could be sanctioned with fines and lose their right to bid on federal contracts. In 1978, the Office of Federal Contract Compliance Programs (OFCCP) was created as an umbrella agency for all federal compliance agencies (Tomaskovic-Devey, 2007). Currently OFCCP sets the terms for covered federal government contractors' and subcontractors' requirements in compliance with Executive Order #11246 to ensure non-discrimination based on sex in employment (Office of Federal Contract Compliance Programs 1964, 1980; Office of Contract Compliance Regulations 2017). The Civil Rights Center (CRC) is part of the Office of Assistant Secretary for Administration and Management and directs equal employment opportunities for programs and activities receiving federal financial assistance while the OFCCP manages employers who hold federal contracts and subcontracts (U.S. Department of Labor 2017).

Legislation to improve gender oppression and discrimination over the past six decades has done little to further women's chances of entering the building trades. In 2013, the EEOC "commissioned a work group to identify the obstacles that remain in the federal workplace that hinder equal employment opportunities for women" (Equal Employment Opportunity Commission, 2013). The report generated six obstacles for workplace equality including inflexible workplace policies, wage gaps, caregiving responsibilities, underrepresentation in STEM, unconscious gender and stereotypical biases, and lack of agency commitment.

Though this report focused on federal employees, it is assumed similar obstacles exist for women in the private sector as well. Title 7 of the Civil Rights Act and Revised Order No. 4, which implements Executive Order #11246, includes a 1978 federal regulation stipulating federal construction contractors must "make good faith efforts to ensure that at least 6.9 percent of hours worked are performed by women" (Hegewisch 2015, 2). These requirements have not been updated. Construction industry regulations provide guidance on maintaining a harassment-free workplace which includes two women on each worksite, adequate toilets, and assurance management is aware of their responsibilities for women and minorities (Hegewisch 2015).

During the 1960s and 1970s, women's advocacy groups pushed for women's rights to better wages, benefits, and respect in the workplace. As more women found themselves as sole heads of households, higher wages and benefits in the construction industry became increasingly attractive to women. Wider Opportunities for Women, organized in 1966 to promote training for minority women, pushed for poor women's entry into craft jobs; Advocates for Women, a splinter group from NOW which formed in 1972, approached women's entry into non-traditional fields as a poverty issue. The relegation of women to low-paying service and sexualized work led to the creation of the Women's Work Force Network in 1979 and created a Construction Compliance Task Force to facilitate women's entrance into the building trades (Maclean 1999). Using Affirmative Action as a tool, women fought for their right to a decent standard of living by breaking out of normal subservient and sexualized gender roles which relegated them to secondary status. Upsetting the gender dynamic threatened men's masculinity, so they turned to sexual harassment to protect their territory (Maclean 1999, 65).

LITERATURE REVIEW

The enactment of legislation to correct inequalities in the gendered divisions of labor has not achieved the goal of gender equality in the workplace but rather has driven the maintenance of the status quo into cultural veins to justify exclusionary decisions (Tomaskovic-Devey, 2007). Processes of stereotyping (Reskin, 2000; Dovidio, 2013), cognitive bias (Fiske, 1998), and in-group preference (Bielby, 2000) are cultural attributes which contribute to gender inequality by condoning and solidifying existing biases against protected classes and consequently reifying organizational structures and practices. Several reasons for the maintenance of the status quo are inertia, the resistance to change (Tomaskovic-Devey, 2007), external environmental pressure such as lawsuits, governmental regulation, outside cultural, or human resource practices (DiMaggio, 1983; Mansfield, 1991), and internal organizational pressure to change leadership (Baron, 1991), human resource agendas (Cockburn, 1991; Mansfield, 1991), and demands from women and minorities (Smith, 2002).

The purpose of anti-discrimination law is to provide some form of remedy in cases where equity-seeking individuals are deprived of opportunities (Bagenstos 2007). Anti-discrimination laws can mediate the effects of overt discrimination when the discrimination is recognized as individual intentional "self-conscious, irrational animus" (Bagenstos 2007, 477), yet it is more likely subtle unconscious or implicit bias that results in limited opportunities and negative evaluations for women and minorities. Because implicit bias remains beneath human consciousness, its existence is difficult to pinpoint, but its effects are often pronounced. Shaped by external stimuli over extended periods, implicit bias remains a social problem which "has systematically harmful effects on the life chances of members of particular socially salient groups" (Bagenstos 2007, 480). Bagenstos (2007) notes it makes little difference to the equity-seeking individual whether the discrimination is overt or implicit because the outcome is equally detrimental. Most policy actors do not recognize implicit bias as a cause of discrimination and usually argue against its existence because of political or judicial backlash (Bagenstos, 2007). Implicit bias insidiously affects institutional organizational structures and policies in subtle and nuanced ways which affect racial and gendered training, job opportunities, retention, and job security. In this chapter we look at the effects of implicit bias on institutional and social discrimination.

Implicit bias leads to institutional bias, the tendency to discriminate, which leads to institutional discrimination, the act of discrimination. *Discrimination*, "the treatment of a functionally irrelevant status (such as race of sex) as relevant for the distribution of some reward or penalty" (Merton 1972, 20), is a socially constructed process which historically and legally favors white males over others. Discrimination "involves the *disparate treatment* of similarly situated individuals because of their sex, race, color, national origin, religion or some other protected characteristic" and includes the *disparate impact* of discrimination or the "use of sex- or race-neutral practices that systematically disadvantage members of a protected class . . . regardless of employers' intent." (Hirsh 2008, 1397) Discrimination implies "inappropriate and potentially unfair treatment of individuals due to group membership" (Dovidio 2013, 6). Claims of discrimination must be proven and are encouraged or restricted based on the worker's perception of workplace practices and fairness. In sex/race-neutral practices, claims decline while in sex/race-conscious practices, claims rise (Hirsh, 2008).

DISCUSSION

How Implicit Bias Contributes to Institutional Discrimination

Institutional discrimination historically was used to justify racial and gendered group-based inequities which favored white men (Henry, 2013); it is defined as the "adverse treatment of women and minorities" via societal and institutional explicit and implied rules and policies (Albelda 2013, 162). Federal laws prohibiting explicit discrimination exist under Title 7 of the Civil Rights Act of 1964, the Americans with Disability Act of 1990 (ADA), the Rehabilitation Act of 1973, the Age Discrimination of Employment Act of 1967 (ADEA) (1964b), and the Genetic Information Nondiscrimination Act of 2008 (GINA) (2008). Institutional discrimination masks as normal operational behavior because existing ideologies support its maintenance. It is only unmasked when disparate outcomes and/or negative consequences between groups/individuals surface (Henry, 2013).

Some scholars recognize the source of group-based disparate treatment as a result of the group's own attributes which disadvantage the group (Kluegel, 1986). The view in these cases is that equity-seeking groups are responsible for their own inequitable status, and this imbalance can only be rectified through group responsibility. This conservative viewpoint sees inequalities as caused by the groups themselves and not as systemized institutional failures. Other scholars recognize a "victimizing society" (Henry 2013, 427) as, at least in part, the source of group-based disparities and believe institutional policies can be biased against disadvantaged groups even when individuals within those institutions have no intentional animus toward disadvantaged groups.

Class Struggle, Job Competition, and Organizational Adaptation

Institutional discrimination is perpetuated via the effects of class struggle, job competition, and organizational adaptation. Class struggle emboldens divisiveness within the collective and impacts the bargaining power and solidarity of workers. Groups or organizations maintain their identity, distribution of income, and control of work processes by covertly discriminating against "other" (women or minorities) in order to protect their economic gains/stance/power/control (Albelda 2001, 184). This divineness is perpetuated when white males benefit from the effects of job competition by "discriminating" against others in order to lessen competition and have the "best" jobs, higher wages, and more promotions (Albelda 2001, 185, 2013). The impact of institutional discrimination affects the solidarity and bargaining power of workers.

Examples of institutional discrimination surface in the building trades' hesitancy to hire, retain, and promote women to good paying positions. Implicit bias reinforces the sexual division of labor which favors the unwritten rules governing male and female behavior and physical strength and size (Peterson 2006). The belief that women are less able tackle the heavy lift associated with construction or their presence is a result of affirmative action that follows from this sexual division of labor.

Caregiving responsibilities as a reason women are infrequently hired and retained is an example of implied discrimination encouraging disharmony and discord. Implicit bias exists against women who leave their homes/families in the care of others to work in construction. The nature of construction often requires varied hours and distant worksites which place an undue burden on women as primary caregivers. Assumptions exist that younger qualified women of childbearing age may exit the firm to bear or raise children.

Implicit bias pays dividends to the dominant white male power structure and affects the "distribution of income and the organization of work" (Albelda 2001, 184). The economic incentives for white males to discriminate serves to maintain their dominant position within the labor/management and the worker/subordinate dyad. This self-reinforcing behavior rewards those who discriminate with influence, money, and power. When labor collectively unites against management, employers face greater costs and lower profits, so management's incentive is to "divide and conquer" in order to maintain profits and control of the work process (Albelda 2013, 164).

Discrimination also occurs within the collective itself. Racial and sexual differences between workers contribute to discrimination, and management capitalizes on this conflict for profitability. Intra-discriminatory practices within the collective are reflected in various racial and sexual coalitions which reify the institutional structures of white male prerogatives and serve to benefit management's control of work processes and maintenance of power. White workers may form coalitions against black or Latino workers or black female workers may form coalitions against their female Latino counterparts. This results in a weakened collective because of workers' prejudices, the "individual-level attitude (whether subjectively positive or negative) toward groups and their members that create or maintain hierarchical status relations between groups" (Dovidio 2013, 5).

Individuals carrying biases and prejudices into the workplace reflect society at large. Women and minorities have difficulty in achieving equitable benefits because the American work ethic, which highly values individualism and competition over the collective, disincentives solidarity. This form of organizational adaptation surfaces in management's preferment of white males over "other" because of the social impact promotions have on the firm's profits. Boards of directors who answer to shareholders question and reprimand management's decision to promote women and minorities to top-ranking positions because of their perceived "fit" within corporate, financial, and capitalistic circles. The historical exclusion of "other" benchmarked by low status, low pay, and disenfranchisement contributes to indirect biases' effect on institutional discrimination from the perspective of the firm as the firm mirrors class struggles in the external environment and intragroup discrimination among workers trying to protect their status, economic benefits, power, and control.

Institutional bias is also affected by social and cultural bias through the dominants' use of legitimate power via avenues of institutional structures. Women's and minorities' performance is measured against a standard white, European, male model of performance creating a perpetual loop of failures for equity-seeking groups who do not conform to the model. Non-conformance to the model positions women in a catch-22 situation in which their behavior and reactions are perceived by the dominant group as inferior or substandard and result in negative outcomes which reveal institutional bias.

How Implicit Bias Contributes to Social and Cultural Discrimination

Implicit bias impacts social structures, patterned arrangements of socioeconomic institutions which act as a framework for human and organizational interaction, and makeup the social networks in which all human engage. Within social structure spaces, human choices are constrained by and acted upon by dominant groups. The influence of dominant group power to define and transmit generational societal values and policies for less powerful groups hails from an American belief that less powerful equity-seeking groups are fairly treated because they disproportionately are less responsible or deserving that dominant groups. Dominant power groups, who control institutional structures, encourage social and cultural bias through sanitizing history to reflect a "collective forgetting" (Henry 2013, 428) of the historical marginalization of women and the restriction of women's entry into jobs requiring physical strength, math and engineering skills, and construction abilities.

These co-opted social structures have a discriminatory impact on women's entry and retention in the building trades. Maclean (1999) suggests male identity is "derived in good part from the maleness of their work cultures" (p. 30), so males protect their gender role and identity by protecting their workplace turf. Ridgeway and Cornell (2004) submit, "gender is an institutionalized system of social practices for constituting people as two significantly different categories, men and women, and organizing social relations of inequality on the basis of that difference" (p. 510). Gender, socially constructed and embedded in everyday interactions, is a multidimensional system recognizing and supporting differences and providing justification for the inequitable treatment of women in the building trades (Denissen, 2010; Risman, 2004; Ridgeway, 2004).

Gendered roles influence our work lives as occupational identities are constructed. The building trades' masculine nature excludes female participation though mandated by federal and state policies (Denissen, 2010). Exclusion is orchestrated via an organizational culture which covertly sanctions gender-specific behaviors by rewarding men primary positions and women secondary positions. Socially constructed gender boundaries reinforce gender inequality and maintain male-gendered dominance by stereotyping tradeswomen as unfeminine, incompetent to do men's work, and devoid of self-worth.

Women are often compliant in reinforcing gendered social structures (Ridgeway, 2004). Our cultural belief system predicates our identity as a composite of our relationships to others and compels us to exhibit certain behaviors within difference situational contexts. The paternalistic and patriarchal nature and trajectory of history values white male dominance as "status worthy and competent overall" (Ridgeway, 2004) and devalues female roles as less competent, secondary, and communal. These cultural beliefs cede power to dominant groups who "shape[ing] women's own actions and responses" (Denissen 2010, 1053) so tradeswomen have to constantly (re)negotiate their gender, status, and power within situational interactions. Women subsume their own identity in order to achieve the higher pay and benefits afforded to their male counterparts or face sanctions such as "harassment, sabotage, intimidation, and exclusion" (Denissen 2010, 1052). Women's agency can redefine gender as an asset within their occupational identities through these occupational challenges and opportunities.

Social structures make up the social institutions of family, home, church, culture, and society. Within these social institutions, one's social life revolves around a mix of economic and non-economic factors (Granovetter, 2005). This means that non-economic factors can influence economic factors to some degree. For instance, employers in the building trades who wish to hire new workers may rely on social networks such as family, friends, associations with business partners, and so forth from which to cull potential new hires. This allows employers to circumvent usual forms of filtering potential employees through intermediaries such as third-party firms whose job it is to vet potential hires and may result in a cost-savings to the employer. Employers rely on confidence grounded in their relationships between trusted family, friends, and partners which no amount of money could purchase. Granovetter (2005) writes, "Such trust and obligations arise from the way a society's institutions pattern kin and friendship ties, and any economic efficiency gains resulting from them are a byproduct, typically unintended, of actions and patterns enacted by individuals with non-economic interests" (p. 3).

The Dominance of Group Power

Maintaining dominance is necessary to reaffirm the hierarchical structures within social institutions. Social dominance theory, developed by Sidanius and Pratto (1999), provides a theoretical framework predicated on "group-based social hierarchies"(p. 31), the "social power, prestige, and privilege that an individual possesses by virtue of his or her ascribed membership in a particular socially constructed group such as a race, religion, clan, tribe, lineage, linguistic/ethic group, or social class" (p. 32). The theory predicts a social hierarchy emerges, is embraced by male-dominated workplaces, and allows recognition and reinforcement of gender differences to rationalize stratification and justify gender inequality. Positive social value is "material and symbolic things for which people strive . . . such as political authority and power, good and plentiful food, splendid homes, the best available health care, wealth, and high social status" (Sidanius 1999, 31) while negative social value is "such things as low power and social status, high risk and low-status occupations, relatively poor health care, poor food, modest or miserable homes, and severe negative sanctions (e.g., prison and death sentences)" (p. 31). Without this gender inequality would disappear and the dominant male group would lose power, prestige, and money (Maclean, 1999; Henry, 2013).

The power of cultural discrimination relies on the dominant group's ability to justify the inconsistencies in inequities through "legitimizing ideologies" (Henry 2013, 431) such as stereotyping the poor as lazy and indolent and women as uninterested in science to shape the interpretation of group reaction to disparities through compliance which maintains the status quo. These ideologies then find their way into policies which have detrimental effects on equity-seeking groups (Yavorsky, 2017). Examples of false consciousness include individual merit-based promotions which rely on individual rather than collective action and obscure the existence of discrimination and the differential treatment of women and minorities in hiring and retention policies.

Another "system-justifying ideolog[y] propagated by the dominant cultural group that distract[s] attention from group-based disparities and inequities" (Dovidio 2013, 9) is known as false consciousness. False consciousness, derived from Marxist theory, suggests unequal power structures in groups are reified through a hierarchy supporting the prerogatives and maintenance of the ruling elite who exercise control through social dominance of the working class which offers little resistance because they believe in the legitimacy of the ruling elite and often cooperate by justifying their ideology (Sidanius, 1999). The ruling elite maintains a dominant position by "promoting social attitudes and policies that advantage themselves" (Sidanius 1999, 21) and protects their status by resisting laws which restrict the redistribution of power and privilege to others.

Recommendations to Reduce Implicit Bias

In the broadest terms, institutional, social, and cultural discrimination in the building trades will only end when implicit bias encouraging and benefiting discrimination ends. Achieving equitable outcomes in the hiring, retention, and promotion of women in the building trades means dismantling existing institutional and social structures which support the maintenance of the white male European model as the standard by which all others are judged. Political economy theory suggests collective action as a means to this end. More work in this direction needs to be done. The literature documenting the failure of existing anti-discrimination law to affect the outcomes of implicit bias is robust (Bagenstos, 2006; Flagg, 1995; Green, 2003; Kreiger, 1995). But the outcomes of discrimination, whether the bias is explicit or implicit, are equally disturbing, and curbing implicit bias is a more difficult task.

Current recommendations to correct the institutional discrimination in the building trades include developing a more holistic approach devoted to an awareness of overt and covert discriminatory practices embedded in leadership practices, organizational culture, and recruitment, retention, and training policies (Dainity, 2004; Dasgupta, 2013; Staats, 2014). Implicit bias doesn't have to be permanent. Tetlock and Mitchell (2009) hypothesize the elimination of indirect bias is not yet possible because competing camps provide a paucity of evidence for its reduction or eradication. They argue legal pressure through state interventions to level inequalities, called statist intervention, counters market competition to eliminate inequality, called market purity (Tetlock 2009). These camps agree inequality in outcomes (as measured objectively) exists but disagree how to facilitate its reduction/elimination. Statist interventionists claim indirect bias, learned over a lifetime of individual subjective associations, cannot entirely be eliminated, while market purists claim market competition will eventually rout out irrational bias. Tetlock and Mitchell (2009) contend neither side makes a compelling winnable empirical argument resulting in a "mismatch between empirical accomplishments and policy prescriptions" (p. 5). They advise both sides to collaborate through "adversarial collaboration" (Tetlock 2009, 5), an approach to sharing data, agreeing/disagreeing on certain pivotal information, and adhering to scientific rigor.

Another plan to eliminate implicit bias is known as "debiasing" (Jolls 2006, 977), reducing implicit bias by mediating the outcomes. Known as "direct debiasing," this strategy outlines four techniques using anti-discrimination laws to reduce implicit bias (Jolls 2006): (1) creating a diverse workforce may increase the probability of positive judgments by affecting cognitive thoughts and behaviors (Jolls 2003, 2006; Dasgupta, 2004; Lowery, 2001; Richeson, 2003; Gilovich, 2012); (2): banning derogatory or sexually explicit visual images which create a hostile workplace and presenting positive images may move the cultural needle toward a less hostile environment in which workers feel less threatened (Dasgupta, 2001); (3): reinforcing the firm's stance against discrimination through the provision of policy handbooks, raining videos, and penalties for violating policy (Jolls, 2006); and (4): promoting affirmative action policies because they promote diversity in hiring and retention practices.

Kang and Banaji (2006) similarly suggest debiasing could be achieved through affirmative action plans by "creating legal structures within which actors may choose to adopt debiasing mechanisms" (p. 987). Change agents within the workspace who choose to engage in implicit bias-reducing behaviors and processes could work to change hiring, training, and retention policies and processes which encourage implicit bias (Kang, 2006). According to Sturm (2001), recognizing "sex-based disparities in [job] assignments" (p. 986) would lead to an awareness of implicit bias propelling employers to "adopt general decision making structures or processes that reduce the intensity and frequency of implicit bias, implicitly biased behavior, or both" (p. 986).

Anti-discrimination laws and affirmative action policies are less effective in reducing implicit bias since proving intentionality of actions is difficult and sanctions against violators may simply affect outcomes (Kreiger 2006). To complicate matters, the lingering indirect bias associated with male-dominated workplace cultures which preserve workplace norms may satisfy a firm's productivity even at the expense of exclusion and harassment of female workers (Selmi, 2005). According to Selmi (2005) this suggests firms are willing to forego profits based on an efficiency rationale and tolerate discriminatory practices. "Management's inability to root out inefficient practices stems from its own perceptions and biases . . . that frequently mirror those of their male employees" (p. 44). Dominant groups defend their positions (Sidanius, 1999; Tajfel, 1982) so it is usually the subordinate groups who initiate change. According to Wright (2013), the subordinate group's membership must identify with the collective identity of the group to inspire collective action to improve the group's status or fend off threats to the group. This is particularly evident in maintaining the status quo through male dominance.

If well-intentioned employers and workers are unaware they engage in implicit bias, how then can they move toward changed thinking and behavior to curb implicit bias? How can indirect debiasing decrease implicit bias if courts generally defeat claims of intentional discrimination against protected groups because the honest belief rule, a defense in which the plaintiff claims he or she honestly believes no discrimination occurred even if that approach is inconsistent with empirical findings about implicit bias and stereotypes (Krieger, 2006)? Addressing these deficiencies requires a strategy for decreasing masculine dominance of workers in the building trades in four areas: governments, markets, unions, and employers.

Governments: Federal agencies must create, enforce, and evaluate policies which strengthen women's access to training, entry, and retention into construction. Policy outcomes are reflected by more women trained/hired/retained in the building trades. Graves (2013) recommends increasing oversite and monitoring by federal agencies charged with overseeing contractor compliance, providing financial and technical assistance to women in apprenticeship programs, coordinating information between federal offices, training programs, and private industry, ensuring civil rights laws are enforced, and strengthening accountability measures in compliance with federal and state laws.

Unions: Facilitating the transition of masculine dominance in construction by an inclusive acceptance of women as equal coworkers requires an equitable power structure between labor and management and men and women through collective action. More money and training must be devoted to apprenticeship programs preparing women for construction jobs. Management and labor must contractually include provisions for women's mentoring programs into collective bargaining agreements. The inclusion of a mentoring component in apprenticeship programs supplies the needed support women find non-existent in the building trades where they are often the target of bullying, intimidation, and sexual harassment in uncomfortable and unsafe workplaces and contributes to "best practices" (Moir, 2011) to retain women in trades. Providing mutual support in a mentoring relationship for women has reduced the number of women leaving the construction industry (McCormack, 1998) and fostered career-related and psychosocial benefits such as "organizational rewards in the form of promotions, increased financial security, and increased job satisfaction and commitment" (Hegstad 1999, 387).

Markets: Amend the current economic system which values profits over people and encourages institutional discrimination through class struggle, job discrimination, and organizational adaptation with a more equitable economic system which values people over profits. This means that within our current capitalist economic system, we must move more toward social justice for equity-seeking groups and farther away from a strictly profit-oriented society. This process depends on the balance of economic power between labor and management, whites and minorities, and males and females. Altering the economic balance of power means shifting the implicit bias associated with favoring one group over another into neutral territory. Employers should add economic incentives/rewards for reduced implicit bias evidenced by the number of women moving into and staying in the construction industry.

Employers: Recognizing the institutional, social, and cultural biases embedded within a firm's practices with respect to hiring, training, and retaining competent female workers and making concerted efforts toward implementation of more gender neutral, family-friendly, and work-life balance policies would be a good start. Research by Hirsh and Kornrich (2008) suggests an organizational approach to studying workplace discrimination and reveals workers are more likely to seek legal redress for discriminatory claims if the firms' personnel policies favor sex/race consciousness, grant fewer promotions for women and minorities, encourage the composition of management positions which reflect less authoritative roles for women and minorities relative to social status, and establish control structures in the form of close supervision in which workers feel a loss of autonomy. Redesigned jobs, flexible working hours, retraining programs, and different attitudes toward women in construction align with cultural changes which recognize there is no place for segregation, inflexibility, and inequality within the construction industry.

CONCLUSION

We have explored the issue of indirect bias as a root cause of institutional, social, and cultural discrimination in the building trades. Situated in political economy theory which uses groups as a basic unit of analysis, historical marginalization and oppression of women and minorities results from unequal power relations and unequal access to resources and results in discrimination in the absence of collective action. I surmise the situational context of women's hiring, retention, and promotion in construction is thwarted by a pervasive masculine-dominated workplace culture which is profitable for construction firms even at the expense of discrimination against female workers.

The current situation pertaining to the reduction or elimination of implicit bias as a root cause of discriminatory treatment is a long way from being satisfied. Years of scholarly research, diversity training, and education have not achieved the intended outcome of equality in the building trades for women and minorities. Though there has been some legislative movement toward creating policies for gender-neutral workplaces, the enforcement mechanisms for those policies have been weakened. The prescriptions to resolve explicit bias, though embedded in anti-discrimination laws, often result in minimal remedy, and the invisible nature of indirect bias makes its persistence likely to reify the long-standing structural institutional, social, and cultural status quo. This then begs the question of how serious governments, markets, employers, and unions are about routing out indirect bias as a cause of discrimination. Though well-intentioned individuals, groups, and organizations work to reduce/eliminate indirect bias and achieve equitable outcomes through education, training, and apprenticeship programs, the process moves at a glacier pace. Our contention is that as long as indirect bias as a root cause of institutional, social, and cultural discrimination remains profitable for the building trades and the social and cultural mores associated with male domination in the workplace remain strong, indirect bias will continue to plague the hiring, retention, and promotion of women in construction.

REFERENCES

1964a. "Civil Rights Act of 1964." In *P.L. 88-352;78 Stat.241*, edited by US Congress. Washington, DC.

1964b. "Rights and protections under title VII of the Civil Rights Act of 1964, Age Discrimination in Employment Act of 1967, Rehabilitation Act of 1973, and title 1 of American with Disabilities Act of 1990." In *2*, edited by US Congress. Washington, DC.

2008. "Genetic Information Nondiscrimination Act of 2008." In *42*, edited by US Congress. Washington, DC.

2016. "Federal women's program." Accessed 3.24.2016. https://www.few.org/our-focus-2/federal-womens-program/.

2017. "National Organization for Women." National Organization for Women. http://now.org/about/.

Albelda, R., & Drago, R. W. 2013. *Unlevel playing fields: Understanding wage inequality and discrimination*. Boston, MA: Dollars & Sense.

Albelda, R., Drago, R. W., & Shulman, S. 2001. *Unlevel playing fields: Understanding wage inequality and discrimination*. Cambridge, MA: Dollars and Sense.

Bagenstos, S. R. 2006. "The structural turn and the limits of antidiscrimination law." *California Law Review* 94:1–47.

Bagenstos, S. R. 2007. "Implicit bias, 'science,' and antidiscrimination law." *Harvard Law & Policy Review* 1:477–494.

Baron, J. 1991. "Organizational evidence of ascription in labor markets." In *New approaches to economic and social analyses of discrimination*, edited by R. Cornwall & Wunnava Cornwall, P. Westport, CT: Praeger.

Bielby, W. 2000. "How to minimize workplace gender and racial bias." *Contemporary Sociology* 29:190–209.

Cockburn, C. 1991. *In the way of women: Men's resistance to sex equality in organizations*. Basingstoke: Macmillan.

Dainity, A. R. J., Bagilhole, B. M., Ansari, K. H., & Jackson, J. 2004. "Creating equality in the construction industry: An agenda for change for women and ethnic minorities." *Journal of Construction Research* 5 (1):75–86. doi: 10.1142/S1609945104000061.

Dasgupta, N. 2013. "Implicit attitudes and beliefs adapt to situations: A decade of research on the malleability of implicit prejudice, stereotypes, and the self-concept." *Advances in Experimental Social Psychology* 47:233–279.

Dasgupta, N., & Asgari, S. 2004. "Seeing is believing: Exposure to counterstereotypic women leaders and its effect on the malleability of automatic gender stereotyping." *Journal of Experimental Social Psychology* 40 (5):642–658.

Dasgupta, N., & Greenwald, A. G. 2001. "On the malleability of automatic attitudes: Combating automatic prejudice with images of admired and disliked individuals." *Journal of Personality and Social Psychology* 81 (5):800–814.

Denissen, A. M. 2010. "The right tools for the job: Constructing gender meanings and identities in the male-dominated building trades." *Human Relations* 63 (7):1051–1069. doi: 10.1177/0018726709349922.

DiMaggio, P., & Powell, W. 1983. "The iron gate revisited: Institutional isomorphism and collective rationality in organizational fields." *American Sociological Review* 48:147–160.

Dovidio, J., Hewstone, M., Glick, P., & Esses, V., eds. 2013. *Prejudice, stereotyping and discrimination*. Thousand Oaks, CA: Sage.

Equal Employment Opportunity Commission. 2013. *EEOC Women's work group report*. Washington, DC: Office of Federal Operations.

Fiske, S. 1998. "Stereotyping, prejudice and discrimination." In *Handbook of social psychology*, edited by D. Gilbert, Fiske, S., & Lindzey, G. New York: McGraw-Hill.

Flagg, B. J. 1995. "Fashioning a title VII remedy for transparently white subjective decision-making." *Yale Law Journal* 104 (8):2009–2051.

Gilovich, T., Griffin, D., & Kahneman, D. 2012. *Heuristics and biases: The psychology of intuitive judgment*. Cambridge, MA: Cambridge University Press.

Granovetter, Mark. 2005. "The impact of social structure on economic outcomes." *Journal of Economic Perspectives* 19 (1):33–50.

Green, T. K. 2003. "Discrimination in workplace dynamics: Toward a structural account of disparate treatment." *Harvard Civil Rights-Civil Liberties Law Review* 38:91–157.

Greenwald, A., & Banaji, M. 1995. "Implicit social cognition: Attitudes, self-esteem, and stereotypes." *Journal of Personality and Social Psychology* 102:4–27.

Greenwald, A. G., & Krieger, L. H. 2006. "Implicit bias: Scientific foundations." *California Law Review* 94 (4):945–967.

Hegewisch, A., & O'Farrell, B. 2015. *Women in the construction trades: Earnings, workplace discrimination, and the promise of green jobs.* George Washington University, Institute for Women's Policy Research.

Hegstad, C. 1999. "Formal mentoring as a strategy for human resource development: A review of research." *Human Resource Development Quarterly* 10 (4):383–390.

Henry, P. 2013. "Institutional bias." In *The SAFE handbook of prejudice, stereotyping and discrimination*, edited by J. Dovidio, Hewstone, M., Glick, G., & Esses, V., 424–437. Los Angeles: Sage.

Hirsh, C. E., & Kornrich, S. 2008. "The context of discrimination: Workplace conditions, institutional environment and race discrimination charges." *American Journal of Sociology* 113 (5):38.

Jolls, C. 2003. "Anti-discrimination law's effects on implicit bias." In *Behavioral analysis of workplace discrimination*, edited by M. J. Gulati & Yelnosky Gulati, M. J. The Netherlands: Kluwer Law International.

Jolls, C., & Sunstein, C. R. 2006. "The law of implicit bias." *California Law Review* 94 (4):969–996.

Kang, J., & Banaji, M. R. 2006. "Fair measures: A behavioral realist revision of 'affirmative action.'" *California Law Review* 94 (4):1063–1118.

Kluegel, R., & Smith, E. 1986. *Beliefs about inequality: Americans' views of what is and what ought to be.* New Brunswick: Transaction

Krieger, L. H. 1995. "The content of our categories: A cognitive bias approach to discrimination and equal employment opportunity." *Stanford Law Review* 47 (6):1161–1248.

Krieger, L. H., & Fiske, S. 2006. "Behavioral realism in employment discrimination law: Implicit bias and disparate treatment." *California Law Review* 94 (4):997–1026.

Lowery, B. S., Hardin, C. D., & Sinclair, S. 2001. "Social influence effects on automatic racial prejudice." *Journal of Personality and Social Psychology* 81 (5):842–855.

Maclean, N. 1999. "The hidden history of affirmative action: Working women's struggles in the 1970s and the gender of class." *Feminist Studies* 25 (1):42–78.

Mansfield, P., Koch, R., Henderson, J., Vicary, J., Cohn, J., & Young, E. 1991. "The job climate for women in traditionally male blue-collar occupations." *Sex Roles: A Journal of Research* 25 (1–2):63–79. doi: 10.1007/BF00289317.

McCormack, S. 1998. "Reflections on affirmative action." *Boston Tradeswomen's Network Newsletter* 3 (2):1.

Merton, R. K. 1972. "'Insiders and outsiders' A chapter in the sociology of knowledge." *American Journal of Sociology* 78 (1):9–47.

Modesitt, N. 2010. "Reinventing the EEOC." *Southern Methodist University Law Review* 63 (1237):1–41.

Moir, S., Thomson, M., & Kelleher, C. 2011. *Unfinished business: Building equality for women in the construction trades.* Boston: Labor Resource Center Publications.

Office of Contract Compliance Regulations. 2017. Electronic code of federal regulations e-CFR. In *Title 41, subtitle B, chapter 60, part 60-20.* Washington, DC: US Government Publishing Office.

Office of Federal Contract Compliance Programs. 1964. *Executive order 11246— Equal employment opportunity*, edited by US Department of Labor. Washington, DC: US Department of Labor.

Office of Federal Contract Compliance Programs. 1980. *41 CFR part 60-4: Construction contractors, affirmative action requirement*, edited by Department of Labor. Washington, DC: Department of Labor.

Peterson, T. 2006. "Motive and cognition: Conscious and unconscious processes in employment discrimination." In *Understanding choice, explaining behavior*, edited by J. Elster, Gjelsvik, O., Hylland, A., & Moene, K., 225–248. Norway: Oslo Academic Press.

Reskin, B., & McBrier, D. 2000. "Why not ascription? Organizations' employment of male and female managers." *American Sociological Review* 65:210–233.

Richeson, J. A., & Ambady, N. 2003. "Effects of situational power on automatic racial prejudice." *Journal of Experimental Social Psychology* 39 (2):177–183.

Ridgeway, C. L., & Correll, S. J. 2004. "Unpacking the gender system: A theoretical perspective on gender beliefs and social relations." *Gender and Society* 18 (4):510–531. doi: 10.1177/0891243204265269.

Risman, B. J. 2004. "Gender as a social structure theory wrestling with activism." *Gender and Society* 18 (4):429–450. doi: 10.1177/0891243204265349.

Selmi, M. 2005. "Sex discrimination in the nineties, seventies style: Case studies in the preservation of male workplace norms." *Employee Rights and Employer Policy Journal* 9 (1):1–50.

Sidanius, J., & Pratto, F. 1999. *Social dominance: An intergroup theory of social hierarchy and oppression.* Cambridge: Cambridge University Press.

Smith, R., & Elliott, J. 2002. "Does ethnic concentration influence employees' access to authority: An examination of contemporary urban labor markets." *Social Forces* 81:255–279.

Staats, C. 2014. *State of the science: Implicit bias review 2014.* Kirwan Institute for the Study of Race and Ethnicity.

Tajfel, H. 1982. *Social identity and intergroup relations.* Cambridge: Cambridge University Press.

Tetlock, P., & Mitchell, G. 2009. "Implicit bias and accountability systems: What must organizations do to prevent discrimination." *Research in Organizational Behavior* 29:3–38. doi: 10.1016/j.rob.2009.10.002.

Tomaskovic-Devey, D., & Stainback, K. 2007. "Discrimination and desegregation: Equal opportunity progress in U.S. private sector workplaces since the Civil Rights Act." *The Annals of the American Academy of Political and Social Science* 609:49–84.

Tomlinson, J., Olsen, D., Neff, K., Purdam, K., & Mehta, S. 2005. *Examining the potential for women returners to work in areas of high occupational gender segregation*. University of Manchester, Cathie Marsh Centre for Census and Survey Research and Discipline of Sociology.

United States Department of Labor. 2017. *Equal employment opportunity*. Washington, DC: Department of Labor.

Wagner, H. 2015. "Hiring goals: Are they assisting more women to enter and reamin in the building trades?" Retrieved from the University of Minnesota DigitalConservancy, http://hdl.handle.net/11299/17555

Yavorsky, J. 2017. "Inequality in hiring: Gendered and classed discrimination in the labor market." PhD Dissertation, Ohio State University, https://etd.ohiolink.edu/pg_10?0::NO:10:P10_ACCESSION_NUM:osu1492542664842056.

Chapter 9

Gendered Agribusiness, Feminization of Work, and the Seeds of Empowerment

The Case of Women of the Greenhouse, *Western Anatolia, Turkey*

Zeynep Ceren Eren Benlisoy

INTRODUCTION

Neoliberal restructuring of global agri-food relations has had destructive effects on the small producers. Literature on rural transformation and change, both national and international, agrees that there is a strong tendency toward the proletarianization, since traditional work, that is, agricultural production and animal husbandry, no longer meets the needs of the small-producer masses in rural areas (Appendini, 2010; Barndt, 2013; Kay, 2006; Luz Cruz-Torres, 2004; Deere, 2005; Akram-Lodhi and Kay, 2009; Razavi, 2002, 2010; Öztürk, 2012; Gündüz Hoşgör and Suzuki, 2017, 2018a, 2018b; Suzuki and Miki, 2019). The gender dimension of the process and of the category of peasant-worker has been understudied in the literature on rural transformation in Turkey. Yet, one of the most striking issues seems to be the "structural break," which occurred after 2000 in relation to the radical downturn of agricultural employment. It refers to the swift decline of women's status as unpaid family laborers in small-scale production (İkkaracan and Tunalı, 2010: 123). Dayıoğlu and Kırdar reveal the common characteristics of labor force participation rate in rural areas for women: "Women become less likely to participate in the labor market as they age" and "younger cohorts of women in rural areas are less likely to participate in the labor market" (2010: 24). In line with this, rural women withdraw from production, while only a limited number replace their previous status as unpaid family laborer with paid labor in Turkey.

This chapter sees a relationship between women's waged labor and a globalized agri-food system. In this sense, I explore the following question: In the age of globally restructured agri-food relations, what are the patterns of the emerging gender labor regime for rural women employed as waged labor in an agribusiness in the Bakırçay Basin?[1] In line with this question, this chapter concentrates on the labor experiences and practices of peasant-worker women employed in one of those greenhouses located in the Basin, which will be referred to in this chapter as "the *Greenhouse*."

As a large-scale and export-based agribusiness located in Izmir, the *Greenhouse* was established in the beginning of the 2000s.[2] It produces various kinds of tomatoes, as well as other products, both in soil-based and soilless (perlite and coco peat-based) units. The facilities also include a nursery and packaging house. After production, the products are packaged and mainly exported to Russia and European countries by the *Company*'s own means of transportation. The *Greenhouse* also sells its products to well-known supermarket chains, such as Tesco (United Kingdom) and EDK (Germany). While the efficiency rate is around 40 tons per decare for soilless units, the profitability rate is approximately 33 percent, a pleasing figure for the manager and the head engineer of the *Greenhouse*.

Although declared to be a story of business success, what lies behind the *Greenhouse* seems to be privatization and misuse of natural resources. Initially, the units designed for soilless production are constructed on extremely fertile agricultural land previously used for the cultivation of tobacco, wheat, and tomatoes. The lands were neither *barren* nor *infertile*, as the manager of the *Greenhouse* asserted during my field research. I met women and men who had cultivated that land and worked there as daily laborers prior to the establishment of the *Greenhouse*. Similarly, areas on which the greenhouse units and fruit orchards now stand used to be shared pastures used by small-scale animal farmers in a village located next to the *Greenhouse*. Having lost their shared land, the farmers had to squeeze into a smaller pasture that was not big enough for all their animals. Stockbreeders, therefore, had to either sell their animals or reduce their numbers as they could not afford to buy artificial animal feed.

Perhaps the most striking misuse is that of the underground water and geothermal energy resources "rented" by the *Greenhouse* to bring down the cost of heating. The management states that the geothermal energy is used in a renewable way in order not to destroy the resource itself. However, I was also told by the head engineer that at one stage the recycling system was not working efficiently and therefore for four months the *Greenhouse* had to drain away all the water rather than recycling it back to the source. The head engineer also claimed that intense use of chemicals triggers a dramatic change in local insect populations. After unsuccessful attempts at biological control, the *Greenhouse* turned to "contact chemicals" (with potent ingredients) to fight the pests. In sum, sustaining the greenhouse production has led to the misuse of fertile land, geothermal energy, and underground water, as well as the privatization of these resources.

THEORETICAL FRAMEWORK AND METHODOLOGY

This chapter takes a socialist-feminist perspective, based on its critiques on capitalism and patriarchy. Having rejected the privileged position of paid labor, this perspective underlines the significance of women's unpaid labor in diverse forms of reproductive labor, therefore prioritizing gender division of labor in the research and analysis (Hartsock, 1983; Peterson, 2005; Weeks, 2011). Not only does the chapter concentrate on women's labor practices as areas of exploitation and domination, but it also seeks to enable possibilities for struggle and change. The latter approach acknowledges women's positions as agents, giving priority to women's perspectives (Heckman, 2014; Donovan, 2014). In this context, this chapter has two concepts: gender labor regime and women's perspective.

This research is based on a case study in which I follow a feminist methodology prioritizing women's agency and experience as a source of knowledge. While employing qualitative techniques, I primarily gather data through in-depth interviews and participatory observation. Therefore, I conducted fieldwork that lasted for more than two years (2014–2016) with several visits. I participated in the production process at the *Greenhouse*, the daily routines of the women in their homes and villages and during social occasions. I also draw on statistical data—such as female employment rates, income levels in rural areas, agricultural production design, or levels of agricultural production—in order to have a better understanding of structural change in the Bakırçay Basin of Western Anatolia.

I made thirty-three in-depth interviews with peasant-worker women employed in the *Greenhouse*. Out of the thirty-three women, eleven women are between twenty to thirty-four years old; while there are fifteen women who are between thirty-five and fifty, and seven women who are more than fifty years old. Majority (twenty women) is married; besides three widows, three divorced, five single, and two engaged women. The number of women with one or two children is twenty-three. Majority has primary education. They are from different ethnic-religious groups: thirteen Yörük, nine Çepni, four Muhacir, three Manav, two Kurdish, and one Laz women[3]. While ten women are Alevi, the rest (23) is Sunni Muslim. Eight women live in the villages (five mountain/slope and three plain villages), while twenty-five women live in the towns of the Basin. Fourteen of the thirty-three women are land/

animal owners.[4] Age-to-work is approximately seven and in traditional rural activities (tobacco, cotton, and olive production, and small-scale husbandry). Women say that they either helped their families in their own business or got paid as daily laborers in the fields. In addition to agricultural production, they worked in husbandry as shepherds, or in carpet weaving. Only two women started their working lives in non-farm jobs as cashier, factory worker, and greenhouse worker.

THE WORKING REGIME IN THE *GREENHOUSE*

The performance system appears as a general principle of the regime. According to the system, women are expected and forced to finish the assigned number of rows every day. The number can vary based on the difficulty of the work. The engineer in each unit calculates and reports workers' daily performance with reference to rows they complete at the *Greenhouse*. While the performance system controls and disciplines the women, it also creates rigid hierarchies where the working atmosphere is marked by divisions between workers and managers. Moreover, there are two types of workers: *eleman* (technically more experienced and holds more responsibility) and *hasatçı* ("non-skilled" worker who is obliged to do whatever is asked by the engineers). Hardworking *hasatçı* women can be promoted to the more secure and stable position of *eleman*, whose conditions are more privileged in the eyes of the women.

> We sweep up, wash, plant, harvest. I'm a *hasatçı*, not an *eleman*, if they say "clean the toilet" I clean the toilet. "Cause we're only temporary, you know." (Solmaz; twenty years old, university student, single, seasonal worker without insurance)[5]

> Staying in one greenhouse, being an *eleman* is better. You go from one greenhouse unit to the next, it's more tiring. You carry all your things, then you realize you left your cup in the other greenhouse. You forget things. Carrying all your stuff is hard. It's not far, but no matter how close it is, going back and forth is tiring. (Gülcan; forty-seven years old, primary school, married)

Despite the differences between the positions of *eleman* and *hasatçı* women, they are still subject to mobbing as a significant management strategy. It is safe to say that managerial control, crystalized in the authority of the engineers, head engineer, and manager, has never shied away from enforcing the disciplinary policies. Mobbing at the *Greenhouse* comes in the form of shouting, humiliation, threats, verbal rebukes, and mistreatment, and result in the devaluation of the women.[6]

Shouts and screams. I'm surprised, "Why are they shouting like that." They [other female workers] said "That's just what they do." But where we come from you don't shout at people. We also go to work for other people but there's no shouting [referring to working in the fields]. But anyway, we got used to that too. (Nadide; fifty-seven years old, primary school, single)

It is safe to say that flexibility has been an established working pattern at the *Greenhouse*. The notion of flexibility is particularly seen in vague job definitions at the workplace, as well as in the *Company*'s recruitment and dismissal policies. Job definitions at the *Greenhouse* are somewhat flexible. It is common for workers to be moved from one position to another. Workers in the packing department can easily be assigned to cleaning duties (either of the toilets or the greenhouse units) or harvesting. The recruitment and dismissal policies of the *Company* are composed of flexible ways of hiring and firing, as well as uncertain probation periods at the beginning. Although the process of recruitment has been institutionalized and formalized, especially with the establishment of the Human Resources Unit, the high number of women who leave and/or are fired is another sign of the flexibility of the work. More than half of the women that I interviewed left the job within six months or a year. There are only a handful of women who have worked there for more than for five years.

They [the management] always say, "This is the *Greenhouse*, one person arrives, another leaves." They know there are a lot of people looking for work, so that's why they're not worried. They don't give you days off. "If you go, you're not one of us" they say.

Anyone who leaves here is likely heading to Bergama. 80% of Bergama has been through this greenhouse. Even if they didn't stay long, they've tried it out. Seher (forty-two years old, attending to online high school, divorced)

The neglected infrastructure also shapes the experience of women at the *Greenhouse*. The insufficient infrastructure for a decent working life is characterized by limited recreational areas, few water units, poor-quality food, and recently privatized shuttle service for some routes. In accordance with that, work safety is mostly ignored, often resulting in "accidents." Precautions are not taken for those working at heights or in extreme heat. The same is true for the use of chemicals and the intense use of pesticides and bleach, and the *Greenhouse* has detrimental effects on the women's health. There is no doubt that negligence of workplace safety creates occupational diseases in the form of acute and chronic health problems.

However, the *Company* deals with work safety by forcing the workers to lie when labor inspectors visit and by keeping non-insured workers away from dangerous tasks at the *Greenhouse*. The rights of women are also not respected at work. Breaks and leave, controlled by the ultimate authority of the engineers, are given arbitrarily and the women's rights in this area are often violated. The issue of social security seems to have only recently been standardized, meaning that many women worked for such a long time without insurance. In addition, there is a unique payment system, in which workers are paid based on a daily rate, behind the façade of minimum wage.[7] According to an unwritten rule, if a woman takes an additional day of leave for whatever reason, the daily rate for five days is cut from her wage. The arbitrariness and violations that characterize the basic workers' rights at the *Greenhouse* seem to thrive on the lack of unionization of the workers.

FEMINIZATION OF WORK: "THE *GREENHOUSE* AS A WOMAN'S JOB"

Work at the *Greenhouse* emerges as a "woman's job" in which female workers have been predominantly employed from the establishment of the *Greenhouse* in the Bakırçay Basin. The most common response to the question of why it is so is, "Because it is a woman's job." The women present a picture of "woman's nature" based on gendered division of labor to explain feminization of work. Yet, this has never been the only explanation the women give for the domination of the female workers at the *Greenhouse*. They also frequently point to other issues that are as important as woman's nature, that is, the restricted position of rural women in labor markets, education or mobility, and the powerful ideology of men as breadwinners that devalues greenhouse work for men.

The feminization of work with reference to "woman's nature" on the basis of gendered division of labor seems to be based on three main spheres: the characteristics of the *Greenhouse* work associated with woman's nature, the similarity of the job to agricultural work, and finally to reproductive tasks. Its attributed skills and attitudes, that is, women's "innate" capacity to do them with their "nimble fingers and artistic touch" are believed to be a good match to the tasks assigned to women at the *Greenhouse*. The gender division of labor at the *Greenhouse* regulates the allocation of different tasks and positions to women and men.[8] Furthermore, today under the shortage of male labor or for the sake of the work schedule, the gendered division of labor can change at the *Greenhouse*, with the women expected to do tasks usually attributed to men when necessary. The same is not true for the men, however, who embrace the gender labor regime so strongly that they can refuse to carry out "women's tasks" if asked to do so.

In addition, they underline the importance of women's previous and current experiences in agricultural production and husbandry as well as their work at home. The idea of women being more compatible to greenhouse work is based on certain similarities observed in gendered agricultural work with reference to woman's nature. A rigid gendered division of labor characterizes the agricultural activities in the region.[9] The attributed similarity of the women's tasks at the *Greenhouse* to their position in agricultural production seems to legitimize the feminization of work.

> Because it's always women who work on plants, there are women in the greenhouses dealing with tomato. Men can't do it as well as women. And so [at the *Greenhouse*] everyone does the work they know. (Selma; thirty-three years old, primary school, married)

Women's tasks at the *Greenhouse* are re-categorized as an extension of the domestic chores at home. As women are "normally" responsible for those chores at home, the task of deep cleaning at the *Greenhouse* for women is the new normal. This also strengthens the gendered division of labor at the Greenhouse, as in the case of the attributed similarity of women's position in agriculture to their tasks at the *Greenhouse*. Based on this, male workers refuse to do cleaning tasks by referring to the gender stereotype in question.

> You can't make the men sweep. They'll say, "Am I a woman or something?" They won't do it. But because the women do every job, because they can do everything [there are more of them]. (Solmaz; twenty years old, university student, single, seasonal worker without insurance)

When it comes to the woman's nature associated with greenhouse work, I observed that women refer to their own privileged position, advantages, and skills rather than deficiencies or limitations compared to men. It is also seen that "woman's nature" protects women from being assigned to men's work that they would rather not do. In this sense, it plays a tactical role that facilitates their working life at the *Greenhouse*. In this sense, they consider "woman's nature" as an umbrella concept composed of a certain set of skills, attitudes, and tendencies, as well as experiences.

Women mention "the living conditions" that shape and limit their participation to work in the Bakırçay Basin. The lack of education and corresponding occupational opportunities, and restriction on mobility are considered as the main reason for women to be stuck in greenhouse work. According to the women, they, as housewives and former small producers, are uneducated, non-skilled, and unqualified in the labor market, who have only very few opportunities to participate in working life.

The best wage a housewife can have is health insurance. You have no profession, no education, what can you do? Merve (thirty-three years old, married, primary school)

> The plastic plate factory on the outskirts of Kınık was going to take on thirty female workers. Three shifts, ten minutes from home. My husband didn't want it. "A woman shouldn't be coming home at one in the morning," he said. I would have liked to work there. There's no other work for women. (Bedihe; thirty-five years old, married, secondary school)

Finally, the general acknowledgment of the position of men as the breadwinner also serves to strengthen the feminization of work at the *Greenhouse*. Such an assumption implies higher wages for men than women and it is one of the main reasons for women to primarily be employed there: the wages are so low that men generally do not prefer to work there, as they are supposed to earn a "family income." Even though women express that what the women earn is a complementary income to that provided by the men this is not the case for many of the households in this chapter. Twelve out of twenty-nine women earn more money than their husbands/fathers. While sixteen of the males (husbands/fathers) have a regular income, seventeen have an irregular income.

The male workers of the *Greenhouse* used to receive the additional day's pay for the sole reason that they were men carrying out men's tasks. However, this practice has changed recently, the payments of men and women have been equalized. This has become one of the strongest reasons behind the association of the *Greenhouse* work with women: Not only do the men consider equal wages as a threat to their position as breadwinner, but they—and particularly the younger men—also find it humiliating to their social status. As men do not like to be paid the same amount of money as women at the *Greenhouse*, the jobs there are left to women.

> They pay the same. If they paid the men a bit more they'd stay too, but they won't stay for the same money. (Güldeste; thirty-six years old, divorced, one-year attendance to primary school)
> The men leave. They say "We get the same money as women!" (Bingül; forty-four years old, married, illiterate)

WOMEN'S COPING STRATEGIES

Women still have their own *coping strategies* to deal with the regime on the basis of consent and resistance. The strategies of consent mainly refer to a work ethic through which the features of a good and decent worker at the *Greenhouse* are defined. Naturally, the notion of "good worker exists" with its opposite, that is, "bad worker." A bad worker is considered to be someone who lacks good character, that is, who is lazy, dishonest, careless, irresponsible, undisciplined, and slipshod: "This is a place with strict discipline, nothing is said to those who do their work, but some of them either don't work well or don't have the right character." Apart from having manual skills, a good worker also has to have social skills that facilitate her working harmoniously in a crowded workplace. The good workers also criticize the "bad" ones for being incompatible with the rules of the *Greenhouse*. As might a worker who knows that the greenhouse work, by its nature, requires adroitness, yet still does it very slowly. The women complain about the bad workers since they think that because of them, all the workers are exposed to the anger of the managers, regardless of whether they have made any mistakes at work. Being a bad worker also legitimizes mobbing. In this sense, bad workers "deserve" to be "pushed," that is, "motivated" by the engineers since they lack the ability to be a good worker who fulfills the tasks on their own. A good worker knows her job well, and is fast, disciplined, and dexterous at the same time.

> There are good workers and bad workers. Don't make mistakes and you're fine. Once he caught me talking on the phone and yelled "That's not what we pay you for." The guy's right; now I never talk, I don't even answer calls. (Yonca; twenty years old, single, secondary school)

The strategies of resistance adopted by the women at the *Greenhouse* do not include direct challenge to the authorities, that is, strikes or slowdowns, but are generally indirect ways to oppose the system. The managers know a permanent increase in performance is impossible, yet they still do not hesitate to push the workers to do so. At this point, the strategies of resistance lay the groundwork for reconciliation, that is, between the fantasies of the managers and the physical and psychological capacities of the women, as Saadet (twenty-three years old, married, unschooled yet literate) says, "They always want more, but you can't always do what they say."

Not answering back and being silent when insulted or basically to pretend not to hear are the most common strategies adopted by the women. Many of the women say they regularly pretend not to hear the insults and humiliations; otherwise, it would be impossible for them to continue working there. Although this strategy is discussed under the title of resistance, I am also aware of its submissive tone. It naturally does not mean women do not get upset during those moments; many times, they told me how they cried and felt humiliated and depressed after such incidents. Yet it is also seen that the women do not internalize what is said to them and try to ignore as much as possible. However, it is also necessary to point out that such a strategy does not mean the total silence of the women, and there are exceptional cases to the mainstream code of conduct summarized above. Some women seem to "answer back" under certain conditions. Sabriye (thirty-nine years old, married, primary school) once told her friends out loud "I learned how to lie in this *greenhouse*!" during a break since she was forced to lie to the labor inspectors who had come to the *Greenhouse* to check the working conditions, saying that she was supplied with a security belt while working at the top of the greenhouse units. Even though what she said was heard by the engineers sitting close by, nobody said anything to her.

Women also try to create a "collective speed," in other words watching each other to match working speeds so that the slowest worker does not attract the attention, and wrath, of the managers. One interviewee says they warn each other with body gestures or eye contact at the end of the row if the managers are around. They think that if they all start the next row at the same time, nobody will be labeled "slow" or "fast." This is even more common among women from the same village or who know each other well. For example, the women from Karcalı Village told me that they wait for each other and make eye contact to start the next row together. As a result, they all have a "normal" speed. Slowing down the work speed is another strategy through which the women protect the slower workers from the fast ones and protect themselves. If a worker finishes her rows quickly, the next day she is required to exceed her own limits. Therefore, not fulfilling her own potential prevents her from becoming exhausted. The strategy of "Never work too much, even if you are able to" advises women to work slowly but constantly, giving you the image of being a hard worker who never takes a break in the eyes of the managers.

> Don't try to get lots done. Do 12 [rows] and that's it. Don't kill yourself, work slowly. Don't stop, but work slowly and steadily. (Adile; forty-five years old, widow, primary school)

> Make it look like you're working. Make them say, "She's never idle. She works well." I worked myself into the ground, but now I've learned. We all get paid the same, no matter how hard we work. (Servet; fifty-four years old, married, primary school)

Humor is a significant strategy developed by the workers to handle and challenge the conditions in which they work, and making fun of the managers offers some much-needed respite. As Devrim (twenty years old, single, university student, seasonal worker without insurance) states, "It is difficult to work under stressful conditions. So, people make fun of everything, like something the engineer or head engineer said. They keep repeating the sentence to each other. It somehow makes them happy and cheerful." Similarly, losing weight because of the heat inside is another common joke among the women, who say they do not work for money, but just to keep fit. "The *Greenhouse* is our diet," they say.

THE SEEDS OF EMPOWERMENT

This part further focuses on the (dis)empowering aspects of the *Greenhouse* experience for women via the re-organization of reproductive labor.[10] Furthermore, how women themselves perceive working outside the home in general and *Greenhouse* work are important to understand the limitations as well as potentials the *Greenhouse* work provides, when it comes to the complexity of empowerment.

The *Greenhouse* shirks its duty in relation to the provision of kindergarten services, even though this is legally compulsory due to the high number of female workers employed. The lack of such facilities at work forces the women to solve the problem on their own. This primarily means the woman herself or other women in charge—generally the mother-in-law, sister-in-law, woman's mother, or older daughter—taking the responsibility for reproduction. Even though limited, husbands are involved in care labor and domestic chores but always in a certain combination with one of the women mentioned above. When it comes to domestic chores, women deal with them in a more flexible way. Since such tasks are, by nature, deferrable, they seem to take secondary status after care labor in the hierarchy of the tasks attributed to women. That flexibility provides a wide range of options, compared to the limitations on the re-organization of care labor. While other women in charge primarily fulfill domestic chores, male members at home sometimes take on part of this burden, mostly dealing with the basic tasks. However, women still appreciate even this limited help with household chores, saying it is lifesaving when they come back home after a long day at work. Women say they do the chores less than they usually would, but I still observed that they wake up earlier, overwork, and/or spend their days off doing the chores. They also buy ready-to-use products instead of preparing them at home.

Women seem to shoulder the burden of both worlds at the same time, due to the robustness of patriarchal codes regarding "dual responsibilities." In this sense, the overburden of work in question is discussed under diverse conceptualizations in literature, such as "dual employment strategy" (Dolan and Sorby, 2003; Jarvis and Vera-Toscana, 2004), "double and/or multiple burdened" (Garcia Dungo, 2007), "double shift" (my translation, Toksöz, 2014), and "dual employment" and even "triple burden" (Barndt, 2002).

Yet they generally appreciate and approve of the idea of working. In spite of criticisms toward *Greenhouse* work, they seem happy to have a job. Their feelings, however, are complicated—a mix of appreciation, gladness, obligation, and discontent. The gendered context—that is, women's reasons to participate in paid work—is important to understand the women's own perceptions. Economic obligation when faced with the urgent need for cash and social security are the primary reasons for women to go to work, while overcoming personal troubles and collective traumas form other motivations.

A regular income means a lot to these women, especially to those who are divorced or widowed, or who do not have a good relationship with their husbands, as the *Greenhouse* work offers them ways of building a better life for themselves. Likewise, Kevser (twenty-two years old, engaged, primary school) says, "I always say I'm glad I worked. I don't want to rely on any man, not even my husband. Any reasonable person would think this way." I observed that days off were used by women to gain a chance to relax and gain some freedom within their private lives. Due to domestic chores, the women stated that they found their days off more tiring than a workday. Nevertheless, women sometimes misinform their family members and leave home very early in the morning as if going to work at the *Greenhouse*. Yüksel (thirty-nine years old, divorced, high school) pretends she is working then goes to Izmir to spend the day with her daughter who lives there.

At the same time, the realities of the *Greenhouse* overshadow the women's positive ideas about work. Women find the work repetitive and boring, while also mentioning the unbearable treatment they are subjected to. They describe the *Greenhouse* as being like a prison where they work as slaves, and the work leaves no room to socialize or spend time with their children or friends. In sum, it is safe to say that women desire to be part of working life but wish for decent work.

CONCLUSION

The working realities of the *Greenhouse* consist of adverse working conditions. While performance system and mobbing cause control, hierarchy, and exploitation, flexibility, insecurity, and the lack of basic worker rights characterize the precarious working regime at the *Greenhouse*. Women still have coping strategies based on consent and resistance creating a work atmosphere consisted of solidarity and competition. Yet the strategies tend to be individual solutions to the problems at work; I observed a few rare examples of collective movements and/or strategies during my fieldwork.

The case of the *Greenhouse* is compatible with various global examples in which a specific gender labor regime goes hand in hand with women's labor force in large-scale and non-traditional agricultural export-based businesses (Freidberg, 2004; Dolan, 2005; Barrientos, 2007; Pedreño et al., 2014; Dey de Prick and Termine, 2014; Appendini, 2002). Flexible forms of workforce are closely related to the increase in women's participation in the labor force as "employers turn to women to satisfy their need for large numbers of low-cost, disciplined and so-called unskilled employees" (Bain, 2010: 343). The workforce of agribusinesses is created from politically and socially vulnerable groups of migrants, women, or locals. As Pedreño et al. argue "The vulnerability of these segments of the labor force is related to their unequal position in the social structure, a position that depends not only on labor but primarily on gender (women) and citizenship (immigrants) inequalities" (2014: 201). When it comes to the women workers at one tortilla-producing hacienda, the managers point out that they liked hiring migrant workers with no family or fewer family ties from the interior (of Mexico) since "they are less likely to know their rights" and "they know less, so they complain less" (Muñoz, 2008: 100). Having been displaced from their lands in rural areas, the women have been obliged to move to the border regions to find work. They form half of the workforce employed in tortilla production.

Likewise, the women of the *Greenhouse* belong to highly indebted (former) small-producer households, of which the male members are mainly irregular workers and/or unemployed. The labor force preferred by the *Greenhouse* is particularly disadvantaged and trapped at home with limited job opportunities in the rural labor market. The findings of two studies from Turkey also reveal a similar dominance of women in such fields (large-scale and non-traditional agricultural export-based businesses). The workers of the sea-snail processing factory in the Western Black Sea Region are mainly women from mountain villages (Gündüz Hoşgör and Suzuki, 2018a, 2018b, 2019). In addition, fifty of seventy workers at the Bey Fide Greenhouse—where they grow, package, and transport produce to Central Anatolia—are rural women (Atasoy, 2017). Allen and Sachs (2007) conclude that global commodity chains take advantage of women as disadvantaged workers in processing and packing houses based on the gendered division of labor.

Crystalized in the domination of the women workers at workplace, the *Greenhouse* work has already been stereotyped as "women's work," despite the short history of the greenhouse business in the area. Feminization of work draws its strength from women who are the pioneers of the reserve army in the rural markets as cheap labor force, from the male breadwinner ideology, and the idealization of "woman's nature" on the basis of gendered division of labor. The labor regime at the *Greenhouse* also brings horizontal and vertical job segregation for women. While the former means the women are stuck in fewer and certain sectors and occupations, the latter determines the nature of work carried out by women as lower-skilled and manual work. Considering these, this chapter argues that the feminization of this work is a process of construction based on dominant patriarchal and capitalist codes. In addition, the agents—female and male workers and *Company* representatives—have actively participated in the construction of the feminization of the work based on their own dynamics, motivation, and/or criticisms. As Bain argues, "Social relations within the labor market do not merely evolve over time, nor do they simply reflect preexisting inequities and prejudices. Rather, they must be actively produced and reproduced" (2010: 25).

Women of the *Greenhouse* still create the niches through which they transform and change their lives. They challenge the patriarchal barriers and increase their power to bargain. They undermine the role of males as breadwinners, make future plans, feel self-confident, or establish an alternative social network of their own. Although they wish for decent work, the *Greenhouse* work is still appreciated and seen as *better* from women's previous lives in the villages as unpaid family laborers. When it comes to the potentials the *Greenhouse* work provides women to change, reverse, and transform their lives, the women mention the economic and social gains. Having cash, even if only in the form of pocket money, makes women feel stronger and boosts their self-esteem. As mentioned previously, in some cases, their work may generate a humble separate budget in which young women become more independent and less vulnerable to the authority of their fathers. Women who are divorced or widowed feel empowered as they have money not only to rebuild their lives but also to take care of their children.

Defining the relation between paid work and empowerment as not direct, mechanic, or unilinear, I rather attempt to understand the complex nature of empowerment in the process of gendered proletarianization for peasant-worker women at the *Greenhouse* that reveals itself in mixed forms of achievements and limitations. Not being involved in collective action that would allow them to make structural and cultural changes, what the women of the *Greenhouse* have experienced through work has been rather the "seeds of their empowerment" (Erman, Kalaycıoğlu, & Rittersberger-Tılıç, 2002: 407).

To conclude, there has been a radical change on use of women's labor in the small-scale producer households of Bakırçay Basin, Western Anatolia studied in this research in the age of neoliberal restructuring of global agri-food relations. Women's unpaid family labor has shifted to waged labor, while women's regular income has become more vital than their unpaid family labor for households in economic deprivation. Income from the *Greenhouse* work takes precedence over income from rural activities. The patterns of the gender labor regime and feminization of work, that is, the *Greenhouse* as a woman's job and women's own coping strategies, show that neither the category of peasant-workers nor the process of proletarianization is gender free. On the contrary, women's experiences and practices, since their own perspectives, are considered as constitutive dynamic and response to the grand narrative of neoliberalism and rural transformation.

NOTES

1. "The Bakırçay Basin is one of the most significant sub-basins in the North Aegean Basin (For the location of the Bakırçay Basin, please see the figure in the Appendix A). It is located in Western Anatolia and primarily composed of the land irrigated by the Bakırçay river. It includes both urban and rural areas of the districts of Bergama, Dikili, Kınık and Aliağa, located in the province of Izmir. The area's mountains extend from east-west. As well as small river valleys and lowlands, its topography is generally rolling, ravine and hilly" (Velibeyoğlu, 2015: 29). The reason behind the selection of the Basin to focus on in this chapter is its historically early integration to global capitalism, the drastic change on its traditional small-scale agricultural production (i.e., the change from tobacco, cotton, and olive production to sunflower, tomato, and maize production) due to the neoliberal restructuring and the proliferation of agribusinesses.

2. The *Company* behind the *Greenhouse* is a very powerful agglomeration, and greenhouse production is only one of its diverse interests. It has actively made significant investments in the same region in sectors such as stockbreeding, poultry, export-oriented fruit growing, online food sales, and finally agri-tourism, making the company one of the biggest buyers of land in the Bakırçay Basin.

3. *Yörüks* are traditionally a nomadic pastoral group. They were forced into settled lifestyles during the late Ottoman and early Republican period. The terms *Muhacir* and *Manav* are used in this research on the basis of local people's own definitions. In contrast to the generally accepted use of these two terms, in which they have the same meaning, *Muhacir* refers to migrants from Balkan countries, mainly Bulgaria and Macedonia, while *Manav* people identify themselves as local to the Bakırçay Basin. *Muhacir* and *Manav* are generally Sunni Muslim, while *Çepnis* are Alevi who used to be a pastoral group like *Yörüks*.

4. This does not necessarily mean that the woman in question holds the title for the land or animal, but she is counted as an owner if her family or her husband is the official owner. In addition, I come across cases in which the woman has no title deeds yet she has received assurances that she will be given them in the near future. In such cases, I checked whether or not she receives any benefit from the land/animal. If she does, then I define her as an owner, too.

5. For the privacy of my informants, I will not expose their names.

6. Mobbing is legally defined in Turkey according to private rather than public law, and is included under the "Law of Obligations" rather than the Labor Law. Mobbing may include a number of different violations of employees, such as psychological and sexual harassment, violation of the decency of the employee, and even the integrity of his/her body.

7. According to the most recent information provided by the interviewees (2020), this was changed in 2019. Since then, women are formally registered and paid as daily laborers employed at the *Greenhouse*.

8. In the past, there used to be *another* division of labor at the *Greenhouse*, in which women shouldered most of the tasks that are today known as "men's work." Certain changes have been made to the allocation and definition of the tasks, yet the tools used to legitimize the feminization of work have remained the same: The gendered division of labor. Muñoz (2008) describes this as the "paradox of gender," through which she explains how the same work of tortilla making at Hacienda CA in the United States and Hacienda BC in Mexico can be constructed respectively as men's work and women's work. While Hacienda CA is a capital-intensive business with high technology run by male workers, Hacienda BC is a labor-intensive one where cheap labor is important to keep costs down. In the former factory, men frequently deal with machines and heavy lifting, in contrast to the latter factory, which is based on women's manual labor. In addition, Hacienda CA has night shifts that are dominated by men and not preferred by women, since the "immigrant and undocumented" men successfully adopt themselves to the flexible conditions of the work (2008: 117–119).

9. What women are responsible for changes from one agricultural product to another. Due to the gendered division of labor in agricultural production, some women's labor has been mainly used for harvest, as well as for other activities such as hoeing or picking corn. Tomato, pepper, and corn harvests are primarily based on women labor, as the cotton and tobacco harvest used to be in the past. The mechanization of agricultural activities has caused some of the women's tasks to be transferred to the men. For example, women would traditionally plant the cotton seeds, regularly hoe the field, and harvest the product. However, cotton sowing and/or picking machines have already removed female agricultural laborers from the fields, when the landowners can afford to such machines. Now these tasks are carried out by men driving these machines. One of the women agricultural engineers employed in the General Directorate of Provincial Food, Agriculture and Livestock in Kınık expresses the unequal division of labor on the basis of gender as follows: "Men are only responsible for irrigation, so they just turn on the faucet. Yet all the rest is the women's responsibility!"

10. In this chapter, I analyze reproductive labor based on domestic chores and care- giving. However, I am aware that reproductive labor cannot be confined to these tasks alone, but also includes the social organization of life and the emotional labor of women for other family members. In this sense, it is not only related to the domestic sphere, but also affects the non- domestic sphere.

REFERENCES

Akram-Lodhi Akram, Haroon & Kay, Cristobal. (2009). *Peasants and Globalization: Political Economy, Rural Transformation and the Agrarian Question*. London, New York: Routledge.

Allen, Patricia & Sachs, Carolyn. (2007). Women and Food Chains: The Gendered Politics of Food. *International Journal of Sociology of Agriculture and Food*, 15(1), April, 1–23.

Appendini, Kirsten. (2002). "From Where Have All the Flowers Come?" Women Workers in Mexico's Non-Traditional Markets. In S. Razavi (Ed.), *Shifting Burdens: Gender and Agrarian Change Under Neoliberalism*. Bloomfield, CT: Kumarian Press, 93–108.

Appendini, Kirsten. (2010). On Feminization of the Countryside. In *Economic Liberalization, Changing Livelihoods and Gender dimensions in Rural Mexico* (pp. 126–136). Rome: FAO.

Atasoy, Yıldız. (2017). *Commodification of Global Agrifood Systems and Agro-Ecology: Convergence, Divergence and Beyond in Turkey*. Routledge Studies in Governance and Change in the Global Era. UK: Routledge.

Bain, Carmen. (2010). Structuring the Flexible and Feminized Labor Market: Global GAP Standards for Agricultural Labor in Chile. *Signs: Journal of Women in Culture and Society*, 35(2), 343–370.

Bank Muñoz, Carolina. (2008). *Transnational Tortillas: Race, Gender and Shop-Floor Politics in Mexico and the United States*. Ithaca: Cornell University Press.

Barndt, Deborah. (2002). *Tangled Routes: Women, Work and Globalization on the Tomato Trail*. Maryland: Rowman & Littlefield Publishers.

Barndt, Deborah. (2013). On the Move for Food: Three Women behind the Tomato's Journey. In C. Counihan & P. van Esterik (Eds.), *Food and Culture*. London, New York: Routledge, 3rd edition, 472–485.

Barrientos, Stephanie. (2007). Female Employment in Agriculture: Global Challenges and Global Responses. In T. Johnson (Ed.), *Small Changes or Real Change?: Commonwealth Perspectives on Financing Gender Equality*. London: Commonwealth Secretariat, 173–189.

Dayıoğlu, Meltem & Kırdar, Murat. (2010). *Determinants of and Trends in Labor Force Participation of Women in Turkey*. State Planning Organization of the Republic of Turkey and World Bank Welfare and Social Policy Analytical Work Program Working Paper Number 5.

de Pryck, J. Dey & Termine, P. (2014). Gender Inequalities in Rural Labor Markets. In A. R. Quisumbing, R. Meinzen-Dick, T. L. Raney, A. Croppenstedt, J. A. Behrman, & A. Peterman (Eds.), *A Gender in Agriculture, Closing the Knowledge Gap*. Dordrecht: Springer, 343–370.

Deere, Carmen Diane. (2005). *The Feminization of Agriculture? Economic Restructuring in Rural Latin America*. Geneva: United Nations Research Institute for Social Development.

Dolan, Kristina & Sorby, Catherina. (2003). *Gender and Employment in High Value Agriculture Industries*. Agriculture and Rural Development Working Paper, No. 7. Washington, DC: World Bank.

Donowan, Josephine. (2014). *Feminist Teori*. Istanbul: İletişim Yayınları.

Erman, Tahire, Kalaycıoğlu, Sibel & Rittersberger-Tılıç, Helga. (2002). Money-Earning Activities and Empowerment Experiences of Rural Migrant Women in the City: The Case of Turkey. *Women's Studies International Forum*, 25(4), 395–410.

Friedberg, Susanne. (2004). *French Beans and Food Scares: Culture and Commerce in an Anxious Age*. New York: Oxford University Press.

Garcia Dungo, N. (2007). *Negotiating from the Margins: Dynamics of Women's Work in a Globalized Agricultural Economy*. Diliman Quezon City: University of the Philippines Press.

Gündüz Hoşgör, A. & Suzuki, M. (2017). Feminisation of Rural Work and Young Women's Empowerment: A Case Study of Mountain Villages in the Western Black Sea Region of Turkey. *Kadın/Woman 2000*, 18(1), 1–22.

Gündüz Hoşgör, A. & Suzuki, M. (2018a) Karadeniz Kırsalında Yaşlı Kadın İstihdamı: Balık Üretim İşletmeleri Vaka Analizi. In Ö. Arun (Ed.), *Yaşlanmayı Aşmak*. Ankara: Phoenix Yayınları, 55–73.

Gündüz Hoşgör, A. & Suzuki, M. (2018b). Japonya Pazarı ile Türkiye Karadeniz Arasındaki Küresel-Kırsal Bağlantı: Rapana Venosa'nın Metalaşma Süreci Vaka Analizi. *Sosyoloji Araştırmaları Dergisi*, 21(2), 285–316.

Hartsock, Nancy C. M. (1983). *Money, Sex and Power Toward a Feminist Historical Materialism*. New York: Longman.

Hekman, Susan J. (2014). *The Feminine Subject*. Cambridge: Polity Press.

İlkkaracan, İpek & Tunalı, İhsan. (2010). Agricultural Transformation and the Rural Labor Market in Turkey. In B. Karaçınar, F. Adaman, & G. Özertan (Eds.), *Rethinking Structural Reform in Turkish Agriculture: Beyond the World Bank's Strategy*. New York: Nova Science Publishers, 103–149.

Jarvis, Lovell S. & Vera-Toscana, Esperanza. (2004). *The Impact of Chilean Fruit Sector Development on Female Employment and Household Income*. Policy Research Working Paper No. 3263. Washington, DC: World Bank.

Kay, Cristobal. (2006). Rural Poverty and Development Strategies. *Latin America Journal of Agrarian Change*, 6(4), 455–508.

Keyder, Çağlar & Yenal, Zafer. (2011). Agrarian Change Under Globalization: Markets and Insecurity in Turkish Agriculture. *Journal of Agrarian Change*, 11(1), 60–86.

Keyder, Çağlar & Yenal, Zafer. (2013). *Bildiğimiz Tarımın Sonu, Küresel İktidar ve Köylülük*. Istanbul: İletişim Yayınları.

Luz Cruz-Torres, Maria. (2004). *Lives of Dust and Water: An Anthropology of Change and Resistance in Northwestern Mexico*. Tuscon: University of Arizona Press.

Öztürk, Murat. (2012). *Agriculture, Peasantry and Poverty in Turkey in the Neo-Liberal Age*. Wageningen, The Netherlands: Wageningen Academic Publishers.

Pedreño, Andrés, Gadea, Elena & de Castro, Carlos. (2014). Labor, Gender and Political Conflicts in the Global Agri-Food System: The Case of the Agri-Export Model in Murcia, Spain. In A. Bonanno & B. Cavalcanti (Eds.), *Labor Relations on Globalized Food (Research in Rural Sociology and Development)*. Emeral Publishing, Volume 20, 193–214.

Peterson, Spike V. (2005). How (the Meaning of) Gender Matters in Political Economy. *New Political Economy*, 10(4), 499–521.

Razavi, Shahra. (2002). *Shifting Burdens: Gender and Agrarian Change Under Neoliberalism*. Bloomfield: Kumarian Press.

Razavi, Shahra. (2010). Engendering the Political Economy of Agrarian Change. In S. M. Borras Jr. (Ed.), *Critical Perspectives in Rural Development Studies*. New York: Routledge, 185–215.

Suzuki, Miki & Gündüz Hoşgör, Ayşe. (2019). Challenging Geographical Disadvantages and Social Exclusion: A Case Study of Gendered Rural Transformation in Mountain Villages in the Western Black Sea Region of Turkey. *Sociologia Ruralis*, 59(3), 540–599.

Toksöz, Gülay. (2014). Türkiye'de Kadın İşgücü Profili ve İstatistiklerinin Analizi. T.C. Aile ve Sosyal Politikalar Bakanlığı Kadının Statüsü Genel Müdürlüğü.

Velibeyoğlu, Koray. (Project Manager). (2015). *Gediz—Bakırçay Havzası Sürdürülebilir Kalkınma Stratejisi*. İzmir Büyükşehir Belediyesi, İzmir Yüksek Teknoloji Enstitüsü, Ege Üniversitesi.

Weeks, Kathi. (2011). *The Problem with Work, Feminism, Marxism, Antiwork Politics, and Postwork Imaginaries*. Durham: Duke University Press.

Weeks, Kathi. (2014). Labor, Standpoints and Feminist Subjects. In S. Harding (Ed.), *The Feminist Standpoint Theory Reader, Intellectual & Political Controversies*. New York: Routledge, 181–193.

Chapter 10

Gender Dynamics in Midwestern Building Trades

Tokenism and Beyond

Lynn Duggan, Gracia Clark,
and Marquita R. Walker

INTRODUCTION

Current studies of women's gendered experiences in U.S. building trades confirm that longstanding sexist patterns and organizational culture discourage women's entry and retention in these occupations. Institutional barriers to women's participation in construction work include hiring discrimination, gender and sexual harassment, and the blacklisting of whistleblowers (Moir 2011). Low entry requirements and wages significantly higher than traditionally female blue-collar occupations continue to attract women to building trades, but women remain a small fraction of workers. The share of women among new construction trades apprentices reached a high point of five percent in 1992 and subsequently fell to 1978 levels (Berik 2006, 324–335).[1]With growing demand for labor in construction, women's share has risen rapidly since 2011, but their overall ratio is still only 3.4 percent of building trades workers (Hegewisch 2019).

Our study of barriers to women in central Midwestern building trades began in 2002 with interviews of 35 tradeswomen.[2] The study findings showed stereotyping, sexism, sexual harassment, and willful endangerment of women comparable to the results of similar studies elsewhere in the U.S. (LeBreton and Loevy 1992). More surprisingly, the interviews generated striking information on dynamics among women workers, related to the low ratio of women to men. The following analysis revisits this qualitative interview data from 2002–2003 to show the ways in which tokenism (defined as skewing in relative subgroup sizes) influenced these tradeswomen's interactions and relationships with their coworkers.

We apply tokenism theory to our data by drawing parallels between Kanter's (1977a, 1977b) analysis of tokenism-driven perceptual phenomena and these Midwestern tradeswomen's accounts. We find strong evidence of worksite tokenism in the form of increased visibility, polarization among subgroups, and caricatured role assignments required for assimilation into building trades' culture. We conclude that tokenism reduces solidarity and collectivity among tradeswomen and between women and potential allies who might also benefit from fighting sexism and organizing for other improvements in working conditions. Theories of tokenism shed light on its implications for coalition-building against discrimination, unsafe work practices, and general exploitation in the construction industry. However, while tokenism clarifies sources of tension between subgroups and among tokens, gender- and class-based analyses of privilege must supplement tokenism for a fuller account of gender dynamics in construction work.

We begin with a brief review of tokenism theory and short discussion of our 2002–2003 descriptive findings. This is followed by our 2019 analysis of the same data, which reframes tokenism theory in dialogue with theories of discrimination

from political economy and feminism. We conclude with observations on the implications of tokenism, discrimination, gender performance, and class conflict on potential interventions for cultural change in the U.S. building trades.

TOKENISM

Theories of tokenism seek to explain the group dynamics found when low relative numbers of particular categories of persons within organizations lead to problems for members of these small subgroups. Tokenism theory usually defines "token" persons as those meeting the official criteria for inclusion in an organization but who are never fully embraced and are frequently ostracized, especially if they fail to conform to the dominant group's expectations. Among other contexts, tokenism has been used to analyze women's and minorities' problems in academia (Laws, 1975), building trades (Riemer, 1979; Whittock, 2002), the military (Rustad, 1982), the police force (Martin, 1980; Gustafson, 2008), highway trades (Kelly et al., 2015), desegregation in the South (Marden, 1973), and innovation in the chemical industry (Poulanen and Kovalainen, 2013).

Definitions of *tokenism* vary among researchers. Some sociologists define *tokens* by their function for the dominant group, for example, "persons (usually women or minorities) who are hired, admitted or appointed to a group *because* of their difference from other members, perhaps to serve as 'proof' that the group does not discriminate against such people" (Zimmer 1988, 65). Laws's psychological research on women in academic settings also defines *tokenism* functionally, as "the means by which the dominant group advertises a promise of mobility between the dominant and excluded classes . . . mobility which is severely restricted in quantity [and] quality" (Laws 1975, 51). These definitions imply discrimination; the number of tokens hired is smaller than the number of those qualified.

Zimmer (1988) notes that for some scholars, "token" refers to a woman or minority person who may be unqualified and is hired to conform to laws or social expectations (65). This last approach focuses on supposed limitations of the tokens rather than limitations placed on them.

Other theorists, including Rosabeth Kanter (1977b) define *tokens* strictly in terms of relative numbers. They need not be "placed there deliberately for display" (968).

> It is sufficient to be in a place where others of that category are not usually found, to be the first of one's kind to enter a new group, or to represent a very different culture and set of interactional capacities to members of the numerically dominant category. (965)

In her research on male-dominated industrial sales, Kanter (1977b) directed attention to the specific effects of relative group proportions, contending that tokenism occurs when category proportions are "skewed" (with subgroup ratios exceeding 85:15). Her usage followed Laws, except that she uses gender-neutral language, referring to "dominants" and "fews" instead of men and women. According to Kanter and other critical mass theorists, an organization or industry that increases the number of "fews" enough to move from skewed to "balanced" (with ratios of dominants to fews less than 60:40) can create a cultural shift. Greed (2000) notes that balanced relative numbers may be pursued via top-down (government regulatory) or bottom-up (equal opportunity advocacy) efforts.

Kanter's analysis centered on three "perceptual phenomena driven by tokenism: visibility, polarization and assimilation" (1977b, 971). With lower relative numbers, the visibility of tokens increases, as these individuals "capture a larger share" (971) of dominants' awareness and carry "the burden of representing their category" (973). Polarization occurs as dominants react to tokens' increased visibility, exaggerating contrasts between the subgroups. Tokens are expected to demonstrate loyalty to dominants in exchange for greater inclusion, making themselves psychological hostages of the majority group. As Kanter noted, the price token women pay for being "'one of the boys' is a willingness to turn occasionally against 'the girls'" (979). Dominant groups easily defeat alliances between tokens by setting up "invidious comparisons" that designate one individual a success and the other a failure (987).

The third perceptual phenomenon, assimilation, occurs through stereotype-based "role entrapment," in which "characteristics of tokens are distorted to fit preexisting generalizations about their category . . . to force them into playing limited and caricatured roles in the system" (Kanter 1977b, 980). Kanter found designated roles for female tokens in industrial sales that included "mother," "seductress," "pet," and "iron maiden" (981–984). Assimilation without role entrapment is rare, as a stereotyped role "offers a comfortable and certain position" (984).

Several researchers have used the concept of tokenism to understand gender dynamics among construction workers (Whittock, 2002; Riemer, 1979; Paap, 2006; Kelly et al., 2015). Paap provides a clear illustration of polarization-related boundary heightening based on her own experience as an apprentice carpenter.

> I soon found . . . that I, as female on site, would be the object against which the men's masculinities would be measured and against which their masculinities would be proved. This meant that men who felt they needed to assert their heterosexuality would 'come on' to me publicly. Men who felt they needed to assert their masculinity as being 'above women' would be publicly hostile or insulting. All of this became as much a part of my job as swinging a hammer or running a saw. . . . [T]hese battles were painfully personal. . . . They generally involved unwanted discussion of or contact with my physical body or my private life. . . . This symbolic "job within a job," representing the Anti-Masculinity, was tiring. (2006, 3–4)

Using role encapsulation categories similar to Kanter's (1977b), Paap notes the prevalence of such assimilation processes in construction, coining a "bitch, dyke, whore" taxonomy (2006, 79).[3]

I had been working in the industry for about two weeks when a friendly-looking older carpenter . . . said casually but provocatively "Well, you're either a bitch, a dyke, a whore, you're looking for a boyfriend, or you're looking for a lawsuit.". . . [H]is argument was identical to others that I saw enacted across worksites and companies over the next few years. . . . The assertion that women in construction are not really there to do the work but are just there to find a man, get laid, or cause trouble is important because it means that no woman's presence can seriously challenge the industry's male identity. (79, 82)

Paap points out that the role stereotype of lesbian ("dyke") for women in construction (likely because the work requires physical strength) can facilitate assimilation in certain ways, although it does not mean women seen as lesbians are welcome (89).

[Lesbians] were seen as less immediately threatening to the gendered rules about men's and women's abilities: that is, to the gendered beliefs that men can do the work and women can't. Women coded as lesbians could be seen as "unnatural" women whose abilities were therefore interpreted by the culture is unrelated to what "women in general" can or should do. The success of these women...was not believed to address the rules and abilities of *men in general*. Thus, these alleged lesbians might have disturbed the men as individuals, but they could not disturb the gender order. (87)

Whittock (2002) documents tokenism processes in her study of non-traditional women's occupations in Northern Ireland through participant observation of a basic skills training course for construction workers as well as interviews with women directly involved in the industry. She notes interviewees' shock at their high visibility, which in turn generated pressure to avoid isolation by tolerating male humor (at their expense) and by achieving top grades on assessments.

A group of men, mainly staff, would congregate at the glass doors of the brick-room where the women worked, laughing and passing comment, necessitating the covering up of the glass panels. (Whittock 2002, 451)

As examples of polarization, Whittock documents a high incidence of sexual innuendo within their male instructors' training (452). She notes assimilation-related role entrapment in the roles of daughter and seductress (454).

Critics of Kanter

In the four decades since her high-profile 1970s research Kanter (1977a) has also drawn criticism from feminist scholars.

Gender Neutrality

Zimmer (1988) objects to Kanter's (1977a) gender-neutral stance, arguing that, while avoiding the "victim-blaming trap," Kanter did not sufficiently acknowledge larger forces behind tokens' racial or gender position in society. Studies of male tokens in traditionally female occupations lend support to this criticism, showing tokenism to have fewer consequences for men. Male nurses, for example, experience opposition but never "severe enough to present an obstacle to men's continued employment" (Zimmer 1988, 69). Male primary school teachers and grocery clerks are promoted faster than their female counterparts. Comparative studies have found that women in more balanced workplaces sometimes actually experience greater gender harassment than women in similar but more skewed workplaces (Zimmer 1988, 69).

Yoder (1991) argues that Kanter's (1977a, 1977b) research omitted key factors that contribute to gender discrimination, including gender status, occupational appropriateness to gender, and the intrusiveness of growing numbers of low-status newcomers (189). As a result, Kanter failed to identify forms of discrimination predicted by intrusiveness theory, including sexual harassment, wage inequities, and blocked mobility (189).

In Kanter's defense, her analysis of tokenism did not purport to replace analyses of gender and race. She asserts that a focus on group structure allows generalization beyond male-female patterns, "making possible the untangling of what exactly is unique about the male-female case" (Kanter 1977b, 967).

> These dynamics are similar regardless of the category from which the token comes, although *the token's social type and history of relationships with dominants shape the content of specific interactions.* (Kanter 1977b, 972, italics added)

Zimmer (1988) faults researchers who build on Kanter's work and fail to acknowledge these other systems of oppression, implicitly assuming that relative numbers alone determine group dynamics and attributing their assumption to Kanter (64, 67).

Cultural Shift

Importantly, Zimmer and others point out a flaw in critical mass theory that Kanter did fail to acknowledge. Societal sexism may need to change *before* relative numbers of women in male-dominated occupations can attain the prescribed 40:60 balance that Kanter believed necessary for a cultural shift (Zimmer 1988, 71). Greed (2000) notes that critical mass "is highly optimistic if used as a predictive social concept without acknowledging the cultural and structural obstacles present [in construction]" (183). As obstacles, she cites "high job turnover, occupational isolation, and limited promotion pros- pects, all factors which work against the build-up of critical mass and culture change" (181). Kelly et al. (2015) note that while critical mass interventions are needed, including pre-apprenticeship programs and financial assistance for women and racial/ethnic minorities in highway trades, "further attention must be paid to addressing the processes that perpetuate inequality in work organizations" (Kelly et al., 2015, 435).

Lewis and Simpson (2012) explain one line of reasoning regarding the ambiguous effect of greater numerical balance on tokens.

> Rather [than lessening tensions and exclusion], [tokens] may encounter less co- operation and more discrimination, hostility and competition. . . . Read through the [Invisibility] Vortex, these behaviors and practices can be explained in terms of the insecurity of the "dominant centre" and how its incumbents seek to preserve advantage and privilege through defensive action as well as the mobi- lization of beliefs regarding who should rightfully occupy positions of power. Relatedly, . . . increasing numerical balance can reinforce rather than destabi- lize the normative power of men, as women 'take up' masculine practices and values. (153)

Dahlerup (1988) suggests that growth in the relative or absolute numbers of women in politics may not encourage diversity, constitute a critical mass, or bring about the cultural shift Kanter posited. Such changing practices result instead from "critical acts," "[based] on the willingness and ability of the minority to mobilize the resources of the organization or institution to improve the situation for themselves and the whole minority group" (Dahlerup 1988, 279). Childs and Krook (2008) similarly focus on "critical actors in women's substantive representation" (734), including both males and females who promote women's inclusion.

Tokenism Revisited

Kanter's (1977a, 1977b) research was completed at a time when gender was primarily considered a biological category. Since then, tokenism theory has been updated and extended. Poutanen and Kovalainen (2013), for example, have used theoretical compatibilities between tokenism, intersectionality, gender, and qualitative methods to examine the gendering of innovation at a chemical plant, "subtle and sticky relations that produce gender relations and the gender order," generating a "modernized" version of tokenism they call "processual tokenism" (270).

Lewis and Simpson (2012) reread Kanter (1977a), using her descriptions and analysis of tokenism to augment their post-structural "invisibility vortex" model of turbulent power relations through which gendered power is perpetuated and concealed. They draw on Kanter's work to flesh out the dynamics through which women are restricted and ridiculed to protect the (invisible) male norm from challenge. These authors argue that "while Kanter retreated from explanations based on the gendering of organizations or from recognition of gendered power, these dynamics can be identified in her text" (Lewis and Simpson 2012, 141).

STUDY OVERVIEW

Recruitment /Design

Participants for our 2002 study of obstacles to women's entry and retention in building trades were recruited through construction labor unions in a medium-sized Midwestern town and nearby areas.[4] Of the eventual thirty-five women interviewed, twelve were apprentices, twenty-two were journeywomen, and one worked freelance outside a union.[5] They included carpenters, drywall hangers, electricians, glaziers, laborers, operating engineers, painters, plumbers, pipefitters, steamfitters, roofers, and sheet metal workers. Each participant chose an off-jobsite location for her confidential interview, lasting thirty to ninety minutes. A questionnaire covered work history, positive and negative aspects of their work, and interactions with coworkers, employers, and union officers, including open-ended questions to elicit examples and explanations.[6]

Descriptive Results

The majority of interviewees (77%) originally heard about construction work through a friend or family member in the trade; almost half (43%) reported a relative currently in the same trade. Only 28 percent had completed a pre-apprenticeship training program; none of these were aimed at women. The work interested them (including multiple answers) because of pay (69%), satisfaction with the work itself (54%), independence (22%), flexibility (18%), and work hours (11%). Childcare did not seem to present a major barrier to entry.[7]

> "I love working with my hands. To me, fixing things and working on things is easy . . . I can fix just about anything." #16

Study participants had worked in their trades for two to thirty years, averaging eleven. A typical workday was eight to ten hours (average 8.5), plus an average commute of 31 miles. Most (77%) reported mandatory overtime. Eighty percent earned more than they did in previous (non-construction) jobs, and 69 percent had better benefits. In 2002–2003, when the minimum wage was $5.15 per hour, these tradeswomen's hourly wages ranged from $14.05 to $27.96, averaging $21.85 (equivalent to $31.18 in 2019). Their average yearly income in 2002–2003 was $37,257 (equivalent to $53,160 in 2019) and depended on the hours they had worked.[8] Forty percent of these women said they did not get as much work as they wanted, and 59 percent reported that men find work more easily than women.

The aspects of building trades work these women reported enjoying included the challenge and satisfaction of producing something they can see and take pride in (51%), the physical work of the job (26%), the people they work with (23%), learning new things, variety (20%), pay and benefits (17%), working outdoors (14%), and the flexibility and choice in this trade (14%).

When asked which aspects of the job they did not enjoy, they mentioned hard, dirty, dangerous work (40%), attitudes toward women (31%), bad weather (26%), inadequate bathrooms and lack of sanitary conditions (11%), insecurity (6%), and work hours up to sixteen to eighteen per day (3%). The main drawback to their trades, based on a separate question, with multiple responses possible, was "hard physical work, danger, and injuries" (63%). Drawbacks severe enough to consider changing to a different kind of work included harassment, hostility, and disrespect, as well as physical limitations, injuries, or risk of injury. Many reported having been severely injured.

Unwelcome Treatment

The questionnaire deliberately avoided the legally charged terminology of "sexual harassment" and "gender discrimination," asking instead whether interviewees had experienced unwelcome treatment they attributed to being a woman. This proved an important distinction. Several reported aggressive acts they did not want to call sexual harassment because they felt they could deal with them. A notable 86 percent reported experiencing "unwelcome treatment related to being female."

Practices commonly classified by researchers as sexual or gender harassment that these women had experienced in the preceding ten years included unwelcome sexual remarks (74%), pornographic pictures in work areas (74%), unwelcome touching (49%), explicit requests for sex (34%), men refusing to work with them (40%), being called a lesbian (22%), physical threats (20%), and actual physical violence (11%). Fifteen (43%) specified other gender-hostile events, ranging from daily being called "stupid cunt" to being set up for an accident, resulting in broken ribs.

"I worked with a crazed maniac for about 8 months and I was ready to quit the
trade. He stalked me . . . followed me [off work]. . . . They need to kick him
out. . . . Back then I was a first year apprentice—I didn't say anything to anybody. . . . I mean you're scared and you're working around all men." #1

The other legally charged category of "discrimination" lurks beneath these tradeswomen's hiring- and promotion-related interactions with employers. Forty-six
percent reported experiencing discrimination in hiring and 11 percent in promotion; yet 40 percent expressed reluctance to report any form of discrimination to
supervisors or their union, mostly for fear of being branded a troublemaker.

"It's like, okay, I file charges. I file charges one time—that's going to follow me
the rest of my life with companies. Now why would anybody want me on their
job if they know I'm going to file sexual harassment charges?" #4

This fear was well founded, judging from the experiences of several interviewees who had filed sexual harassment or pay discrimination complaints
or lawsuits. Two were blacklisted for a year. A third reported deliberate
endangerment.

"I learned, don't ever let the union get your job back because you might end up
dead. Because then they worked the hell out of me; people treated me like crap.
. . . The union couldn't protect me." #28

Nonetheless, 53 percent of interviewees rated their union representation as
"excellent" or "good," while 35 percent chose "OK" or "could be better," and
only 12 percent chose "not good at all."

Departures

Study participants were selected from women who had continued working,
however, 69 percent had known other women who had left their trade. Half
were believed to have left due to discrimination (including sexual harassment) and a quarter, due to the physical demands of the work. Some had quit
but later returned.

"It's not the work but the environment that you're in, the people you're
around." #33

"Every three or four years, some guy is so horrible that I just hate all men
and want to kill them...and then I will look for another job and it doesn't pay
enough." #27

"It's like a waitress in a bar. There's just some men that are obnoxious pricks and there are certain men that are nice and fine." #18

Women of color faced more physical threats, whether upon arrival or in retaliation for a complaint.

"In fact, there's like three black women I know of that have left the trade because they never had a chance . . . being a black woman, that was even worse." #11

There was one woman who escaped the usual isolation entirely.

"I guess I've just been really lucky to work with the guys that I've worked with. Because I think that you go into a field like this kind of expecting to be treated differently, and I've been pleasantly surprised . . . I like that people in the field are very honest. . . . I'm treated much better in this field than I was as a social worker." #19

Fellow Women

Ambivalence regarding the benefit of additional women on worksites emerged from two interview questions in our interviews. While more than half (57%) said that the small number of women in their trade created problems for them, less than half (46%) believed that having more than one woman at their jobsite would be beneficial (see table 10.1). Fewer (34%) said this would make no difference, and one woman (3%) said it would make things worse. For 9 percent, it would depend on the woman. Those who expressed indifference or ambivalence had most commonly reported that the small number of women caused them no problems.

Table 10.1   Tradeswomen's Attitude toward Additional Women on Job Sites

	Question: Do you believe it would it be beneficial to have more than one woman on each job site?				
Question: Does the fact that only a small number of women are doing this kind of work ever create problems for you?	Number	Better	It depends on the person; it can be better or worse	It doesn't matter	Worse
No, never	14	3	1	10	0
Yes, occasionally	16	11	2	3	0
Yes, often	3	2	0	0	1

Source: Interviewees' statements.

Many interviewees volunteered descriptions of fellow tradeswomen's actions that they believed aggravated their own situation. (We will discuss the stereotype-based adaptations and role options emerging from these interviews below.) Certain behaviors were seen to reinforce men's stereotypes about women, undermining the efforts of committed tradeswomen to carve out a viable persona at work. A frequent trope described problematic women as "not there to do the work" but to find husbands or file harassment /discrimination charges. As one interviewee explained,

"You know, it's not no 'women going out to lunch' thing. . . . Most women don't like other women on the job. . . . It depends what they're there for. If they're there to work, I like them fine, but if they're not there to work, then yeah, I get irritated about it. Because I'm over there working, earning my money. They need to be earning theirs." #28

Another described a positive experience.

"Sometimes it's been a benefit, because it's real nice to have someone to talk to and you've got someone to work side-by-side. . . . I've had two women together working . . . and it was wonderful." #6

APPLYING TOKENISM THEORY TO MIDWESTERN TRADESWOMEN

Stage two of this research project, completed sixteen years after stage one, involved applying Kanter's (1977b) tokenism theory to the interview data collected in 2002–2003. In this second iteration, the interviewees' responses demonstrate the perceptual processes highlighted by Kanter.

Visibility

The tradeswomen we interviewed were well aware of their high visibility as a small minority. Each woman walks a fine line in her daily actions, aware of intense scrutiny. The behavior of other women—even rumors about them— can impact any woman's reputation. Interviewees' perceptions of their visibility and its symbolic consequences are illustrated in comments such as:

"I just know when I get women like that on job sites I start puffing up like an old banty rooster, because I want them off the job site. You're disrespecting me . . . you make me look bad. You make every guy on the project think he can talk and look and act to me the way he does you. I won't tolerate it." #10

"It makes the rest of us women look bad because . . . [the men] they'll say 'that's why we don't need women in the trade, because of that right there.' And then they put us all in the same boat, and we're not that way. The men aren't that way— you've got good men and bad ones. You've got good women and bad women!" #1

Because the actions of women are sharply visible in the highly skewed settings of construction projects, men view these actions as true of trades-women in general. Some women attempt to distance themselves from certain others, but this risks further marginalization. Since hiring frequently takes place through personal networks, isolation can result in lost work hours and unemployment.

By contrast, undesirable behaviors among white men have no symbolic consequences for other white men. A double standard applies to women, with another for black men.

"I can't say I'm cold and I'm wet. I'm whining. A man can say they're cold and they're wet and it's okay. . . . There's times that I've noticed that two guys wouldn't do what I was doing on a daily basis, but I did what I had to do to keep my job." #8

"Now you have guys that are just the same way, that don't work and stuff like that, but it's rarely pointed out." #6

"There's a lot of men out here that's not capable of doing this job. I've worked around them and they've worked for me." #5

"They had a black guy that got laid off because he didn't call in . . . they discriminated against him and they knew they were discriminating. . . . You got a bunch of white guys who've done that." #12

One of the Guys

Women frequently feel compelled to prove their value in masculine contexts, sometimes by "acting like men" (Addleston, 1996; Cockburn, 1991; Franzway, 2009; Le Feuvre, 1999; McElhinny, 1994; Watts, 2007). This path is also often an attempt to become less visible, and some try to make men more comfortable with their presence by mimicking typical male behavior.

"And you have to pretty well put them at ease . . . and if they dump water on you, dump it on them. . . . That loosens them up a little." #20

Some interviewees criticized fellow women for overly masculine behavior.

"That person was a total opposite from me. She was more wild. . . . She just got a bad rep is all it was, by the way she acted . . . I don't try to act like the guys when I'm on the roof . . . like the cussing. . . . It seems like the women that's in this . . . they don't care. They're worse than a lot of guys are." #34

"[T]his is a man's world and if you're going to come into this world with all these men . . . you're going to cuss, cut up, tell nasty jokes, whatever, which some of these gals do . . . cause you're fitting in." #1

They described limits to fitting in, on or off the jobsite.

"You think you have a friend and you see them somewhere and they won't even talk to you because their wife's with them. . . . Or they pretend to be your friend and then they try to pick you up." #4

Excessively feminine behavior or appearance was also criticized by interviewees. Smith suggests that fingernails are particularly symbolic because manual workmen's hands represent tools (Smith 2013, 866).

"Like some women, they come out and they have fake nails and you know, you see someone automatically with fake nails and you know that's not going to work out well." #28

Polarization

Token groups' high visibility gives rise to the phenomena of polarization and boundary heightening, when dominants reemphasize their accepted traits in opposition to perceived (polarized) traits of tokens. A wide variety of the hostile actions interviewees reported, such as unwanted touching, sexual advances, and comments like "you should be at home," were examples of this.

"Like the writing on the port-a-john about me. . . . We call it 'making the shit house wall.' I usually make it . . . but so do the other women." #5

Another interviewee gave this response:

"There was one time where a guy said something about going out with me. And it's like he does it in front of people, so he has the macho image, and it's like not in a really bad way, but . . . 'No thank you, I already got one asshole in my pants.'. . . As long as you don't get too crude, it's like they'll shut up and they'll be all right. It's all how you respond or how you handle it." #4

Loyalty Tests

As noted, in order to overcome polarization and boundary heightening, tokens are expected to demonstrate loyalty to the dominant group. Our interviewees' criticism of other women's behavior sometimes slipped into endorsing stereotypes about women, conforming to Kanter's (1977b) model of a loyalty test.

"I do think a lot of women have been treated very badly, but also there are some of them that bring some of that on themselves." #1

"There's 300 men and you're the one woman. . . . The whole job site's got to change because I'm here? I'm queen for a day, or I'm Queen of Sheba here—I am?" #1

"I can see why a company would want to have more men than women 'cause, not to disrespect women, but most of the women that I meet at work are worthless and can't do the work anyway, and they try to get by on their looks and their personality and the fact that there are state guidelines. And so a lot of women [are] like 'haha, you need a woman and I'm here, so it doesn't matter how crappy I am, I'm going to stay.' That's just what I've noticed, because I actually can work and do work." #28

Like the last participant, another also presented herself as an "exceptional token" (Kanter 1977b, 979).

"To tell you the truth, and I tell it to the guys all the time, it's just . . . this really ain't something that women should get into. . . . I'm just one of the odd ones. There's a lot of lifting and you gotta put up with a lot of the sarcasm that the guys give you . . . because you're not doing as much as they can." #10

Roles

The phenomenon of assimilation via role stereotypes was also a clear trend noted in the tradeswomen's statements. Women "fit in" and form alliances with majority workers by accepting a carefully negotiated and fragile role assignment, which also serves to separate women from each other psychologically and in the minds of men. The similarity of building trades roles to those available to women in other male-identified occupations suggests these roles are firmly rooted in gender stereotypes. Fellow tradeswomen often subscribe to these stereotypes, as may be seen in the following examples.

Mother

One interviewee approximates Kanter's (1977b) "mother" stereotype:

"That F-word, I can't stand it. The guys know it, and the ones that don't know it, that haven't worked with me before, they learn it real quick. And they do try to stop it." #34

She finds it difficult to take this same role with fellow women.

"To me, two women shouldn't be on the same roof because the guys, they can handle their language more. But if a woman tells another woman to quiet down, then it just causes trouble . . . I don't know if they want to act big and bad because they're on the roof, or what." #34

Pet

The large number of interviewees who reported having relatives in the trade (43%) suggest that something approximating Kanter's (1977b) "pet" role gives these women access to male social networks that promote employment and retention, although some found other relatives uncooperative.

"I talked to my brother about it . . . I had to go through the process of trying to get in without telling my father, because he wasn't too keen on women being in the electrical field." #25

Seductress/Slut

Kanter's seductress role (Paap's "slut") inspires the most vivid language:

"She didn't want to get dirty. She didn't want to do the work. She made it obvious she was out there to find a boyfriend and have a good time and make money, and at lunchtime she would strip off her clothes and sunbathe in a bikini. . . . The guys were just falling over themselves." #31

Iron Maiden

An expression among our interviewees of Kanter's (1977b) "tough and dangerous" (984) iron maiden role was stoicism regarding inhospitable aspects of the work atmosphere along with an assumption that coarse male behavior was biologically driven or inevitable.

"You've just got to . . . put yourself in the man's shoes. This is their world, and you just gotta deal with it. You can't change it. They've been doing it a lot longer than what we've been doing it. . . . And that's the way I see it with other women. . . . They shouldn't take it away from them. It'll just make it hard on you and hard on everybody else. It'd be like a guy coming into a women's locker room and wanting us to change things. You can't do that." #10

"As a woman you shouldn't have to put up with sexual harassment, but you do." #9

Paap's (2006) category of "bitch" also roughly correlates with Kanter's (1977b) "iron maiden." Some interviewees' comments demonstrate that not only men but also women subscribe to "bitch" stereotyping in reference to women who press legal charges.

"I mean, there's some women that's been through there just for trying to get— you know—file sexual harassment charges to get money off of them. . . . A lot of them [women] have them [men] gun-shy." #17

"I know of instances where different gals in the trades have made a huge big deal out of stuff, and to me they were just looking for a lawsuit and a way out." #1

The threat of being stereotyped as a bitch/troublemaker was used to talk women out of filing complaints.

"I went up to discriminating, I mean I had it all filled out. But [name} told me to take care of it and he got me back to work. He told me just let it go and it will be OK. Otherwise you're gonna get blackballed and you'll never work." #12

One interviewee's supervisor put her name on a sexual harassment complaint without her knowledge, apparently hoping to make trouble for her.

A Critical Act

Despite the boundary-heightening dynamics of tokenism, acts of male–female solidarity do occur in this industry, as one interviewee vividly described:

"The foreman, . . . Well, he didn't like women on the job . . . he'd give me a bunch of crap and . . . he'd give me the wrong equipment . . . he'd just give me a hard way to go. And I was sitting there [on a bulldozer] pushing up to a [back] hoe, and you have to wait because a hoe is loading trucks. And the owner of the company came by and he goes 'I'm [name] . . . I'm the one who signs your checks.' And the next morning, the superintendent came down and wouldn't let me on my dozer. He started giving me this big old speech that the dozer shouldn't ever be stopped. And it's like, okay, I'm pushing up to a hoe, I can't get in the hoe's way. By all rights you stop and then you start again. We sat there for an hour . . . got nose to nose. And pretty soon—there was like 24 of us on this job—I mean 24 different pieces—and everybody stopped. Everybody, all the guys stopped. And . . . pretty soon he was coming—he just apologized. I mean, it was just unbelievable that the guys stood up for me like that. Because they knew I knew what I was doing. It may not sound like much, but you would have had to have been there. But to have that many men stand behind you—to me, that was incredible." #4

Critical acts and actors contribute to the success of gender equity strategies. Tokenism provides insights into certain dynamics that can undermine the trust, relationship-building, and solidarity that are required for such acts, both across subgroups and among tokens.

CONTEXTUALIZING TOKENISM

We turn now to several alternate theoretical frameworks, not based on tokenism, which provide a useful context for analyzing solidarity and collective action among women and men in building trades and other male-dominated fields. The class- and gender-based frameworks noted below shed light on forces that contribute to discrimination and harassment. Midwestern tradeswoman's accounts are used to illustrate the ways in which discrimination works to interrupt solidarity and collective action as laid out in each of these theories.

Political Economy of Discrimination

Based in institutional economics, the field of political economy addresses class, race, and gender systems of oppression, focusing on

> the relationships of the economic system and its institutions to the rest of society and social development. [Political Economy] is sensitive to the influence of non-economic factors such as political and social institutions, morality, and ideology in determining economic events. (Riddell 1998, 4)

Institutional economics and political economy highlight "rules and incentives that govern the behavior of economic institutions," rather than the decisions of individuals (Shulman 1996, 49), contending that discrimination has its roots in collective behavior. Firms, markets, and governments systematically disadvantage certain groups, making use, for example, of de-facto segregation, irrelevant voter tests, and banks' redlining of African American neighborhoods (in spite of the National Labor Relations Act and the Civil Rights Act). Below we discuss three political economy theories of discrimination.

Organizational Adaptation (OA)

OA theory focuses on businesses' adaptations to the social context within which they exist, such as conventions embedded within family, home, school, church, and other institutions. As Shulman (1996) clarifies:

> Firms may be innovators with respect to technology, work organization, marketing strategies or product development. But to do so they need stability and predictability with respect to their external relationships. . . . The neoclassical belief that managerial decision-making would be irrational if it took factors such as race and sex into account fails to consider the firm's need to fit harmoniously into its larger environment. (50)

Among our interviewees, OA can be seen in the following: certain women reported that construction employers deliberately hired certain women to prove that all women were incompetent. OA suggests a different interpretation of these comments. In the society surrounding construction firms where such hires have allegedly taken place, women are assumed to be incapable of "manly" work and better suited to caring for men and children. As part of this society, employers believe that they may as well hire women based on looks, sexual availability, or filling quotas, since such hires make little difference to the firms' profits.

Divide and Conquer

Divide and conquer theories of discrimination make the case that disparate treatment of subgroups disrupts worker solidarity and is profitable to employers because it reduces workers' organizing strength (Albelda and Drago 2014, 151). Disunity within a racially divided workforce has been shown to undermine unions (Reich, 2015).

By favoring a dominant group of employees, management gains greater control over the whole workforce (Albelda and Drago, 2014; Shulman 1989, 1996). For example, firms reduce overall labor costs when they brand women as unfit for the job in order to avoid safety-related improvements that would improve both men's and women's working conditions. Male workers' investment in their reputations for courage and strength obscures their actual job insecurity, chronic endangerment, and lack of respect in society, while giving them a degree of psychological compensation.

> "Lots of men don't want a woman on the job, and they don't think you can do the job, and some of it you can't do because you're not as tall or strong. . . . But the point is really, they shouldn't be doing it either. Yeah, you can pick up a piece of plywood and carry it all the way across the job site, but . . . should you

do that to your back? But if you ask for help to do something like that . . . they think you're asking because you can't do it. You know, it's just normal things you would expect! Lots of men don't want you there." #15

The arbitrary nature of work evaluations caused self-doubt and self-censorship among the tradeswomen we interviewed.

How come I'm always on the first layoff? . . . They're saying because I wouldn't go over nights. But there's guys there that I know are not qualified. . . . They say it's not my work. But then they want to say "Maybe it's the way you talk." #24

When unions distance themselves from gender and race discrimination, they fuel animosity among subgroups, allowing divide and conquer to prevail (Crain 2007, 116).

Job Competition

Job competition theories of discrimination argue that employers and workers of the dominant group benefit both individually and collectively from discrimination. Darity (1989) theorizes that workers of different races, genders, and ethnicities compete for the best jobs in a stratified hierarchy of occupations. He posits that job competition will perpetuate workplace discrimination as long as the hierarchy exists. Harassment, isolation, and social exclusion of women and racial/ethnic minorities solidify white males' monopoly of better jobs.

As an illustration of job competition, our participants reported that hostile foremen or partners deliberately undermined their competence and confidence.

"You may have some materials come up missing so that you can't finish your job. Your brushes may be missing so you don't have a brush to use, so you have to call your boss or go to the paint store and that takes time . . . you'll find them maybe two weeks later." #8

"He . . . gave me the materials to do it and I said, 'I won't do it . . . because this is not the product that you use on that. . . . He thought he'd send me up there and I'd put this material on the wall and these doors, and it would ruin them and then he could say, 'Well look what she did.'" #10

Similarly, journeymen assigned to train both male and female apprentices sometimes refused to train women, ensuring a low skill level.

"When they'd get ready to do something they'd turn their back so you couldn't see how it was done, or they'd keep it from them some way or another." #24

"You spent your entire apprenticeship running a roller or oiling, which is ... very minimal and it's the lowest pay. So they will intentionally pass you over for, like, going out on a backhoe or a dozer or a forklift." #32

Male Dominance/Hegemony

We turn now to a feminist discrimination theory, hegemonic masculinity. In contrast to tokenism theory, feminist approaches to gender discrimination are generally grounded in a broader concept of patriarchy in which social practices categorize people as male or female with distinct social roles and personal attributes. Gendered beliefs relegate women to subordinate status, upheld by systems that protect men and justify unfair treatment of women. Male dominance permeates social and cultural structures, reducing women's resources and options. Masculinity attracts privileges and rewards, while the "diffusion of feminine values such as altruism, sensitivity and empathy" is devalued and penalized (Smith 2013, 862).

Hegemonic Masculinity

Male dominance is described as hegemonic when both women and men accept and internalize it, allowing employers to consciously favor men without expecting open rebellion or contradiction. In this way, culturally constructed masculinity becomes naturalized, equated to biological male-ness. The male body is "yoked to strength, skill and violence, which are necessary in manual work and trades" (Donaldson 1992 in Smith 2013, 862).

This hegemonic definition expands into an ideal that includes

whiteness, location in the middle class, heterosexuality, independence, ratio-nality and education, a competitive spirit, the desire and the ability to achieve, controlled and directed aggression, as well as mental and physical toughness. (Howson 2006, 60)

The construction industry features as a prime location for such ideal mascu-linity. "Traditionalist site culture . . . portrays construction work as uniquely tough, masculine and practical, while celebrating the freedom it can offer" (Ness 2012, 662).

The hegemonic roughneck image of men in construction facilitates male tolerance of insecure employment, with frequent layoffs for unverifiable reasons. Macho displays by men are considered appropriate on construction sites, and men who conspicuously refrain from them may be penalized or picked on (Denissen 2010, 1056).

As noted above, many of the tradeswomen interviewed emphasized that building trades were a "man's world," some considering this male hegemony to be legitimate. Nonetheless, not all building tradesmen conform physically to the masculine stereotype, as seen in the following example.

> "That's pretty heavy conduit to be running, and it was me and another little guy. And I told him, I said 'We'll get this in here but it's going to take the two of us, and I'm not quite as strong as you are.' Well, it turned out I was stronger than he was and could lift it." #3

Safety

Widespread neglect of safety in Midwestern construction work reflects this hegemonic ideal of masculinity. Our 2003–2003 interviews showed worksites regularly violating the safety codes required by the federal Occupational Safety and Health Agency (OSHA), which rarely inspected them. Supervisors did not hesitate to penalize workers for not working fast enough. Slower ones were verbally abused and laid off first, as were those with too many injuries. Hiring levels vary widely with the stage of a project as well as seasonally, giving layoffs hefty influence on annual incomes. Both workers and supervisors frequently treated insistence on safe practices as a sign of weakness and fear, resulting in a paradoxical connection between hegemonic masculinity and self-exploitation.

> "We kept saying he needed to go to the hospital, and of course he's one of those big, tough, brave men. . . . He went ahead and worked the rest of the day." #27

Proper safety procedures and equipment reduce the risk of injury and the cumulative toll of manual labor. Union contracts often specify safety standards, but declining membership, strength, and safety inspections have contributed to lax enforcement (Paap 2006, 35, 39, 156).[9] In 2002–2003, unions often cooperated with contractors, who benefit from safety shortcuts by avoiding the costs of buying and maintaining safety gear (which often slows the pace of work), as well as tasks and procedures to keep worksites secure. The concept of "working smart" received lip service from contractors, employees, and union representatives alike.

> "The place that this [male fatality] was had the huge safety manual, but in a crunch they'll bypass their own safety practices—you get the job done. And that was one of those times." #5

> "You get put in dangerous situations that shouldn't be. . . . A contractor will get to where they don't care how dangerous it is for you, they just want the job done so they can get their money." #8

Safety has improved somewhat the over the last two decades; however, the construction industry continues to be ranked as one of the most dangerous industries (Eisenberg 2018). Fatal injury rates among roofers, electric power-line installers, and structural iron and steel workers were from five to twelve times higher than the average rate for (full-time equivalent) U.S. workers in 2017 (Laws 2019, 2). Eighty U.S. construction workers were killed on the job each month in 2017 (Jones 2018, 2). With the economic recovery, Indiana's construction industry fatalities have risen each year from 2016 on, culminating in 31 in 2018, a 121 percent increase over 2017 (Indiana Department of Labor 2019, 3).[10]

As Zou (2011) notes, "Developing a safety culture for a construction project or organization does not occur overnight; it is a journey rather than a destination, and it requires a commitment from top management right down to the individual employees over an extended period" (19). Despite improvements, women face continuing challenges in construction. Eisenberg (2018) writes:

> In a dangerous industry a hostile workplace can be fatal or cause lifelong injury. The difference between a responsible warning and a veiled threat can be in the tone of voice or facial expression. Situations intended to cause harm can be disguised as accidents that can happen in a moment and without witnesses, or with witnesses who are complicit. I have often been asked to confirm that violence against tradeswomen has lessened over the years, and probably it has. It is important to note, however, that jobsite violence was part of the blowback to the strong push under Carter to open these jobs to women; if there is another strong effort, a similar blowback should be anticipated and addressed proactively. What made situations more dangerous was the lack of recourse for tradeswomen if the immediate chain of command failed to protect them; inadequate union protocols are largely unchanged, and apprentices are still particularly vulnerable. (xiii)

Apparently, there is still much work to be done.

CONCLUSION: OVERCOMING DIVIDE AND CONQUER

Is the root of tradeswomen's problems in construction their low relative numbers, as implied by tokenism, or is it systemic sexism, as implied by theories of male dominance? The comments and responses of women in central Midwestern building trades give support to both bodies of theory, as well as to class-based theories of discrimination that focus on the exploitation of disunity to undermine worker organizing, disempower workers, and reduce labor costs.

Tokenism exerts pressures on relationships among workers, making it harder to overcome discrimination rooted in divide and conquer (by employers), job competition (by dominant group managers and coworkers), organizational adaptation, and hegemonic masculinity. Although based on relative numbers rather than class, tokenism constrains class solidarity across gender, race, and other divisions. Critical acts of solidarity would be more common if not for tokenism.

But while theories such as Kanter's (1977b) provide significant explanations of the strategies women report using to survive in construction occupations, class issues and gender dynamics complicate relative numbers. Men also adopt roles, such as the "hotshot," explicitly to survive layoffs and they too must pass loyalty tests, whether by making misogynous remarks or by their willingness to work fast and for long hours. Those who complain are stigmatized as losers.

> "[Overtime is] not mandatory, but, like I said, if you don't work it then you'll be the next one laid off." #15

Like women, men are also not supposed to take employers or union officials to court.

With layoffs arbitrary and frequent, retaliatory firing is easy to conceal; deliberate endangerment is likewise difficult to prove due to the ordinarily dangerous conditions on construction sites. Network hiring, subjective evaluations of work quality, and the constant threat of layoff weaken both men's and women's bargaining position vs. contractors, simultaneously preventing women from effectively resisting gender discrimination.

Class commonalities suggest that cross-gender solidarity would facilitate improvements in safety, bargaining power, wages, unjust firings, and other abusive conditions. Perhaps for this reason, gender discrimination plays a vital role in controlling the construction workforce. Harassment, retaliation, and tacit encouragement of discrimination, fueled by tokenism and hegemonic maleness, undermine solidarity and organizing across genders and racial/ethnic groups.

Hegemonic maleness plays a significant role in this constellation of divisions. Even within their families, working-class men associate themselves with roughness, while associating women with respectability and middle-class aspirations (Willis, 1977). Male independence is contrasted to women's orderliness. Dirty work is not generally high on the status ladder, and construction workers' status is ranked lower than that of men or women in cleaner jobs, so contractors gain leverage from boundary-heightening valuation of bravery and risk, exploiting men's pride in order to ignore safety standards.[11]

Tokenism and hegemonic masculinity undergird each other in construction. Different definitions and valuations of toughness for male and female workers underlie gender hierarchy. Toughness in women means enduring abuse and unpleasantness without complaint, while in men, by contrast, toughness means giving abuse, as well as tolerating verbal abuse, mandatory overtime, and unsafe working conditions. All assimilation role options for tradeswomen require that they refrain from returning abuse.

> "Once I actually got fired because a guy wouldn't keep his hands off me, and I finally threatened to whop him with my pliers, and I ended up getting fired after two years [at that company]." #2

> "I had a boss one time that almost hit me several times, and when I said something to him about it . . . he goes, 'next time it will be a 4'x8' sheet of plywood' and I said 'If it is, then I will kick the shit out of you.' So I ended up getting fired off of that job." #27

As other scholars have argued, despite class similarities among women and men working in building trades, men's status depends on the masculinity of this job. Many of the specific forms of harassment and discrimination commonly reported can be traced to men's perception that women's presence in their trade threatens their status via their masculinity. Their work has lent them special confidence and pride in their gender identity, and this depends on retaining a highly masculine workplace.

Strategic Options

Unions

Tradeswomen interviewees recounted both negative and positive experiences with their unions and tended to generalize from these to the labor movement as a whole. Paap (2006) observed declining white male support for building trades unions because unions are required to represent tradeswomen when they file charges against tradesmen and contractors. Our interviewees reported that several unions declined to represent them, while other business agents were reliable allies.

> "They literally threatened to kick him completely out of the union because of his behavior. . . . That's the difference between being union and non-union is the fact that there is somebody that you can go [to]." #22

Union contracts usually defend standardized pay rates and some apportion work through hiring halls, two principles that are particularly helpful in preventing discrimination against women.

> "[In a non-union shop] the difference between mine and the journeyman plumbers was at least ten dollars an hour. . . . Some of the ones that were in training that was a couple years behind me were making more money than me." #71

> "[In a union shop] your name goes on a list and . . . moves up the list as other people get hired. So right now, I'm number one on the apprentice list because I've been laid off the longest. Well he [the business agent] did call me right before I left to come here and tell me that they had a two-week job for me." #35

Statistics show an overall favorable impact of unions on female apprentice recruitment and retention.

> [Union-contractor] joint programs feature higher shares of women in the incoming class and higher odds of completion in comparison with unilateral contractor programs. While White women have higher completion rates than Latinas and Black women, the union impact on completion rates is the largest for Black women and the lowest for White women. (Berik 2006, 321)

Several interviewees appreciated their unions' formal training classes, which gave them fair access to valuable skills and union-backed credentials.

Affirmative Action

Statements by women in construction demonstrate both the value and the limitations of affirmative action hiring targets. In the absence of these, very few of our interviewees would have been hired at all. Construction trade unions and employers both have long histories of openly refusing to hire women.

> "Someone told me once that the white male is the minority now. . . . That's why they're working and I'm not . . .—I've been laid off for a month, but I get a job just because I'm a woman?" #15

However, affirmative action has done little to dispel hostile attitudes or make jobs more bearable for women. Workplaces without support for women increase departures and contribute to a vicious cycle, reinforcing their low numbers. With goals starting as low as 7 percent, women will remain tokens for many years, even if targets are enforced and gradually increased. Also, male dominance need not dissipate just because women enter in larger numbers.

Organized mentoring opportunities are a realistic intervention, even with small numbers of women overall.

Mentoring/Organized Support

Most of our interviewees did not think having more women on their jobsites would solve their problems; however, several women did describe as useful meetings or support groups outside the jobsite.

> "They have like a women's carpenter thing. . . . It's a huge thing, I guess . . . I was going to go . . . to help me feel that I'll get to stay and succeed . . . I thought that maybe I needed to see the companionship of knowing that there are more women, because I do feel so alone because I'm the only one." #15

> "I've not had problems. . . . I was thinking more of the younger girls that don't have a background in it. . . . I was up there with first year apprentices this year and there were probably 7 or 8 women in that class. . . . There was that deer in the headlights look. . . . I'd like to see something where the women could go in and . . . pick up a phone and call and say 'you know I was on the job today and they were doing this, and it just didn't look right to me—why are they doing it?'" #14

As Moir (2011) explains, tradeswomen have historically created "pre-apprenticeship programs for women and networking in several U.S. cities have contributed to slight increases in women's recruitment and retention, as have advocacy groups and taskforces in the United Kingdom, including male and female awareness-raising" (Greed, 2000; Berik and Bilginsoy, 2006; Whittock 2002, 455–456). Mentoring programs have reduced attrition among women apprentices from a third to under 10 percent (Moir 2011, 13).

Cultural Change

The Policy Group on Tradeswomen's Issues (PGTI) in Boston is a critical actor that demonstrates notable success in steering the Massachusetts construction industry toward best practices in diversity through technical assistance and training. This organization notes two best practices as "gamechangers:" diverse core crews (the workforce carried by a construction firm from job to job) and frequent external monitoring of compliance for workforce diversity (PGTI 2016, 4). PGTI partners with unions, apprenticeship programs, contractors, managers, owners, and developers, emphasizing women's growing significance to the industry due to several economic drivers. These include a projected shortage of labor in construction, the growing importance of women's earnings, the increasing numbers of women veterans trained in building trades, and the creation of jobs in emerging green technologies. PGTI's success in organizing for cultural change is clear; Massachusetts now leads the nation in the ratio of women in contruction apprenticeships at 9.2 percent, nearly three times the national average.

Progressive change in society needs to be well underway before either the percentage of women in construction or their treatment on worksites dramatically improves. Dismantling the hegemonic masculine ideal in construction will involve eliminating the penalties currently visited on strong, assertive women in general, while also placing higher value for both men and women on virtues presently regarded as feminine. A shortage of critical acts perpetuates skewed numbers in this industry, while skewing in turn promotes polarization and boundary heightening, reducing critical acts.

Tradeswomen thus continue to bear the cost of reflexively juggling role shifts between feminine, masculine, and gender-neutral presentations of themselves (Denissen 2010). Not only are gender ratios in construction exceptionally small, but building trades have a special symbolic charge, as many men and women see them as the last bastion or refuge of the unreconstructed "real man" (Ness 2012). This suggests that they will be among the last to fall. The construction industry seems likely to cling to the material benefits of hegemonic masculinity, divide and conquer discrimination, job competition, and tokenism-driven tensions until rewards are removed for the same kinds of behavior in other influential arenas.

NOTES

1. In 1965 Executive Order #11246 prohibited "federal contractors and subcontractors and federally-assisted contractors and subcontractors that generally have contracts that exceed $10,000 from discriminating in employment decisions on the basis of race, color, religion, sex or national origin" (U.S. Department of Labor EO 12486). Affirmative Action targets, set in 1978 at 6.9 percent for women in federally funded construction projects, were not enforced after 1980 when the U.S. government slashed Equal Employment Opportunities Commission (EEOC) funding (Berik and Bilginsoy 2006, 324, 329–335).

2. This study was supported by a Multidisciplinary Ventures and Seminars Fund grant from Indiana University.

3. Another illustration comes from coal mining, where women are categorized as "ladies, flirts and tomboys" (Yount 1991).

4. Interviewees identities are withheld.

5. The falling percentage of union labor in construction makes this sample less than completely representative, although women are more likely to enter union than nonunion apprenticeships. Women who remained in construction (including study participants) were also likely to have fewer problems than those who left. In addition,

interviewees doubtless self-censored their responses due to concerns about continuing relationships with coworkers, employers, and union representatives.

6. The complete questionnaire can be obtained by contacting lduggan@indiana. edu.

7. Twenty women (57%) had at least one child under age twelve for some years after joining the trade. Of these twenty, seventeen were able to compare childcare problems in construction with those in prior jobs. Of these seventeen, 53 percent reported facing the same degree of childcare problems in construction as in their earlier work, 18 percent reported fewer childcare problems, and 29 percent reported more problems.

8. The Bureau of Labor Statistics, Consumer Price Index was used to adjust wages and incomes for inflation between July 2002 and December 2019.

9. The U.S. Bureau of Labor Statistics (2020) reports union membership in the construction industry as 12.6 percent of employees in 2019 and approximately 87 percent in 1947.

10. Falls, slips, and trips accounted for the highest number of deaths (Indiana Department of Labor 2019, 3).

11. Nursing and childcare, though objectively dirty, fall into the category of naturally female jobs, thus carry more gratitude than reward. Female-identified dirty, heavy jobs include waitressing, cleaning, and laundry.

REFERENCES

Addleston, J. S., & Stiratt, M. (1996). The last bastion of masculinity: Gender politics at the Citadel. In C. Cheng (Ed.), *Masculinities in organizations* (54–76). Newbury Park, CA: Sage.

Albelda, R., & Drago, R. (2014). *Unlevel playing fields: Understanding wage inequality and discrimination* (4th ed.). Boston, MA: Economic Affairs Bureau.

Berik, G., & Bilginsoy, C. (2006). Still a wedge in the door: Women training for the construction trades in the USA. *International Journal of Manpower, 27*(4), 321–341. doi: 10.1108/01437720610679197.

Cockburn, C. (1991). *In the way of women: Men's resistance to sex equality in organizations.* Basingstoke: Macmillan.

Crain, M. (2007). Sex discrimination as collective harm. In D. Cobble (Ed.), *The sex of class: Women transforming American labor* (99–116). Ithaca, NY: Cornell University Press.

Dahlerup, D. (1988). From a small to a large minority: Women in Scandinavian Politics. *Scandinavian Political Studies, 44*(1), 275–298. doi: 10.1111/j.1467-9477.1988.tb00372.x.

Denissen, A. (2010). The right tools for the job: Constructing gender meanings and identities in the male-dominated building trades. *Human Relations, 63*(7), 1051–1069. doi: 10.1177/0018726709349922.

Eisenberg, S. (2018). *We'll call if we need you: Experiences of women working construction* (2nd ed.). Ithaca, NY: Cornell University Press.

Franzway, S., Sharp, R., Mills, J., & Gill, J. (2009). Engineering ignorance: The problem of gender equity in engineering. *Fontiers: A Journal of Women's Studies, 30*(1), 89–106.

Greed, Clara. (2000). Women in the construction industry: Achieving critical mass. *Gender, Work and Organization, 7*(3), 181–196.

Hegewisch, A. (2019). Women gain jobs in construction trades but remain under-represented in the field. Institute for Women's Policy Research Fact Sheet, C479.

Howson, R. (2006). *Challenging hegemonic masculinity*. New York: Routledge.

Kanter, R. (1977a). *Men and women of the corporation*. New York: Basic Books.

Kanter, R. (1977b). Some effects of proportions on group life: Skewed sex ratios and responses to token women. *American Journal of Sociology, 82*(5), 965–990.

Kelly, M., Wilkinson, L., Pisciotta, M., & Williams, L. (2015). When working hard is not enough for female and racial ethnic minority apprentices in the highway trades. *Sociological Forum, 30*(2), 415–438.

Laws, J. (1975). The psychology of tokenism: An analysis. *Sex Roles, 1*, 51–67.

LeBreton, L. W., & Loevy, S. S. (1992). *Breaking new ground: Worksite 2000*. Chicago, IL: Chicago Women in Trades.

Le Feuvre, N. (1999). Gender, occupational feminization, and reflexivity: A cross-national perspective. In R. Crompton (Ed.), *Restructuring gender relations and employment* (150–178). Oxford: Oxford University Press.

Lewis, P., & Simpson, R. (2012). Kanter revisited: Gender, power and (in)visibility. *International Journal of Management Reviews, 14*, 141–158.

Marden, C. M. G. (1973). *Minorities in American society*. New York: D. Van Nostrand.

Martin, S. (1980). *Breaking and entering: Policewomen on patrol*. Berkeley: University of California Press.

McElhinny, B. (1994). An economy of affect: Objectivity, masculinity and the gendering of police work. In A. Cronwall & N. Lindisfarne (Eds.), *Dislocating masculinity: Comparative ethnographies* (159–171). London: Routledge.

Moir, S., Thomson, M., & Kelleher, C. (2011). *Unfinished business: Building equality for women in the construction trades*. Boston: Labor Resource Center Publications. University of Massachusetts.

Ness, K. (2012). Constructing masculinity in the building trades: 'Most jobs in the construction industry can be done by women'. *Gender, Work & Organization, 19*(6), 654–676. doi: 10.1111/j.1468-0432.2010.00551.x.

Paap, K. (2006). *Working construction: Why white working-class men put themselves and the labor movement in harm's way*. Ithaca, NY: Cornell University Press.

Policy Group on Tradeswomen's Issues (PGTI). (2016). Finishing the job: Best practices for a diverse workforce in the construction industry, *6*(1).

Poutanen, S., & Kovalainen, A. (2013). Gendering innovation process in an industrial plant: Revisiting tokenism, gender and innovation. *International Journal of Gender and Entrepreneurship, 5*(3), 257–274.

Reich, M. (2015). Racial inequality. In V. Kippit (Ed.), *Radical political economy: Explorations in alternative economic analysis* (197–204). New York: Routledge.

Riddell, T., Shackelford, J., & Stamos, S. (1998). *Economics: A tool for critically understanding society* (5th ed.). Reading, MA: Addison-Wesley.

Riemer, J. (1979). *Hard hats: The work world of construction workers.* Beverly Hills: Sage.

Rustad, M. (1982). *Women in Khaki: The American enlisted woman.* New York: Praeger.

Shulman, S. (1989). Racism and the making of the American working class. *International Journal of Politics, Culture & Society, 2*(3), 361–367.

Shulman, S. (1996). The political economy of labor market discrimination: A class-room-friendly presentation of the theory. *The Review of Black Political Economy, 24*(4), 47–64.

Smith, L. (2013). Trading in gender for women in trades: Embodying hegemonic masculinity, femininity and being a gender hotrod. *Construction Management and Economics, 31*(8), 861–873. doi: 10.1080/01446193.2013.833339.

U.S. Bureau of Labor Statistics. (2020). Union members—2019, News Release, January 22, 2020.

Watts, J. (2007). Porn, pride and pessimism: Experiences of women working in professional construction roles *Work, Employment & Society, 21*(2), 299–316.

Whittock, M. (2002). Women's experiences of non-traditional employment: Is gender equality in this area a possibility? *Construction Management and Economics, 20*, 449–456.

Willis, P. (1977). *Learning to labor: How working class kids get working class jobs.* New York: Columbia University Press, Morningside Edition.

Yoder, J. (1991). Rethinking tokenism: Looking beyond numbers. *Gender and Society, 5*(2), 178–192.

Yount, K. (1991). Ladies, flirts, and tomboys: Strategies for managing sexual harassment in an underground coal mine. *Journal of Contemporary Ethnography, 19*(4), 396–423.

Zimmer, L. (1988). Tokenism and women in the workplace: The limits of gender-neutral theory. *Study for the Society of Social Problems, 35*(1), 64–77.

Zou, P. (2011). Fostering a strong construction safety culture. *Leadership and Management in Engineering, 11*, 11–22.

Index

About the Editor

Marquita R. Walker is interim chair and associate professor in the Department of Labor at Indiana University Purdue University Indianapolis. Policy research involves workers' (re)integration into the workforce and workers' education. Her publications focus on the labor-management relationship, global supply chains, and female narratives from working environments.

About the Contributors

Asli Şahankaya Adar is a lecturer in the Department of Management and Organization at University of Beykent, Turkey. Her research interests and publication include topics on women's work, welfare and migration, work-life balance, and childcare economy. Her research is founded by ILO, EBRD, and World Bank.

Per Bauhn is professor of practical philosophy at Linnaeus University, Sweden. Dr. Bauhn publishes in English on ethical issues relating to political terrorism, nationalism and morality, the virtue and value of courage, and the concept of normative identity. He also publishes in the field of aesthetics.

Zeynep Ceren Eren Benlisoy is a post-doctorate researcher at Kadir Has University for the Gender, Justice and Security UKRI GCR Hub, London School of Economics. Research interests include gendered dynamics of the labor migration, forced migration and displacement in Turkey, agri-food relations, rural transformation, migration, and woman labor and ethnography.

Armand Chevalier is a first-generation, triple bachelors seeking working-class scholar at Indiana University, Indianapolis whose academic aspirations span the intersections of labor studies, latino studies, psychology, and sociology. His research interests encompass the social organization of work, occupational behavior, industrial relations, and inequalities linked to social stratification.

Gracia Clark is professor emerita in anthropology at Indiana University, Bloomington. While a union apprentice plumber in Washington, DC (1973–1976), she negotiated affirmative action goals for women in federal

229

construction contracts with WIC. Fieldwork since 1978 in Kumasi, Ghana informs her two books, three web galleries (search aodl.org), and other publications.

Ana Luíza Matos de Oliveria, PhD, is an economist in the Latin American College of Social Sciences (FLACSO) São Paulo, SP, Brazil, a consultant, visiting professor at FLACSO and coeditor of *Brasil Debate* and *WEA Commentaries*, and a member of the International Association for Feminist Economics.

Saniye Dedeoglu is professor of social policy in the Department of Labour Economics and Industrial Relations at Mugla University, Turkey. She is the author of *Women Workers in Turkey: Global Industrial Production in Istanbul* (2007) and *Migrants, Work and Social Integration: Women's Labour in the Turkish Ethnic Economy* (2014).

Lynn Duggan is a professor in the Labor Studies Department, Indiana University Bloomington. Her research on social policy and labor relations is published in *Comparative Economic Studies, Feminist Economics*, the *National Women's Studies Association Journal,* and multiple anthologies. She is co-editor of *The Women, Gender, and Development Reader, Zed Press.*

Anil Duman is an associate professor at Central European University. She received her MA and PhD in economics from UMASS, Amherst. Her research interests include political economy, industrial relations, welfare state policies, and redistribution. Her recent research specializes on the interrelations between labor market status and socioeconomic inequalities.

Lygia Sabbag Fares, assistant professor in economics—STRONG ESAGS. Visiting researcher at the Institute of Brazilian Studies, University of São Paulo, and organizer for the Young Scholars Initiative Gender Working Group, has a BA in international relations, labor economics certificate, MA in labor policies and globalization, and PhD in development economics.

Elizabeth Hoffmann is an associate professor of sociology at Purdue University. Dr. Hoffmann authored *Co-operative Workplace Dispute Resolution—Organizational Structure, Ownership, and Ideology* from Routledge Press and currently researches and writes on employment issues, legal consciousness, and workplace ideologies.

Mariam Philipose is a doctoral candidate in the School of Economics, University of Hyderabad in India, whose mixed method approach to research employs a feminist perspective and focuses on the dimensions of fieldwork conducted on tea plantations in Munnar, Kerala. Other interests include gender, political economy, and human geography.

Chris Sahley is a professor in the Department of Biological Sciences, director for the ADVANCE-Purdue Center for Faculty Success, Special Advisor to the Provost for Gender Equity, and is coeditor of the "Working Papers Series on Navigating Careers in the Academy: Gender, Race and Class."

Fatma Fulya Tepe is an assistant professor of sociology at the Faculty of Education, Istanbul Aydın University, Turkey. Within gender studies, Dr. Tepe publishes research on Turkish academic women, essentialism and women, the Turkish media representations of women, and Turkish women as Mother Citizens.

Nisha Viswanathan currently practices as an extensivist physician and clinical instructor of medicine at University of California, Los Angeles. She previously published work on intimate partner violence in the Dominican Republic and now focuses her research on gender-based inequities in medicine and alternative care models for patients with complex needs.